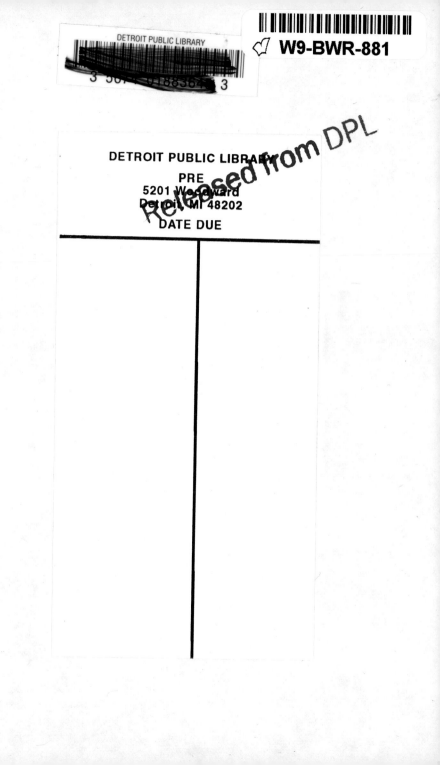

Group
Marriage

Group Marriage

A STUDY OF CONTEMPORARY MULTILATERAL MARRIAGE

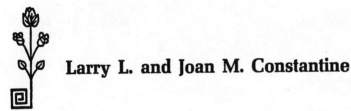 **Larry L. and Joan M. Constantine**

COLLIER BOOKS

A Division of Macmillan Publishing Co., Inc.

NEW YORK

All names and professions attributed to the
people described in this book are
entirely fictitious.

Macmillan Publishing Co., Inc.
866 Third Avenue, New York, N.Y. 10022
Collier-Macmillan Canada Ltd.

Library of Congress
Catalog Card Number: 72-87157

Group Marriage is also published in a
hardcover edition by
Macmillan Publishing Co., Inc.

First Collier Books Edition 1974

Printed in the United States of America

Contents

Preface

Behind this book is an adventure, a radical, perhaps even courageous, entry into a new form of marriage. It is the adventure on the part of about a hundred people we came to know and many more we will never meet. And it is our adventure. With two people whom we grew to love and care about very much, we left the mainstream of American family life and entered deep water. Our short-lived group marriage was turbulent and difficult but not without its joy and some profoundly intimate moments. Our months spent with two people we could love but could not live with changed us, though. Doggedly we built a new and even better marriage for ourselves out of the material we had gotten from our experience. And we embarked on another adventure which was the research on which this book is based. As we learned, we saw that though our own particular experience in group marriage was not common, neither was it absolutely unique. As a result, we carry with us a personal sensitivity for the issues and a sense of the reality of group marriage which can only come from having stepped out into deep water ourselves.

This book is based on nearly three years of research into almost every aspect of group marriages and the people in them throughout the country. Our principal aim is to present a comprehensive picture that is the sum of many experiences rather than the story of a few whose adventures might not be at all representative. Those trying new forms of marriage and family living will need to relate in detail their personal adventures, but this is not such a book. We do not deny feelings or avoid opinions, nor try to invalidate the importance of the elaborations of subjective reality, but we are primarily interested in relating factual, representative information on emerging forms of marriage, an area of the contemporary scene in which real information is absent and rhetoric is abundant.

Knowledge should be a tool for the alleviation of fear, alienation, and prejudice, an implement on the road to insight, understanding, and acceptance. We want to write for many different people for whom knowledge of marriage alternatives could be a tool. Principally, the book is designed for anyone whose horizons might be extended. We hope it is also a document of scientific worth on which more valuable investigations can be built. Indeed, if we have failed to provide the stepping-stone for continued research and the stimulus to mount it, we have failed in a central reason for our own research. Equally important, we want to reach the large body of professionals who labor in service to families, giving them the essentials of new family patterns as well as the basis for looking in new ways at the options in conventional marriages. We hope the book will be valuable to anyone interested in knowing what group marriage is really like, whether as a potential participant, observer, or even opponent.

Our multiple purposes may make it harder for any audience to read the book. The casual reader will not find a single complete story of anybody's experience in group marriage, for no real story would be representative; a representative composite would be fiction, and there is already too much fiction on the subject. The casual reader will find his/her attention repeatedly interrupted by percentages and footnotes. The professional may be similarly perturbed by the intrusion of values and feelings in the midst of data.

To serve both masters, we have organized the book into text and appendices. The text is intended to be essentially self-contained and useful to almost any intelligent person regardless of background. We do feel it is important to cite the sources of information, references, and further reading, but we have endeavored to do this in an accessible yet unobtrusive manner, leaving the reader free to ignore these "scholarly" embellishments.

We have departed in one very important way from accepted practice in writing for a general audience. In this context it is not customary to refer to the statistical significance of findings. Facts pertaining to particular people or practices are often reported without a point of reference or comparison. It means nothing to report that 43 percent of residents in an urban housing project exhibit neurotic symptoms unless one has the incidence of such symptoms in general or in, say, suburban neighborhoods. Even should we know that only 41 percent from a suburban neighborhood had these symptoms, the difference may not be statistically significant; that is, it may be well within what may be expected by chance alone. We need to be told whether even this small difference is extremely improbable and hence significant. This is a simple and easily understood concept, but one which is essential if the reader is to be able to interpret for himself what the authors are telling him. It not only seems unnecessary to shield intelligent readers from this bit of mathematics, but somewhat misleading to do so.

Throughout this book, whenever the word "*significant*" or "*significantly*" or the phrase "*statistically significant*" appears *in italics* in the text it means that accepted statistical procedures were used in analyzing the results and that, on the basis of those statistical tests, there is no more than one chance in twenty that the observed results could have occurred due to chance alone. In many cases the odds for results being a chance occurrence are much less than one in twenty.

The appendices contain complete summaries of all data used in reporting on our research as well as details of the particular statistical procedures employed and the exact levels of significance. Appendix I is devoted to a technical discussion of statistical issues in the study.

The text of the book has been further subdivided. The first three chapters describe, as we see it, the matrix of contemporary American marriage and family life and its relationship to other styles of marriage: in other cultures, in the past, and on the horizon. The next four chapters describe the study, who the respondents are, something of what they are like, and some essential features of the group-marriage experience.

Chapters 8 through 19 take us from the process of formation through the process of separation, each chapter dealing with a distinct aspect of the group-marriage experience. The final chapters move from the highly specialized area of group marriage into human love and sexuality in the broadest sense and from the contemporary to the future scene. These chapters emphasize implications that experiences within group marriages have for other human relationships, including more conventional marriages.

Acknowledgments

Oᴜʀ ꜰɪʀsᴛ ᴛʜᴀɴᴋs go to the people about whom this book is concerned, for their sharing of themselves. Our gratitude to them is boundless; the entire book is an expression of it.

It was a privilege to work for a summer with Angela Hunt, whose study of children in group-marriage families she has generously permitted us to include with our own material. She has become more than a colleague; to all our family Angela will always be a very real member, wherever she goes. We are deeply indebted to Dr. Louis J. Gerstman, who found time within an always busy schedule to assist us in the use of tests and measurements. Without his confidence in our professional competence we would have been barred from using standard psychological tests and deprived of an important part of our understanding of group-marriage participants. His feedback on statistical procedures has been invaluable.

Numerous professionals in the family field, through their encouragement, interest, and acceptance of us as their colleagues, sustained us through frequent attacks of self-doubt. Roger Libby of Washington State University was especially generous in giving us feedback. We have received valuable feedback from others who reviewed portions of the manuscript for this book: Dr. Lester Kirkendall, Ronald Mazur, Dr. James Hawkins, Dr. Robert Whitehurst.

In the last hours, our neighbor, Vivian Sayre, gave us some much needed help with the typing, and with giving our children some extra care and attention.

To our editor, Clement Alexandre, goes more than the expected amount of credit. He approached us with support when we thought that we might have to abandon the project.

We would like to be able to thank the Midwest businessman who expressed his concern for our project in the form of a thousand-dollar check, but he has asked to remain anonymous.

Perhaps the greatest thanks go to our beautiful and very grown-up daughter of three, for being such good company on long days of driving, and for understanding far beyond her years the importance of her parents' "work-work." Joy and her new sister, Heather, are what it is all about.

Group
Marriage

PART I

CONTEXT

1

The Myths of Monogamy

THE ORIGINAL "Kinsey reports"[1] on human sexual behavior could only have been surprising to a society out of touch with itself. The enormous impact of the late Dr. Kinsey and his collaborators is a measure of the incongruity between the images and the actualities of America's marriage, family, and sex relations. Twenty years later, we as a society are little better in touch with the realities of marriage and the family. We prefer, it would seem, to maintain the myths.

The myth in America is of monogamy. In a strict sense, monogamy means one mate for a lifetime. In its American embodiment, monogamy means lifelong sexual fidelity as well. The picture is embellished with details from an old Norman Rockwell magazine cover; husband and wife, perennial close companions, lovingly herding their several shiny-cheeked children to worship together. If this family fights at all, members are quick to acknowledge their transgressions and make up. Its members have sharply delineated roles. It always has the same configuration (man, woman, 2.85 children; the oldest child is a boy). Mom and Dad were married in church (Mom rightfully wore white!) because they loved each other.

Society expects its members not only to subscribe to this glossy magazine portrayal, but to emulate it. Before kindergarten, children have been sufficiently socialized to believe that marriage for them is a foregone conclusion. The questions they pose concern whom they will marry and when—not if. And what kind of marriage do they expect it to be? You guessed it, right off the cover of *Saturday Evening Post*.

At the center of this picture is sexual fidelity or exclusiveness. Our Judeo-Christian code, petrified in law, calls for sexual relationships only in the context of a marital bond with one spouse. Of course, we have had to admit that premaritally our model has broken down. Acknowledgment of sexual reality comes slowly. Even in the 1920s only half the brides were virgins.[2] Nevertheless, we continue to enthrone "premarital chastity." Loaded words in need of redefinition—like "chastity" and "fidelity"—reveal that ultimately this is a religious issue. It is out of vogue to wield religious weapons, so society recasts the model in sociological and psychological terms, emphasizing the maturity necessary to handle sexual relations and *sotto voce* references to risking future marital happiness. Psychological labels such as "acting out" replace condemnations of "immorality"; yet from a scientific standpoint, all we can say is that the effects—positive or negative—of premarital sex vary with the nature of the experiences and the goals of the marriage.

Premarital sexual patterns and changes in them are well documented by both science and journalism. The sexual patterns of the young (or black, or "deviant") make good copy. But what about the Rockwellian father smiling at his fellow parishioners? Kinsey found that the chances are better than half that he has had some extramarital sexual intercourse. By age 40, more than a quarter of the women have done the same thing. More recently, Paul Gebhard, head of the Institute for Sex Research founded by Kinsey, estimated that extramarital sex involved three out of five men and two in five women.[3] In short, on the basis of the data, strict sexual monogamy is the exception rather than the rule.

We once made that statement to a small gathering of friendly suburbanites in Minnesota. They granted that it *might* be true somewhere, perhaps for the kind of people who participated in the Kinsey studies, but certainly not for most people, absolutely not in their community. Coincidentally, research on extramarital intercourse in that very community had just been published.[4] In that sample, more than a third of the couples interviewed were affected by at least one affair, and there are reasons to believe this understates the incidence. As usual, men were found to have more extramarital experience than women, but they also reported having more opportunity. Where there had been opportunity, the percentage of affected couples rises to 40 percent. And in response to a hypothetical situation in which the spouse is out of town, more than two-thirds of all men and 56 percent of the women would put themselves in situations ranging from spending an evening alone with a close friend of the opposite sex to becoming sexually involved.

The thesis that extramarital sex occurs because something is wrong with the marriage is one of the myths of sexual monogamy. Yet Johnson found that high marital adjustment was as frequent among those positively inclined to extramarital intercourse as among those who were not. Similarly, Neubeck and Schetzler[5] found no significant difference in extramarital involvement between highly satisfied and highly unsatisfied married couples.

There are other indicators which suggest that monogamy with complete sexual exclusiveness is exceptional. The growing middle-class phenomenon of sexual mate-swapping ("swinging") and new attitudes toward exclusiveness among young people are suggestive.

TYPES. When sociologists John Cuber and Peggy Harroff did their pioneering study[6] of sex among the affluent, they were more interested in context than in counting incidence. They found that there are many kinds of affairs just as there are many kinds of marriages. Some affairs compensate for defective marriages, but others become fulfilling adjuncts to marriages which are no less sound than ones unaffected by extramarital involvement. Cuber and Harroff observed long-lived "affairs" that had all the hallmarks of good marriages and that continued with the knowledge, and sometimes even the blessing, of the spouse. Their debunking of stereotypes in extramarital affairs has since been repeated by others.[7] No longer can extramarital intercourse be labeled simply as either sick or a sign of sickness.

Cuber "discovered," further, that people enter marriages for different reasons and that the entire relationship is structured according to those goals. It is not reasonable to speak of the success or failure of a given marriage without reference to the goals of its partners. Cuber's typology recognized five types of marriage: Some conflict habituated, providing sparring partners, fulfilling important needs for conflict; passive-congenial, instrumental in career development or providing simple, congenial companionship; the vital, characterized by vital, intense mutual involvement; devitalized, lacking their former vitality; and so-called total marriages, marked by total, almost symbiotic, mutual immersion. There may be additional distinct types. Marriage, obviously does not have a single universal meaning, even in our culture. We can expect things related to marriage to have different meanings to you and to your neighbor. Where one person may see extramarital sex as a violation of faith, another may see it as instrumental in achieving other goals—continued congeniality, career progress. The marriage that primarily satisfies conflict needs may be a mutually satisfying relationship to the two adults involved, although an outsider might term it "unsuccessful."

SUCCESS AND FUNCTION. Success in marriage is elusive of achievement and of evaluation. If success is merely hanging together, then more than one in three marriages fail. But the divorce rate understates the real catastrophe, for many deeply unsatisfactory marriages remain undissolved; Few continue to contribute to the growth and fulfillment of both partners. The Roys' analysis of several sources suggests that fully three-quarters of intact marriages are a failure in this sense.[8] Figures on abandonment are more difficult to develop than on divorce, but there is reason to believe that they are at least as high.

The family, built around a marriage, has many purposes. It is an essential economic unit. It divides the labor, often by disregarding the human resources involved. The family creates children, and it socializes them into acceptable patterns of behavior. It is a recreational facility for all members. In recent history it has become a primary source of emotional gratification, and even more recently, a means to individual self-realization. But, increasingly, all these functions are being usurped by other social entities, or otherwise lessened in centrality for the family. With growing emphasis on population control and popularization of day-care, this is becoming true even for reproduction and child-rearing.

Our educational systems—both the schools and the media—promulgate stereotypes which deny underlying diversity. While single parents at least have their representatives on TV, divorce is unknown except during the diurnal parade of "soap operas." Indeed, nowhere are the American contradictions and confusions over marriage more evident than on TV, which lacks simple, affectionate, marital sex but little else.

It is ultimately easier to say what marriage in America is *not* than what it *is*. Marriage is not, in reality, a strictly one-man/one-woman, deep-love, lifetime-commitment type of thing. Marriage is not any *one* thing. It is different things to different people, and even different things to the same people at different times. The cycle of married life from child-rearing through the "empty nest" is a motion picture rather than a color slide. Some people do have marriages which conform, more or less, to our monolithic model. Those who conform are not necessarily better off, nor are the nonconformists to be blamed or pitied.

THE NUCLEAR AGE. It is not known whether the families of America's past were ever really of the large extended form in which a single household included several generations, including Uncle Charlie and a cousin of dubious connection. Family sociologist William Goode calls this "the classical family of Western nostalgia."[9] Some families took this form, but there always seem to have been an abundance of small, independent, parents-and-children families, the kind today called nuclear families. The truth is that even today the relative proportion or importance of isolated families versus ones with extensive kin involvement is unknown.[10] The autonomous nuclear family, though it may be an indigenous species in middle-class suburbia, is found elsewhere as well;[11] and extended families are not localized in the Italian North End of Boston.

More and more, however, members of today's families experience a sense of isolation and containment in a miniscule enclave. Functional ties with kin, though still real in a sociological sense, are decreasing; they are not undergirded by a residential or economic basis and are experienced as psychologically tenuous.[12] Not only is this experience real, but a sense of isolation tends to create isolation; if we think there is no one to reach, we will not reach out. Housewives find the roles of mother and manager and the walls of small, separate houses equally confining. Teenagers look for someplace else to go, their choices narrowed to remaining in siege, running away, or getting married. Husbands turn *from* their outside involvement in work that is boring or overdemanding only to find the family too small and too constrained to supply the elusive balm, which they may then be more likely to seek elsewhere.

For many, old and young from all social strata, the magazine picture is beginning to loosen at the edges, revealing an unfamiliar but starkly real image beneath.

We can romanticize a lost past populated with extended families that we may never have had. We can enshrine and mystify the insular families we now create. Or we can examine in critical focus the underlying realities of marriage, of our marriages. Only through seeing what marriage is may we glimpse what it might be.

REFERENCES

1. Alfred C. Kinsey, Wardell B. Pomeroy, and Clyde E. Martin. *Sexual Behavior in the Human Male* (Philadelphia: Saunders, 1948). Also Kinsey, Pomeroy, Martin, and Paul Bebhard, *Sexual Behavior in the Human Female* (Philadelphia: Saunders, 1948)

2. Ira L. Reiss, *The Family System in America* (New York: Holt, Rinehart & Winston, 1971).

3. Quoted in the introduction to Morton Hunt, *The World of the Formerly Married* (New York: McGraw-Hill, 1966).

4. Ralph E. Johnson, "Extramarital Intercourse: A Methodological Note," *Journal of Marriage and the Family* 32, 2 (May 1970).

5. Gerhard Neubeck and Vera M. Schetzler, "A Study of Extramarital Relationships," in Gerhard Neubeck, *Extramarital Relations* (Englewood Cliffs, N.J.: Prentice-Hall, 1969).

6. John Guber and Peggy Harroff, *Sex and the Significant Americans: A Study of Sexual Behavior among the Affluent* (Baltimore, Md.: Penguin, 1969).

7. Lonny Myers and Hunter Leggitt, "A New View of Adultery," *Sexual Behavior* 2, 2 (February 1972).

8. Rustum and Della Roy, "Is Monogamy Outdated?" in Lester Kirkendall and Robert Whitehurst, *The New Sexual Revolution* (New York: Donald Brown, 1971).

9. William J. Goode, *World Revolution and Family Patterns* (New York: Free Press, 1963).

10. An excellent recent analysis of the nuclear family versus the extended-kin network is found in Geoffrey Gibson's "Kin Family Network: Overheralded Structure in Past Conceptualizations of Family Functioning," *Journal of Marriage and the Family* 34, 1 (February 1972).

11. Albert E. Scheflen and Andrew S. Ferber, "Critique of a Sacred Cow— the Nuclear Family," in Andrew Ferber, Marilyn Mendlsohn, and Augustus Napier, *The Book of Family Therapy* (New York: Science House, 1972).

12. Talcott Parsons, "The Normal American Family," in Arlene S. and Jerome H. Skolnick, *Family in Transition* (Boston: Little, Brown, 1971).

2

The Family of Human Families

Like the blind men exploring the elephant and perceiving the same object in contradictory ways, we all have a propensity for examining parts rather than wholes and seeing what we want to see, including nothing. The sociologist, M. F. Nimkoff, in reviewing the facts on marriages throughout the world, observed the surfeit of cultures favoring multiple wives and the rarity of ones favoring multiple husbands. These figures, he maintains, "buttress the thesis that men are generally governed by internal sexual drives and are disposed toward sexual variety much more than are women."[1] Ford and Beach, from the same set of data, conclude that "it has not been demonstrated that human females are necessarily less inclined toward promiscuity than are males. What the evidence does reveal is that in a great many societies the woman's tendencies to respond to a variety of sexual partners are much more sharply restricted by custom." Most importantly they note that "in those societies which have no double standard in sexual matters and in which a variety of liaisons are permitted, the women avail themselves as eagerly of their opportunity as do the men."[2]

What are we to believe about human marriages and families when equally reputable anthropologists deliver differing reports on the same tribe? Can we isolate facts from the fictions and fractions or, like the blind men, are we doomed to fragmentary and misleading images? Is monogamy the epitome of social evolution, the epiphenomenon of capitalistic decadence, or an archaic feudal residue?

In arriving at a summation which may hint at mankind's marital proclivity, it makes a great deal of difference how we gather and label the evidence and how we perform the addition. Were we to poll every person on earth today we would most assuredly find the vast majority of married people have only one mate. We do not feel that such a poll would be very enlightening. Most people are products of their culture. Their marital and sexual patterns are functions of cultural conditioning at least as much as of individual manifestations of human nature. Each individual's vote is pledged, as it were, to the norms of his society. Each distinct society, however, represents one human experiment in giving social form to human propensities, in developing a culture to suit individual and collective needs. Trends in the outcomes of these "experiments" are more meaningful as data from which to infer something of those propensities than are nose counts of individual members. It can still be disturbing to count a tiny African tribe and the United States each as a single culture, and we shall have to return again to this issue.

We also recognize the inadequacy of anthropological data. The quality of observation from which summary data is derived varies tremendously. Most historical and early anthropological information would not meet modern standards for adequate data. Countless cultures have been lost forever to scientific scrutiny. Yet we must also recognize that ethnographic information is the broadest data base available and the best data from which to draw inferences of the type in which we are interested.

FORMS. If there is so much as a single solid fact concerning human marital and familial experience it is that the experience is varied. What man has called "family" forms a piebald patchwork with as much that is unique as that which is common. To the Nayars of the Malabar Coast of India, for example, the family was the *taravad*, a permanent, multigeneration clan of relationships traced only through the mother. Marriage was a nightly visit from one of several changing husbands of another *taravad*.

It was the *taravad* that accumulated property and reared children. The official father was an absent man who, prior to a girl's menarche, had tied around her neck a *tali*, a chain symbolic of marriage. Rarely, and only if the girl were older, would the symbolic marriage have been consummated.[3] The nuclear family of father, mother, and children was all but unrecognized among the Nayars. The Hopi of Arizona, by contrast, were rigidly monogamous. Some legal and economic rights were traced matrilineally, while others were traced patrilineally, according to elaborate rules. But theirs was a brittle monogamy characterized by rampant divorce that required fathers to live separately from their children who, like the house they lived in, belonged to the mother.[4] The Nayars, polygamous and permissive, and the Hopis who were monogamous, lived in similar but easily distinguished family patterns.

From an ethnocentric perspective, Americans tend to think of marriage in terms of monogamy—oh yes, and in terms of the other kind, polygamy. In informal (especially male) use, polygamy means multiple wives or is equated with wife-swapping. Traditionally, those who study the family have recognized four kinds of marriage. Polygamy refers to two of these forms: polygyny and polyandry. *Polygyny*, in which one man is mated to more than one woman, on a cultural basis is by far the most common form of marriage, being preferred in 415 of the 554 cultures in the World Ethnographic Sample.[5] In marked contrast, *polyandry*, or one woman with more than one husband, is very rare: 4 cultures in the World Ethnographic Sample.* The remaining cultures, less than 25 percent, are officially monogamous. As we shall see, the official may seriously misrepresent the actual.

To complete his summary of types of marriage, Nimkoff introduces *group marriage* (two or more men married to two or more women), then dismisses it as "only a theoretical possibility, not an

* Our own efforts uncovered eight: Toda, Marquesan, Tibetan, Nepalese, Kandyan of Ceylon, Tiya, Kammalaus, and formerly the Nayars of India. Undoubtedly there are others.

actuality, presumably because it has no special advantages and entails special problems."⁶ Group marriage does not even have an official cultural representative in the World Ethnographic Sample. But group marriage has not been so easily dismissed from the imaginations of men. Group marriage figures in many theories of the origin of the family and was the focus of a decades-long debate among anthropologists in the last century. Whether or not it can be achieved in practice, group marriage has the signal and unique advantage of providing for sexual variety for *both* men and women *within* a stable marital configuration. This may not be its only advantage or the most important one, but it certainly is characteristic of group marriage vis-à-vis other types of marriage.

PROGRESS. All forms of marriage and the family found preserved by cultures are responses to social and personal needs, some transient or situational, others intrinsic to the organization of human society or to individual humanness. Children will always need nurturing, and the existence of society depends on some socialization process. Throughout our lives our sexuality is an essential part of our humanness. But the Nayars' highly developed permissive polyandry fitted very specific occupational requirements of the males of that caste. Their occupation was war. As war on the Malabar Coast became a declining business, *taravads* became the smaller *tavaris*, the association between lovers became less tenuous. Finally Anglicized law intervened, and today single mates and nuclear families are the rule.

The Todas, a small tribe in the Nilgiri hills of southern India, also practiced polyandry, but they were homekeeping herders, not wandering warriors. The norm of multiple husbands was made possible by female infanticide. This pastoral culture encountered modern Western civilization and was forced to abandon the practice that made polyandry possible. As a result, instead of several brothers sharing one wife, they began to marry many wives.⁷

It can be seen that the relationship between "progress" and form of marriage is anything but simple. Over the centuries the concept of a primitive state of promiscuity or group marriage has attracted a variegated crew of followers from Christian apologists for the status quo, to elder male scientists seeking support for fantasies of a more "natural" state of polygamy, to Marxists rationalizing communism and attempting to wrench capitalism at its presumed nuclear-family heart. The facts are rather skeletal compared to the elaborate theories. For one thing we can never know about the actual origins of marriage and family in human prehistory; we can only speculate. Second, at all times for which there is any substantive evidence, many forms of marriage have coexisted, contrasting patterns being found even in neighboring tribes having substantial commerce with each other. Third, many of the most primitive cultures are monogamous.

We also know that any form of polygamous marriage requires a more advanced economic base than monogamy since some individuals must be capable of producing enough output for their multiple mates. In general, "the types of organization which seem remotest [from the monogamous nuclear family] do not occur in the more savage and archaic societies, but in the relatively recent and extremely sophisticated forms of social development."[8]

Social evolution does not move universally from polygamy toward monogamy, though this appears to be the worldwide trend in modern times. Strictly monogamous societies are certainly among the largest and most prolific. Their "success" greatly inflates the total number of monogamous matings. The success of a society integrates so many terms—climate, natural resources, exogenous mobilizing forces, among others—that it is not legitimate to infer that monogamy leads to growth and progress. History records both advanced and highly successful polygamous cultures and short-lived monogamous failures.

Even within cultures favoring multiple mating, actual polygamous marriages are usually in the minority. The reason for this will be clear if we return to the Todas of India. They were able to maintain a primarily polyandrous system of mating only by killing many female babies. Without some such intervention, there will always be about as many men as women. The ratio of male to female babies guarantees that polygamous matings must be the numerical exception, however favored or preferred they may be. Only monogamy and group marriage are compatible with the natural sex ratio and permit a majority of a population to follow the norm of marriage.

It is clear again that, whatever technical objections may be raised to "counting cultures," that which each culture favors is a better reflection of human mating preferences than the marriages of individuals.

As for the current world trend, we should note that both polygyny and polyandry are inherently asymmetric. In a polygynous household it is the man who may chose to marry another woman. Implicit in the freedom of acquisition is power or control which goes beyond other culturally affirmed power relationships in marriages. Of course men retain control even when they share a wife. Because of the power differential implicit in polygamous relationships, as cultures move toward equality of the sexes, they abandon polygamy in favor of monogamy. We have only to look at our own culture to see that this in no way guarantees equality, but it may be a necessary step on a society-wide basis in view of the sexist milieu in which polygamy is usually imbedded.

GROUPS. Besides possibly the Todas, we uncovered only one other culture where group marriage was significant. In the jungles of Brazil live the semimigratory Kaingang. The Kaingang permit both polygyny and polyandry as well as their combination into a form of group marriage. Nevertheless, over an entire century only 8 percent of marriages involved two or more men *and* two or more women. Polygyny and polyandry were about equally common, yet 60 percent of all marriages involved only one man and one woman.[9] But at least among the Kaingang group marriage was more than a theoretical consideration.

The inadequacy of the available ethnographic data cannot be known, and there may have been any number of other societies which practiced group marriage on a significant scale.

One culture which probably did *not* practice group marriage was the Kamilaroi. The Kamilaroi, Kurnai, and other Australian aboriginal societies were among those purported to practice group marriage and on whom attention focused in the nineteenth century.[10] Study of these societies was complicated by the fact that the cultures appeared to have been changing even as they were being studied. Missionaries took their usual cultural toll. Forms of address suggested remnants of earlier relationships no longer practiced. The debate centered on whether the Kamilaroi and others evidenced survival of earlier primitive promiscuity.

The debate ended when Malinowski as an absentee anthropologist reanalyzed the many confusing and conflicting reports.[11] His incisive argument hinged on pointing out the obvious. He maintained that sexual access is not the same as marriage. Under certain circumstances the aboriginal *pirrauru* relationship granted sexual access outside a marital pair to members of well-defined groups in a tribe. Marriage, Malinowski maintained, is much more than sexual access, even if sexual access is socially sanctioned.

The Kamilaroi, it turns out, permitted a restricted, somewhat ritualized form of wife-lending, similar to that of the (now) better known Eskimos. In fact, socially approved forms of extramarital sex are far from rare. Ford and Beach report[12] that 39 percent of the 139 societies in the sample available to them openly approved of extramarital sexual liaisons; 13 percent had essentially no barriers to sexual relationships other than incest taboos. But in one out of five of those societies where extramarital sex is officially taboo, it is common and not seriously punished. Thus more than half of the cultures are actually permissive, regardless of the form of marriage. *Only one in twenty cultures is monogamous and wholly disapproves of both premarital and extramarital sex.* Most cogent is the fact that even within the most restrictive, punitive societies, men and women do engage in premarital and extramarital sexual relations.

MARRIAGE. Malinowski was right, of course, but if sex isn't marriage, what is? That question has bedeviled many a sociologist, anthropologist, and psychologist. To define, or even to characterize, marriage in just the United States is a substantial though not impossible task. The real problem is coming up with a definition that holds across cultures and across time, that covers the Nayar woman's *sambadham* relationship with several men as well as her *tali* relationship with the "father" of her children, that includes Western Europe and the jungles of Brazil, and that will not be superseded by a new definition next year. Legalistic definitions fail for cultures governed without laws, for societies in transition like the Todas, for subcultures like those of the Nayars and the contemporary "gay" community that run counter to their culture, and for "deviant" forms of marriage. Even a minimal sociological definition of marriage would not be applicable to all cultures. In most cultures, marriage includes sharing a common residence, sexual cohabitation, division of labor, and rights in regard to children, yet numerous exceptions to each of these factors can be found.

An adequate, unbiased definition of marriage becomes painfully necessary in any attempt to study a form of marriage that deviates significantly from the norms of a society. Recurring evidence indicates that some Mormons today still enter into polygynous marriages.[13] But what makes a polygynous union in Utah a marriage if it is secret, illegal, officially disavowed even by the Church of Jesus Christ of the Latter-day Saints? Ultimately we may only find out if Josiah is married to both Sarah and Mary by asking them all.

What finally defines marriage is the perceptions of the participants. Social definition and approbation are important but secondary considerations. Marriage is a relationship between individuals in which one person sees himself or herself as committed or bonded to another in a significant way involving some degree of intimacy and assumptions of continuance. Two people are married if, and only if, they perceive themselves to be married—that is, committed in this or an analogous manner. This phenomenological approach is useful in numerous dilemmas though it may appear to be lacking in all objectivity. Should the county courthouse burn down and with it the only copy of your marriage certificate, the phenomenological definition of marriage would seem mighty attractive. It might enable you to discern whether your son and his girl friend are married or just living together. ("Well, son, are you?")

For us, it permits the researching of group marriages in a culture that does not recognize or permit them, while at the same time separating marriages from reporters' fantasies, communes, and mate-swapping parties. Of course, in most cases law, custom, and neighbors all agree; but if in doubt, you ask:

"I see, ma'am, that you just had intercourse with that young man over there. The one with the drink. Are you married to him?"

"Him? Oh no, I've only seen him once before at a swinging party. That's my husband over there, on top of the brunette."

MEN ARE . . . Dorothy Parker is credited with the verse: "Hoggamus, higgamus/ Man is polygamous;/ Higgamus, hoggamus/ Woman's monogamous!" There is no doubt widespread belief in this doggerel declaration. Certainly we socialize women more forcefully into a monogamous norm. It is essential to realize that almost every culture at all times through human history has been male-dominated. Even among matrilineal societies, control is generally exercised by a woman's brother. Polyandry essentially has permitted a woman to take on more than one master. While many cultures permit married women to have sexual relations with men other than her husband, this is often institutionalized as a form of wife-lending. The husband determines where, when, and with whom.

It may be difficult to gain insight into the innate sexual propensities of men and women, but it is not hard to see how male determination and androcentrism in cultural patterns mask and distort the underlying sexual nature. Scientific research which illuminates merely the male-determined surface may only serve to perpetuate the distortions. There are now enough data to say that the double standard dealing with male premarital permissiveness and female virginity is declining, and behavior and standards of behavior for both sexes are converging.[14] Girls, it was long believed, participate in sex for different reasons than do boys. Girls need or want affection and sex together in a committed, ongoing context; boys want sex for its own sake. As standards converge, girls are engaging in sex for reasons once attributed to boys—for fun or curiosity, for example.

Our only hope of transcending these limitations placed on women is to see what happens when men and women are not so differentially socialized or when restraints are removed. We reported Ford and Beach's conclusion at the opening of this chapter; given the opportunity, women are as polygamous as men. The data on the Kaingang, which permit both multiple husbands and multiple wives, would seem to support this. Polygyny was about as frequent as polyandry. We need not go far away for confirming evidence, however. In our own society are permissive subcultures in which female sexuality and interest in a variety of partners are validated. There, too, Ford and Beach's conclusion is borne out.

To be fair, even these data do not necessarily mean that both men and women are about equally polysexual. All that may be indicated is how highly plastic, how modifiable, human sexual nature is. In any event, however, the Parker postulate of sex differences is called into question.

In almost all polygamous cultures, rivalry and friction between spouses of the same sex are reportedly high. Among the Toda, for example, men may resent having to share a wife. The preferred form of marriage is for brothers to share a wife; within these so-called fraternal marriages rivalry is virtually unknown.[15] In fact, a marked preference for sororal (sister) or fraternal marriages is very common in polygamous societies.

Such marriages are seen as happier and more stable than non-fraternal or nonsororal ones. There is a clue here to understanding the form of group marriage being tried in the United States today. It is in the interpersonal bond that exists between the Toda brothers as much as between each of them and their common wife.

On the basic frameworks of monogamy, polygyny, polyandry, and group marriage, human societies have built elaborate cultural systems. More often than not, whole cultures have chosen multiple mates as the preferred form. Yet without selective infanticide or a very large unmarried population, no culture can maintain polygamous marriages for other than a select minority. If, as the data suggest, both men and women prefer to have more than one sexual partner, and will even violate cultural proscriptions to have them, restrictive monogamy hardly seems the solution.

Inarguably, group marriage is more complicated, hence less likely as a marital pattern than either monogamy or polygamy. It *is* a pattern which provides for multiple sexual involvement within committed ongoing relationships. It is intrinsically symmetric with respect to the sexes and is compatible with the ratio in which males and females are born. In a cross-cultural perspective on human marriage, it makes a good deal of sense, though it has rarely been observed. With the inclusion of new interpersonal elements, group marriage and related structures may very well be viable in twentieth-century America.

REFERENCES

1. M. F. Nimkoff, *Comparative Family Systems* (Boston: Houghton Mifflin, 1965) p. 17.
2. Clellan S. Ford and Frank A. Beach, *Patterns of Sexual Behavior* (New York: Harper and Row, 1951), p. 125.
3. Joan P. Mencher, "The Nayars of South Malabar," in Nimkoff, *op. cit.*; and Claude Lévi-Strauss, "The Family," in Arlene S. and Jerome H. Skolnick, *Family in Transition* (Boston: Little, Brown, 1971).
4. Lévi-Strauss, *op. cit.*
5. George P. Murdock, "World Ethnographic Sample," *American Anthropologist* 59, 3 (August 1957).
6. Nimkoff, *op. cit.*, p. 18.
7. Lévi-Strauss, *op. cit.*
8. *Ibid.*, p. 55.
9. J. Henry, cited in Ford and Beach, *op. cit.*, p. 116.
10. L. Fison and A. W. Howitt, *Kamilaroi and Kurnai: Group Marriage and Relationship* (New York: Humanities Press, 1967; reprint of 1880 edition).
11. Bronislaw Malinowski, *The Family Among the Australian Aborigines* (New York: Schocken Books, 1969; reprint of 1913 edition).
12. Ford and Beach, *op. cit.*, p. 121.
13. See "Americana: The Whispered Faith," *Time*, October 11, 1971.
14. For differential analysis comparing Scandinavian and American trends, see Harold T. Christensen, "Scandinavian vs. American Sex Patterns," *Sexual Behavior* 1, 9 (December 1971).
15. Ford and Beach, *op. cit.*, p. 121.

3

New Ways, New Whys

When society has problems the family is among the first scapegoats.[1] The family has never been unimportant. A retailoring or radical change in the family system has figured in virtually every utopian scheme from Plato's *Republic* through Skinner's *Walden Two*.[2] Modern Western civilization places an unprecedented responsibility on the family, especially on the marriage around which the family is built. A marriage was once considered successful if the partners were civil and fulfilled minimal preordained responsibilities to each other while raising their children to adulthood. Now couples expect to feel happy and fulfilled, to enjoy an exciting sex life, to grow through the marriage toward realization of their full individual potential, and to raise successful and emotionally healthy children—all this riding on two ordinary human beings.

Nostalgia over days when men and women (especially women) had to believe themselves happy with less than their human birthright would be misplaced. High goals are not necessarily bad, but they do strain marriage as a traditional system. A society which expects so much from marriage can anticipate more breakups and, increasingly, creative experimentation in attempts to make existing marriages more fulfilling, even when this means violation of cherished family ideals. In our scientific age, experimentation is considered an essential component of progress; yet, ironically experimentation associated with marriage and family life is anathema.

High marital expectations, irrespective of content, can be expected to lead to breakdown and experimentation with new forms. America is simultaneously moving toward acceptance and facilitation of divorce and toward tolerance of variations in lifestyle. High personal expectations from marriage comprise the general force, while liberalized divorce procedures and increasing cultural pluralism are the enabling milieu.

More specific cultural and individual forces are also operating. A real sense of isolation and alienation was cited in the first chapter as common in contemporary families. In an immediate framework, the perception of isolation tends to fulfill itself. But people are innately gregarious; and eventually the rising tension of alienation and isolation, whether real or imagined, must lead to attempts at amelioration. Eventually people alone seek other people; people out of contact seek contact; walled-up people try to break down the walls.

The drive toward full realization of individual potential is both an active force in changing family patterns and a modifier of attempts to compensate for, or eliminate, alienation and isolation. An orientation toward personal growth dictates somewhat the mode of action taken in breaking out of the traditional nuclear monogamous pattern.

Changing ethics of human relations mediate the process of innovation while at the same time accelerating it. Equality in relations between men and women, long an intermittently honored ideal, may for the first time in human history become reality for significant numbers of people.

Freer, more humanistic sexual ethics have a culture-wide impact. The accelerative effects of legislative changes and the mass media cannot be ignored. Combined, sexual equalitarianism and sexual freedom form a most powerful agent for change in marriage and family structure.

SWING LOW. The earliest rumblings of significant purposive departures from traditional marital patterns came in the mid-fifties with rumors of organized mate-swapping. "Men's" magazines—and later special publications devoted to the subject—served to identify the phenomenon, to spread the word, and to act as vehicles for communication among participants. Unintentionally, staid publications became proselytizers even in their pejorative exposés, for the appeal of free sexual exchange tapped deeply felt desires for a variety of sexual partners. For many reasons—among them, the media of publicizing, the emphasis on participation by couples, and the appeal to a bored or disenchanted group—the early participants appear to have been largely lower-middle and mid-middle class couples, married for some time. Only much later, in the mid-sixties, did anything like sexual mate-exchange catch on among younger or single people in the form of the Sexual Freedom League.

No real data on that early period are available. Dr. Gilbert Bartell, an anthropologist whose full report on this phenomenon appeared in 1971,[3] admits to being aware of social mate-swapping in 1957, but he and his colleagues dismissed the subject. Not until 1966 did a serious, though flawed, study of swapping appear.[4]

Today's social mate swappers prefer to use the euphemism "swinging"; consistent with our emphasis on reality as participants organize it, we, too, will use that term. Impact-conscious journalists (and not a few scientists) have been using the more jarring phrase "group sex." Unfortunately, that leaves no convenient term for active sex in a group, regardless of social context; hence it is an unfortunate usurpation.

Swinging may have been the earliest sizable departure from conventional monogamic patterns because its premise is so simple. Swinging is a social process. The participants, usually in couples, meet for parties or informal get-togethers and, after various ice-breaking processes, divest themselves of their clothes, and in two's, three's, or more, in the same or separate rooms, have sex. Allowing for considerable individual, class, and regional variation, sex is about all that is implied. The participant *need* not invest himself in any way except sexually.

Numerous studies of swinging have been published,[5] though if anything, the picture is more confusing than ever. It appears that there are several distinct subgroupings within swinging. Most research suggests that swingers tend to be conservative middle-class marrieds, conventional in every way save one—they screw at parties. Swinging is their form of recreation. Involvement on a non-sexual plane outside their marriages is discouraged. Various wild-guess estimates by otherwise responsible observers have placed the number of people involved in swinging at one or two million.

NET RESULTS. Some research suggests that many swingers gradually move from the uninvolved party-swinging into stable networks of close friends who share various interests and activities but also have sex together.[6] Intimate networks of families also come about by other processes. As an alternative to the conventional family, the intimate network was first proposed by the late Fred Stoller, pioneer of encounter groups.[7] Stoller's proposed networks did not include sexual intimacy but excluded little else.

Of course, most families have friends, even close friends, but it appears that few American couples are genuinely intimate with other couples. We once proposed a quick test for genuine intimacy in relationships between couples. Three of the most private, personal, and *important* things within families are sex, child-rearing, and fighting. But in today's society, if a couple starts quarreling, their visitors usually exit or pretend it isn't happening. It is an unwritten law to refrain from commenting on another couple's child-rearing—in their presence, that is. As for sex, to discuss openly, with both spouses present, one's sexual attraction to a neighbor is much worse by contemporary social standards than doing something about it on the sly. Few friendships are intimate in any interpersonal sense, much less sexually.

Intimate networks of families answer many of the issues raised in opening this chapter. Children who grew up in spontaneously formed networks often report the advantages of having alternate adults to whom they can turn.[8] Where parents can get concerned feedback on their parenting and where children can "run away across the street" for a few weeks when communication stalls, the whole prospect of parenthood and childhood brightens.

In other ways, voluntary intimate networks can fulfill many of the functions of extended families and close communities, providing, for example, alternate resources for temporary needs. Based on choice and involving families in similar stages of the family life cycle, intimate networks can avoid some of the tensions and resented obligations of the extended family based on blood ties.

NEIGHBORHOOD TO COMMUNITY. A commune might be thought of as an intimate network that lives together. Of all the "new ways" in family living, communes have received the most publicity, partly because of their association with younger people and the counterculture, and partly because of a few sensational examples. The Charles Manson of swinging has not yet been found.

One important difference between the commune and other family variants is the focus on the commune, the place, the group. A particular house may remain a commune even though the turnover rate in residents may be high. Group identity and group cohesion are especially important to the survival of the commune.

There are many variations from one commune to another. The number of people in a commune may be as low as five or as high as a hundred. Some participants are in their teens, some fifty and older, though the vast majority appear to be in their twenties. A commune may be a farming, student, political, religious, social-change, therapeutic, or expanded family commune. There are even urban communes made up wholly of professionals.[9] Community standards are not limited to specific marital status or one specific sexual ethic. Sexual practices range from celibacy to free sexual access among all adults. Marriage may be strictly monogamous, or a pattern of short-term, serial, one-to-one relationships may be followed. Often sexual involvement must be with outsiders (exogamy), especially in urban settings where individuals within the house relate much as do sisters and brothers. Of the myriad patterns which have been reported, the most common seem to be exogamy and serial monogamy.[10] Principal responsibility for the children is generally with the entire commune, but in practice lies ultimately with the biological mother, especially should the commune dissolve. The psychological boundaries that separate the commune from the rest of the world may be tight or loose, depending in part on the ethic of the commune vis-à-vis the entry of new members, in part on their skill or luck in defining their existence apart from the rest of the world. Loose boundaries make group cohesion harder to achieve.

The entering communard often finds himself having to reorient his values and practices, learning to share money, possessions, time, and space, for example. Commitment and responsibility may also be problems. Individual needs and desires in conflict with communal ones can result in the breakup of the commune or the exit of the individual.

Sociologist Rosabeth Kanter has noted that some of today's communes emulate the successful communes of the nineteenth century in many of the following ways: they center around common values, group activity, tasks, and goals; pairing off is discouraged (in free access, celibate, or exogamous patterns); children are separated from their parents and raised together by the entire commune (rather than by just the two parents); group rituals and celebration are practiced; there are encounter sessions ("mutual criticism"); property is owned and shared jointly, and goods are distributed equally; there is a central figure and the commune is organized and self-sufficient.[11]

In addition to the nineteenth-century-type of communes, Kanter identifies two new types: anarchistic communes and growth-and-learning communities. The anarchistic commune tends to lack pattern, rules, and group structure. "Do your own thing!" is the ethos. The boundary or separation between who is or is not a member is vague; work and economic support are voluntary. The paucity of commitment and group purpose makes this type of commune short-lived, and it often may not even meet the needs of the group or the individuals within it. Kanter considers the most successful type to be the growth-and-learning community, such as Esalen or Synanon. Encounter, personal growth, and learning form the purpose for members and a temporary community for others.

The anarchistic commune may temporarily meet some of the needs of its members regardless of its short duration (as in crash-pad communes). It has served fortuitously as a kind of halfway house for people who are disappointed with their past life or lifestyle and need or desire to reevaluate their lives and themselves.[12] Many have been rejected by a society which leaves them nowhere to go. For the separated or divorced, the commune may be a temporary practical solution to suddenly being alone. Many single communards are committed to a permanent lifestyle, but others see it as a temporary situation to be replaced by a conventional monogamous marriage.

The number of people living in communes or interested in such a lifestyle is mushrooming. As a result, organizations have been formed such as New Community Projects in Boston,* which serves as clearinghouse, information center, and facilitator in self-awareness, and as a resource for people involved in or interested in alternative lifestyles, but especially communes.

THE OPEN END. In a 1970 address before the National Council on Family Relations, clergyman Ronald Mazur referred to couples who, as an integral part of their marriage, valued and were open to intimate interpersonal involvement with others.[13] His phrase "open-ended marriage" became a buzzword for the entire conference, entering the lexicon almost immediately. Such marriages admit into the marriage an open-ended series of alternate involvements without prior assumptions or limitations on depth of intimacy. The O'Neills' book, *Open Marriage*, appears to embody some of the same concepts.

In practice, most open-ended marriages find the partners sexually intimate in the alternate relationships, though this is not necessarily an expectation. What is valued are interpersonal elements of alternate relationships; sex is an enjoyable side effect.

This pattern, because it is based on the conventional marital dyad, unimbedded in either a large community or an unwieldy network, is probably more compatible with today's mobile, rapidly changing lifestyles. Like the intimate network, but unlike communes, the open-ended marriage avoids the day-to-day difficulties of numbers of adults living in close proximity. No estimates of the frequency of open-ended marriage are available, but some of the young marrieds in an National Institute of Mental Health (NIMH) panel were found to hold at the time of marriage an ethos which could be described as open-ended.[14]

* New Community Projects, 302 Berkeley Street, Boston, Massachusetts.

Because they augment and are integral to an open-ended marriage, these alternate involvements are sometimes referred to as comarital relations. The Roys, in their book *Honest Sex*, were among the first to distinguish comarital from extramarital relations.[15] Extramarital relations as practiced in most countries today are truly *outside* the marriage. In an open-ended marriage, husband and wife often share a mutual interest in and intimate friendship with the same people. A husband's best friend may come over for dinner and lively three-way conversation, go bowling with the husband, then enjoy sex with the wife, all as accepted aspects of their close trilateral friendship.

THE AGREEMENT. The open-ended marriage pattern should be distinguished from another practice which may at first appear to be identical. This is the "agreement" which sophisticated couples may have permitting both husband and wife to indulge separately in extramarital relations. Basically this is "Affairs are okay, but I don't want to hear about yours and I won't tell you about mine. Anything goes as long as you don't bring them here and screw in our bed." Such relationships, even though mutually agreed upon, remain outside the marriage, not a part of the shared experience of the couple. This pattern is best termed "consensual adultery."

Consensual adultery is more compatible with the older American ethic of not talking (at least not at home) about one's sexual relations. It is more likely to appeal to an older group, while open-ended marriage is more likely to be attractive to younger people or to anyone placing a premium on congruence of word and deed.

Of course individual marriages may fall somewhere between open-ended marriage and consensual adultery in the lifestyle they find most personally satisfying, but these are the major trends.

THE MANY-SIDED MARRIAGE. The relationships between members of an intimate network or within the intimate friendships associated with an open-ended marriage may become so close that individuals feel as if they were married to more than one person. A multilateral marriage consists of *three* or more partners, each of whom considers himself/herself to be married (or committed in a functionally analogous way to more than one of the other partners. If each of the "married" relationships is represented by a line, the whole marriage is a many-sided or multilateral figure, hence the name "multilateral marriage."[16]

Group marriage has a long-established definition; it is a marriage of at least *four* people, two female and two male, in which each partner is married to all partners of the opposite sex. Group marriages are thus also multilateral marriages. We reluctantly coined the term "multilateral marriage" to include as a single phenomenon, *all* multiperson marriages in which no partner was monogamously related. Multilateral marriage does not specify the numbers of each sex as does group marriage, hence a four-person relationship of one woman and three men would be a multilateral relationship if each of the men considered himself to be married to the woman and committed in an analogous way to at least one of the other men. If this foursome included only marriagelike relationships between the woman and each man, it would be a polyandrous marriage.

Our initial intent in foisting this neologism on the world was to include triads—three-person multilateral relations—with group marriage, for we were finding them to be closely related contemporary phenomena rather than fundamentally different forms as the terms "polygamy" and "group marriage" suggest. Much the same people were involved for the same reasons and facing many of the same problems.

The fine (or not so fine) distinction is best illustrated by contrasting classic polygyny (multiple wives) with a male-female-female multilateral marriage, a triad. It is the polygynously married man and he alone who marries an additional wife. No commitment or even relationship between the wives is assumed; wives often compete. In some cultures the wives even reside in separate houses. In the contemporary triad there is a strong relationship between the two cowives, and all three partners enter as equals into the relationship. A decision to marry yet another person to make it a foursome, which sometimes happens, would have to be by consensus.

Multilateral marriage is the most extreme form of emerging family patterns. It combines interpersonal intimacy and sexual intimacy with living together and multidimensional involvement in each other's lives—all in the context of an intense, essentially marital, commitment. It is a highly unlikely form of marriage from the standpoint of American history. Why, then, multilateral marriage now?

FICTION. Do men make the times or do the times make the men? Probably the men and the times come together to make the times and the men. Fiction is often the meeting ground of men and times. In 1961 an unlikely piece of science fiction appeared, unlikely because in the virtually sexless science-fiction genre it fairly dripped of sex and because it came from that conservative dean of science fiction, Robert A. Heinlein. *Stranger in a Strange Land*, a rich, space-age *Candide* was immediately heralded as a science-fiction classic. Though many elements contribute to its continued popularity, what stands out in most readers' minds is the protagonist's matter-of-fact assumption that sex is a way of sharing and growing closer and that one can—and should—grow closer to many people. Valentine Michael Smith could be forgiven; after all, he was born and raised on Mars, but many readers took his profoundly naïve, maybe even correct, outlook seriously.*

The Harrad Experiment, a novel by Robert H. Rimmer first appearing in Bantam paperback in early 1967, has had an even greater influence on the course of marriage and man-woman relationships. Though Rimmer undoubtedly did not start the sexual revolution, an accolade conferred on him in one television appearance, his utopian novels dealing with multiple sexual relationships[17] have certainly not held back the "revolution."

The Harrad Experiment established a fictional experimental college in the Boston area whose facilities consisted of a coeducational dorm with male-female roommates and a gymnasium in the Greek sense of the word, that is, where participants wore no clothes. The coed living and an integral, somewhat pedantic "Human Values Seminar" were intended to open students to new

---

* Ironically, for Heinlein's fiction leans toward pragmatic agnosticism, the "religion" founded by protagonist Valentine Michael Smith has been actually implemented as the Church of All Worlds, joining with Feraferia and others as part of the neo-pagan movement. Neo-paganism's main elements seem to be affirmation of life, identification with nature, and atavistic ritual. The Church of All Worlds publishes *The Green Egg* (Church of All Worlds, P.O.Box 2953, St. Louis, Missouri 63130).

possibilities in authentic human relations. By graduation time, the three male and three female protagonists had formed a group marriage of sorts which they christened "In-Six."

The effect of Rimmer's novels may have been due to format as much as to radical subject matter. Each of the three novels which were related to multilateral marriage, though clearly marked "fiction," was written as if the events described were real, hitherto unrevealed happenings. The secret Harrad College and its sponsoring foundation seemed plausible. Many otherwise rational people, their credulity magnified by their fantasies and desire to believe, wrote to Rimmer on the assumption that he was the gatekeeper for access to a world of coed dorm rooms and financial *deus ex machina* with which to underwrite experiments in multiple relationships. The formula continues to work moderately well for Rimmer and has even been imitated.[18]

Rimmer is a novelist whose vantage point is a sizable volume of correspondence with fans and readers. We feel that his fact-mimicking style has sometimes promulgated personal views about the functioning of multiple relationships which do not appear to be valid generalizations from available data. We will have later occasions to contrast fact and fiction.

Almost all of our early contacts and most later ones reported that Rimmer's novels, notably *The Harrad Experiment*, played some role in leading to their actual involvement. Most often, the novel served as an object of discussion, an excuse for talking about threatening new ideas rather than as a progenitor. Of course, for many people talk was never actualized; but for others, the intellectual interest emerging from deeper sources was eventually transmuted into a more emotional commitment.

So significant were the Rimmer and Heinlein novels in serving as releasing mechanisms (or such was the masterful timing) that we have been unable to trace the start of experimentation with actual group marriages prior to 1966. No group in the primary study was formed before 1967 and with a single exception we have been unable to verify any earlier experimentation.*

---

* We regard multilateral marriage as a discrete, twentieth-century phenomenon of recent origins, largely unrelated to utopian group marriage of the last century. The case will be clear from the remainder of the book.

The one verified earlier attempt at a group marriage occurred under circumstances which suggest that there were undoubtedly other isolated experiments, though almost certainly not a general pattern. The group consisted of two young couples and lasted for about six months in 1952. The husbands were both graduate students, studying under the GI Bill. Apartment- or house-sharing arrangements were common in those circumstances, and many led to very close friendships. This one led to a stormy sexual involvement as well. Probably there have been many intimate marriage-like groups growing from the propinquity of similar practical conditions. What makes the present unique in Western history is that alternate marital styles, especially multilateral marriages, are being deliberately sought in a definite pattern rather than as the chance result of isolated events.

The emergence of alternative marriage structures at present is a self-conscious process involving no small numbers of people. This is true even for multilateral marriage, probably the most extreme and consequently the rarest emerging family form. In a survey among readers of *Psychology Today*[19] twenty thousand respondents reported their attitude toward group marriage. Approximately a quarter were either in favor of group marriage or thought they might be interested; nearly a third of the men responded in these categories. Large, active interest groups for people exploring multilateral and expanded family relations have sprung up in Boston, New York, Washington, D.C., Los Angeles, and San Francisco.

What is not known is the actual incidence of multilateral marriages. We have located group marriages throughout the United States and find them to be on the increase. If groups we have identified constituted even as much as 10 percent of all multilateral marriages in the country (and this is highly doubtful), that would represent about a thousand groups. It does not seem likely that there could be as many as ten thousand multilateral marriages without more confrontations with the law and community. A number closer to one thousand is our estimate for early 1972.

Multilateral marriage embodies so many of the attributes found in other alternatives that it is an almost ideal territory for the exploration of the effects of the various attributes of interest.

REFERENCES

1. Reported in M. F. Nimkoff's *Comparative Family Systems*.
2. Behaviorist B. F. Skinner's novel, *Walden Two* (New York: Macmillan, 1960), concerns a utopia implemented through behavior modification; it has become a popular model among some communards and a few group-marriage participants.
3. Gilbert Bartell, *Group Sex: A Scientist's Eyewitness Report on the American Way of Swinging* (New York: Peter H. Wyden, 1971).
4. A somewhat sensationalistic work which nevertheless appears to be based on more than casual observation, *Swap Clubs* by William and Jerrye Breedlove (Los Angeles: Sherbourne Press, 1964)
5. Basic references would be Bartell's *Group Sex*, and reports by Denfeld and Gordon, O'Neill and O'Neill, Smith and Smith in *Journal of Sex Research 6*, 2 (May 1970). The unpublished masters theses of Carolyn Symonds ("Pilot Study of the Peripheral Behavior of Sexual Mate Swappers," University of California at Riverside, 1968), and Charles Varni ("An Exploratory Study of Wife-swapping," San Diego State, 1970) present important views of different types of swingers.
6. This is the thesis of the Palsons, whose anthropologically oriented observations are reported in "Swinging in Wedlock," *Society 9*, 4 (February 1972).
7. Stoller, F. H., "The Intimate Network of Families," in Herbert Otto's collection *The Family in Search of a Future* (New York: Appleton-Century-Crofts, 1970).
8. From personal communications with now-grown members of several such networks.
9. Jay Molishever, "A Commune, Professional Style," *Boston Sunday Globe*, May 16, 1971.
10. Larry L. and Joan M. Constantine, "Group and Multilateral Marriage: Definitional Notes, Glossary, and Annotated Bibliography," *Family Process 10*, 2 (June 1971).
11. Rosabeth Kanter, "Communes," *Psychology Today 4*, 2 (July 1970).
12. Robert Houriet, *Getting Back Together* (New York: Coward, McCann and Geohagan, New York, 1971).
13. Mazur's plenary address, "Beyond Morality: Toward the Humanization of the Sexes" is a still unpublished but eloquent exploration of new-style relationships.
14. J. S. Kafka, R. Ryder, and D. Olson, "A Nonconventional Pattern within the Conventional Marriage Framework"; unpublished research report, NIMH, 1969.
15. Della and Rustum Roy, *Honest Sex* (New York: New American Library, 1968).
16. Larry and Joan Constantine, "Group and Multilateral Marriage: Definitional Notes, Glossary, and Annotated Bibliography," *op. cit.*

17. *The Harrad Experiment* (Los Angeles: Sherbourne Press, 1966). *The Rebellion of Yale Marratt* (Boston: Challenge Press, 1964) concerns a triad of one man and two women. *Proposition 31* (New York: New American Library, 1968) is a novel about two couples who form a multilateral marriage. Rimmer's latest, *Thursday My Love*, (New York: New American Library, 1972) proposes a structured, legally recognized form of extramarital affair.

18. Henry Sackerman's book *The Westbank Group* (Los Angeles: Sherbourne Press, 1970) is blatantly imitative sexploitation. The "plot" concerning a seven-person group marriage merely provides excuses for chapter after chapter of vividly described group sexual activities.

19. Athanasiou, *et al.*, "Sex," *Psychology Today* 4, 2 (July 1970).

PART II

STUDY

4

A Study That Wasn't

Eventually, the intellectual interest launched by a Rimmer novel takes off and the "alternative family structure" that was once theory becomes for a few people reality. As they embark, or having stepped offshore and slipped, the travelers of this marital underground often look around anxiously for well-wishers, seasoned travelers, tour guides, or even an heroic captain.

For us, too, there came a point when we turned to sources outside ourselves, hoping to learn—and understand—more about one particular alternative; multilateral marriage.*

A literature search turned up nothing, save a few largely philosophical papers from a 1966 meeting of the American Psychological Association.[1] We would have to find out from participants themselves. A scattered, *ad hoc* sort of organization had accreted among correspondents of Rimmer, producing the aptly named forum, the *Harrad Letter*, and a series of formless meetings in the New England area. Until it faded from existence, this never-

---

* We prefer the term "multilateral marriage" for the technical reasons given in the preceding chapter, but others also use "group marriage" to refer to this broader phenomenon. Informally, we tend to use them interchangeably.

named nonorganization served a vital function, making potential and actual group-marriage participants aware of each other and providing a means for their meeting. Through them, we contacted the first few bona-fide multilateral marriages with whom to talk.

Though no research results had entered the literature, we thought that perhaps professional research was underway. While seeking groups with whom to meet we also sought active researchers. Consistent rumors led us to one California psychologist. He was not doing research, but did seem to consider our unstructured probings worthy of a colloquium under the aegis of a local professional organization. Although that group withdrew its support of so controversial a topic, the colloquium was held on schedule in La Habra, California. Awed by the prospect of a closed meeting of marriage and family professionals, we drafted a "position paper" setting out what was then a somewhat inflated view of our undertaking.[2]

That night, a respected social psychologist led off the questioning. Memory blurs all but a few phrases, something about "batteries of standard psychometrics" and "results that reach statistical significance." Utterly unprepared, we felt devastated by the onslaught of questions. The colloquium experience was only the first of many encounters with the pros, the public, the potential participants, and the partners in multilateral marriages turning to us as resources. With no one else in sight to take over, we took the plunge, committing ourselves to a major but unspecified undertaking. The essential skills and background we would build as we went along; where totally blocked by inadequate credentials or lack of competence, we would turn for feedback and help to those with the requisite skills.

BIAS. All scientists are biased when it comes to the subject of their researches. Some admit it, some don't. We were uncomfortably aware that our personal experience and our interest in multilateral marriage left us open to fooling ourselves as well as others about the objectivity of any study which we might conduct. We wanted to be sure we knew why we were tackling the project and what we were after; and we wanted our motivations to be open to scrutiny by those who would have to use the results. Most important, we wanted it clear that the research was in service of a larger vision rather than a pointless pursuit of knowledge for its own sake.

Ours is a personal vision of a changed society, one which will offer to our two daughters as they approach young adulthood, not the constricted choice of saying Yes or No to marriage, but an open-ended array of options out of which each can structure a uniquely suited, personal, family lifestyle. We are deeply committed to increasing the acceptance and viability of alternative lifestyles in this society. Knowledge is an instrument of that change. Before individuals and societies can use options, they must know what their options are and what the consequences of taking them will be.

Unlike many entrenched family scientists, we have no stake in the status quo, nor does our personal morality compel us to reject new marital and sexual patterns. We have nothing to sell, neither monogamy nor multilateral marriage. Our interest is in cultural pluralism, and we become adamant only in asserting the *rights* of people to be married conventionally at St. Marks, or to shack up in a homosexual group, or to shun humanity altogether.

INSIDE. The amorphous group around the *Harrad Letter* had no shortage of group-marriage talkers, some of whom met their matches through the group and later became doers. But doers, even in that special-interest club, were few and far between. More often than not a rumored multilateral marriage turned out to be a multilateral marriage only in someone's fantasies. More than once a letter referred to a forming group which came as a surprise to some of the alleged participants when we followed up on the lead. Desire can be so strong that, like the farmer's wife counting eggs as chickens, the dreamed-of relationship is described as closer to reality than it is. Outsiders, too, project their fantasies onto real people and see group marriages where there are none. And a relationship may be real but still be a different relationship to each person involved. We learned the importance of getting individual, private perceptions as a counterpoint to group pronouncements and as absolutely preferable to having only one person's account. One of the earliest rules of the research was that *all* members of a group had to agree to full cooperation, at least in principle.

To illustrate, we once received a letter from a middle-aged woman asking us to visit her group marriage, a foursome, in our next travels. During the visit, her husband described their relationship as "forming." The other man saw a future potential for a group marriage but felt they were definitely short of that. The second woman, recently divorced, responded quite forcefully when asked if she considered herself in a group marriage: "No way! Not group marriage, not any marriage, not marriage! Never again."

TRIPS. But real multilateral marriages did turn up. As we became known, they even began to seek *us* as the only source of factual information. In three years we received more than three thousand letters. We followed up on every clue, such as multiple names on a check and others more subtle. The groups that surfaced were all over the country. They couldn't come to us; we had to go to them.

We hitched the lightest sixteen-foot travel trailer available behind our banged-up Volkswagen Squareback, loaded it with provisions, a couple of tape recorders, bales of disposable diapers, and set out for seven to nine weeks at a stretch, the trailer serving as motel, nursery, and research-center-on-wheels. In all we made six trips coast to coast; the trailer made three, covering more than thirty-two thousand miles. It outlived the VW and the differential of our next car. It would be nice to say we saw the country, but we only passed through it between one group of respondents and the next.

WHAT MONEY. We accepted the driving and roadside living—and sundry other research shortcuts—because there was no money for the project. In a period when whole departments full of Ph.D.'s were being denied funds for innocuous projects, we should hardly have expected foundation help.

Still, every month or so a letter arrives from someone who has heard of our work. Inside will be a check, $10, $15, occasionally more, along with a note saying, "I like what you are doing, keep up the good work!" And we ask for cost-plus donations for the thousands of preprints and offprints we have distributed. But the bulk of the research cost has come out of our pockets.*

On the positive side, we learned how to do good research cheaply. For interviewing, a $40 tape recorder is almost as good as a $100 one. With a pocket calculator and some file cards which have holes drilled in them, one can do almost as well as with a computer, provided one is willing to keep at it until 3:00 A.M.

The financial issue is not just relevant to our bank. In itself, financial limitations reduced the options available to us in terms of the size and scope of the study and the sophistication of the procedures of investigation and analysis. The lack of outside funding also meant we could not devote full time to the research. At this writing six additional intact multilateral marriages have indicated an interest in participating in the Study Project, but there is neither the time nor the money to include them and thus increase the primary sample by 50 percent. Research controls in the form of people of similar age and socioeconomic background from conventional families would have greatly enhanced the meaningfulness of the study, but would have nearly doubled the cost. In one file cabinet is a thick manila folder of interesting hypotheses and possible relationships which could be tested based on the data in hand, but which would take prohibitive amounts of time with the available analytical methods. We anticipate a great deal of legitimate scientific criticism for things which could be no other way because they were economically rather than scientifically dictated. What the study is, it is, for whatever reasons, and we shall let this matter rest.

CREDENTIALS. We are not conventionally credentialed family professionals, and no purpose is served by glossing over that point. Before making a complete commitment to the research project we gave considerable thought to our qualifications and the effect they would have on the outcome and acceptability of our research. We finally judged that we could do the type of work contemplated and

* Rent, groceries, and research were paid for through Larry's "other career" as a computer consultant, which, though it meant as many hours as any job, allowed him to "package" his time differently, with eight-week holes into which field trips could be squeezed.

that the project itself would have to stand or fall on its own merit, serving in a sense as our credentials. We structured our own training program on-the-fly but rejected the tedious traditional academic route as inefficient and in many respects irrelevant.

Hardly a presentation of ours closes without someone challenging our qualifications. Yet there are more than a few recognized professionals in the family field who have accepted us as colleagues. And some who have not. For the real professionals we are really no problem, as they can personally assess the work we have done. For the public, though, a dilemma remains. We recognize credibility as an essential intervening variable in the process of communication. But in the end, we do not know what to do about it except to disclose what we have found and, risking tedium, explain why we did things as we did.

REFERENCES

1. These papers were eventually published in Herbert Otto's collection, *The Family in Search of a Future* (New York: Appleton-Century-Crofts, 1970).
2. A revised version was later presented at the 1970 Annual Meeting of the Indiana Council on Family Relations and was reprinted in Robert Rimmer's *You and I Searching for Tomorrow* (New York: Signet, 1971). A condensed version appeared in *Forum: The Journal of Interpersonal Relations*, 3, 9, (April 1970) in Great Britain and again in the American edition, 1, 1.

5

Methodology and Friends

Wₑ ᴡᴇʀᴇ in the next state before Joan discovered the small envelope in her purse. Larry was driving. "What is it?"

"It looks like a note from the A———s." She opened it. Wrapped in a slip of paper was a new $20 bill! "We wish this could be more. We wanted to help with your trip. We are all glad to be a part of what you are doing." There was a certain touching incongruity in the A———s' giving us money. It was a substantial gift, we knew, for more than once we had crowded around the kitchen table, rapping over coffee as Rita extricated the group from financial collapse by materializing a few extra dollars or delaying a time payment. Since when did research subjects kick in to help finance the research? Or consider themselves to be truly part of what the researchers were doing?

To us the A———s were not subjects in an experiment; they were people, and like quite a few other respondents in our research, they had become friends as well. We have held our breath while they worked through difficulty. We have shared and contrasted our very different worldviews with them, somehow finding a place for meeting and friendship in their conservatism and our radicalism. And we have celebrated with them, even if not always in their presence, as when they recently rejoined into a single household.

We are certain to be criticized for our human caring and personal involvement with respondents. Our scientific objectivity will be questioned, and rightfully so, for we are fully aware of the risks attendant to an open and involved relationship with respondents. We are subjective; we care about what we are researching; as we stated in the last chapter, we have strong feelings about our subject which emanate from our personal values.

It is essential to realize, however, that all research on human behavior is value oriented and subjective; objectivity, especially in areas of strong encounter with concepts of morality, is a myth. There are only two kinds of social-science researchers: those who acknowledge and state their personal values in relationship to what they are studying, and those who, though equally biased, claim objectivity.

The methodology for our study—the technical strategy for finding out what we wanted to know—grew first of all out of our strong personal morality, a humanistic sense of the ethical that is deeply ingrained in both of us and which long predates our research interest. In that sense, we did not make choices as to methodology, for many issues were dictated by a prior commitment to private ethics. We value and strive for honest and open relationships beyond the platitudinous, opportunistic, lip-service honesty of contemporary America. This, for example, meant for us a commitment not to use any research technique which depended on deception for its effectiveness, eliminating many popular and no doubt effective psychological strategems. Our earliest sense of what we were doing also included a dedication to make the research experience mutually worthwhile, to share information with those who helped us develop it, and to choose techniques with intrinsic value to respondents.

TRUST. To be candid, a significant part of what we did in the research grew out of our sense of inadequacy. From the beginning we were aware of our lack of formal qualification for research of the subtlety demanded by this project. We sharply delineated the limits of our abilities. We believed that to have access to the full range of personal information we would have to be trusted by respondents, because we felt incapable of devious derivation of the desired data even had we elected such methods.

Our thinking on trust was and remains rather simple. To learn the realities of multilateral marriage in depth, we needed to be really trusted; to be really trusted we needed to be not only trustworthy but trusting. Neither our trust nor theirs could be faked. Ancillary to our personal trustworthiness were issues of confidentiality. Various means of protecting identities and preserving confidence were worked out, including contingency plans for such unlikely events as the subpoena of our records. We have been just short of paranoid in avoiding chance identification of groups through us and in maintaining confidence. It goes without saying that all names used in this book are fictitious and all potentially identifying details have been altered. No unfragmented case descriptions are presented either, on the outside chance that even disguised material, in sufficient quantity, might lead to exposure of a group.

But the central outcome of our commitment to a trusting relationship was the process of trust-building itself. It is a complex and delicate process which is allowed to proceed at its own pace as much as the practical research realities permit. We start off by trying to get to know potential respondents as a group and as unique persons and to allow them to know us. We may spend an evening or two just rapping and a day hanging around. At the outset we make clear that we are available as resources to the group. We expose our expectations of them, our personal feelings about multilateral marriage, and what we see as the content of their participation. Thus we tell them that we see ourselves as being in a position of special and inviolable trust with respondents, that we will make every effort to make participation valuable to them by sharing information in a mutual learning experience.

Typically we have been interrogated by respondents who are justifiably concerned about our motives. Frequent early questions include: "Why are you doing this? What's in it for you?" "Who's footing the bill?" "Are you in a group marriage? Have you ever been?" "What have you learned so far? Do other groups do thus and so?" "How confidential is what we tell you? What will you do with it? Are you writing a book?" We have tried to answer these questions as openly and candidly as possible, even when they concern our "ulterior" purposes and personal involvement.

Scientifically, our straight-from-the-shoulder approach has been vindicated, though our original rationale was ethical rather than scientific. Sydney Jourard and others[1] have learned that self-disclosure by the experimenter does more than just alter the outcome; it facilitates spontaneous self-disclosure by subjects.

Openness and honesty were not just research techniques, but continuously demonstrated reality. Of course, we slipped sometimes. We knew that relationship had to precede research, that data, given in distrust even if obtainable, are less valuable than information given out of trust. But occasionally, to save time, we were tempted to cut corners.

The B———s were a group tucked away in middle America. It seemed important to get some written data from them, in case we could not make the trip into the heartlands. We sent them some questionnaires to complete before we met them "to save time," thus violating our own rule about first building trust.

The night we were finally to meet them, Joan was having a rough time and we decided that Larry would go alone. We still did not know why we hadn't received all the questionnaires back. Those we had were incomplete. Larry was apprehensive about the meeting. It went badly. Within a few minutes, the group announced that their "therapist" was coming over shortly, a bit of territorial behavior serving to protect their boundaries as a group and to express their distrust of us. It was soon learned that the group had found various parts of the questionnaire threatening or offensive. There were specific, real differences of opinion and philosophy, but ultimately it came down to the fact that they didn't know us, trust us, or feel that they were involved in what we were doing. That was the last time we made an exception to our routine of building the relationship first.

PUBLIC, PRIVATE, AND PERSONAL. In most cases, as trusting relationships grew, we became aware of the multiple levels of respondents' experience that became accessible to us. The first of these we called the public level. At the public level are those group truths which a responding family, like all families, maintains in relation to outsiders. It is the image, real though not very deep or detailed, flawed in emphasis if not content, which a member of the group would be likely to relate in a letter to a public figure or in a discussion before an audience.

At the private level is that summary of experience that a family shares with itself and possibly with close friends. It is difficult to gain access to private meanings without a meaningful relationship or special privilege (such as a therapist or a researcher might have). Finally, there is a level of meaning which is personal and individual, feelings and perceptions which may not even be shared with one's family, conceivably not always acknowledged to oneself.

In a sentence, our entire methodology is an attempt to discover as much of the private and personal realities of multilateral marriage as possible while relating to respondents in a fair, honest, and human way.

QUESTION, QUESTION. The research goals are themselves subordinated to the goal of spreading understanding. Outside informational needs have often guided the design. When we were consistently asked certain questions which impressed us as being important to us or to others, but which could not be answered on the basis of our available data, we set about trying to find the answers. Sometimes these were simple matters of oversight. At one meeting of professional marriage counselors a man asked us, "I just want to know whether these people are happy with what they are doing. Do they like it?" It is such an obvious question, but in the welter of interactional observations, factual questions, and psychological investigations we had never asked it. So we went back and asked how happy they were. (Their answers are reported in Chapter 10.)

We began to identify different informational needs from different audiences. We were directing findings from the study to several distinct populations. Our obligation to those in or considering multilateral marriages came first, but professionals in service to the family—social workers, marriage counselors, clergymen, family therapists, psychologists, psychiatrists—were a close second. These professionals not only influence others concerning marriage and family relations but are in a position to help make attempts at new forms of marriage successful. Speaking to them is very different from meeting with a group of couples who would like to try group marriage or from addressing the general public. Professionals would often request numbers and test results while potential participants asked about feelings and experiences, yet both might be addressing the same issue. Thus we needed different kinds of data supporting the same conclusions, depending on the audience.

What eventually emerged was a philosophy of research which said that everything was data—had some information value—but which tried to cover every major area of inquiry from at least two independent sources. Thus we mixed the subjective and the objective, the personal and the impersonal, the firsthand and the secondhand. Letters, phone calls, and chats with groups added to the fund of knowledge. Questionnaires and tests were augmented by many hours of formal and informal observation. Carefully designed interviews with each individual were sometimes supplemented by the personal diaries that several respondents were willing to share with us. Wherever possible, we devised objective checks on our observations and impressions; thus the quantitative information requirements of professionals served to "keep us honest."

Another source of questions was our own respondents. In making participation a mutual, reciprocal process, we shared information with respondents in various ways. Informally we would pass on the experiences of others and our own distillations of many experiences. We also set a rule of sharing manuscripts with respondents, often early drafts of papers we were writing. This was a time-consuming and mechanically complicated procedure, for it meant retyping drafts onto mimeograph masters, copying and mailing, and then sometimes repeating the whole process for the version that finally went into print. Sometimes we slipped altogether, other times we were more than a little late; but we tried. This is a rare procedure in human research, to give or try to give "subjects" the first look at what came out of their participation. We suspect that much research in human behavior would be reported differently (and improved) if subjects saw the results and were permitted to comment. We gained much in this process, from editorial improvements, to additional data, to suggestions for new questions for investigation.

THE STUDY IS . . . We regard the most significant technical feature of the project to be our use of a precise definition of the phenomenon under study. We repeat here the definition given in Chapter 3.

> A multilateral marriage consists of three or more partners, each of whom considers himself/herself to be married (or committed in a functionally analogous way) to more than one of the other partners.

From this definition is derived a simple operational criterion for qualification as study respondents. Having established a relationship, we ask each member of the group privately, as the opportunity arises, to whom in the group he feels he has a real marital commitment. Each member must name at least two other members. Informality if not outright sloppiness in definitions and inclusion criteria mars much of the research on alternative lifestyles and virtually everything which has appeared on communes and group marriage.[2]

THE BASE STUDY. Following that first encounter with professionals in La Habra and based on the informal interviews that preceded it, we began to design some data-gathering procedures. Working with one group that was within easy reach, we developed and refined a set of questionnaires through several rounds, one for each adult participant and one for the group as a whole. These were not models of good research-instrument design, but their flaws were tolerable and they did deal with some basic facts as well as some issues of considerable subtlety. These questionnaires are summarized in Appendices III and IV.

The 151 items of the Individual Summary are divided into seven sections. These deal with (1) basic personal data (sex, occupation, education, etc.); (2) reasons for involvement; (3) problems in the group marriage; (4) sexual experience; (5) sexual encounters within the group; (6) preferences (sexual, trusting, etc.) for others in the group; (7) relationships with outsiders (friends, business acquaintances, parents, etc.). The sections on reasons and problems are long checklists which have proven to be quite comprehensive. Most of the problems in using the Individual Summary have had to do with the section on sexual experience (which lacks precision) and the one on preferences in the group.

From the very beginning, we have been interested in the *structure* of multilateral marriages, that is, how the various relationships within the group are defined and how they match and do not match. At one point we hoped to be able to relate group structure to group functioning, but this has proven to be much more difficult than it first appeared to be. The section on preferences and other structural data will have to be analyzed in some future project.

It is difficult to admit and express to an outsider that you love one person in your family more than others, that you would rather have sex with Anne than Candy, or that you trust Harold least of all. But such information can be highly revealing and even of considerable value as feedback to a group if it has been given with honesty. We do not know how trustworthy such data are but we do know that being asked can be very threatening. Several groups refused to furnish the information, including the Brookses mentioned earlier.

The B———s objected that such preferences were transient and changing and might be misconstrued as representing stable conditions. They also objected on what amounts to moral grounds, that they *should* all love each other equally and prefer each other equally as sexual partners. Their first point is well taken with respect to any element of data we collect, which is why we insist on repeated visits and continuing contact. Their second point, shared by a few others, will be taken up in detail in a later chapter.

The seven-page Family Summary covers the membership and history of the group, the economic structure of the group (how finances are handled), child-rearing and difficulties the children may have had, sexual structure and sleeping arrangements, and group relationships with the community.

The base study also used separate, individual tape-recorded interviews with each of the adult participants. These interviews did not use an elaborate interview schedule of questions. Instead, we had a series of subject areas on which we wanted to get each participant's personal views, as much as possible eliciting what they saw to be important in the way they organized their experience rather than imposing our organization. In some cases we hardly spoke during an hour-and-a-half interview, but as a rule we brought up each of the subject areas and asked the respondent to talk about it.

Except for introducing the subject areas, our approach was informal, conversational, intuitive, and nondirective. Hendin, Gaylin, and Carr and Cuber and Harroff have shown the power of similar interviews to elicit substantive data.[3] We found that having three to six separate "stories" all but guaranteed that most important aspects of group structure and functioning were included somewhere. Where interviews revealed conflicting or inconsistent pictures, we had data from other channels, plus our own accumulated personal understanding of the group, as a check.

We relied on our intuition when respondents were hesitant or appeared to be blocking (avoiding something), or when important elements were missing. While we do not subscribe to the basic subterfuge in Hendin's psychoanalytic interviews, two essential techniques of his we used extensively, namely, selective silence and alternate paths to the same elements. We developed a distinct technique in which we avoided filling pauses but felt free to probe into areas that the interviewee seemed to be skirting or which our intuition or other knowledge of the family suggested was important. By not compulsively filling silences with our own commentary or moving on to the next question, we found that respondents generally filled the silence by bringing up undiscussed issues they felt to be important.

Five areas were explored in the individual interviews: (1) how the individual sees the process which led him into a group marriage, including personal background and history considered relevant; (2) the greatest benefits and joys; (3) principal problems and disappointments; (4) feelings for/about each of the other participants; (5) the future, what is expected, what is hoped for.

Because interviews were conducted privately and generally only after some trust had been established, we found that very rich and detailed pictures of the multilateral-marriage experience were revealed, especially in terms of the different ways that partners in the same marriage could report the same situation. In many respects, the interviews and the observations have yielded the deepest insights into contemporary group marriages and form an unstructured counterpoint woven into the more quantitative reports of the rest of this book.

Direct "participant observation" forms the final component of the base study. For the short period of our visits we would try to join into the family much as close relatives might, participating in much of the daily routine of family activities. We slept in spare rooms or on a spare couch when there was space and in the trailer when there was not. We shared in cooking and new recipes and dish-washing, changed diapers, and sat through family fights. We got into the act with discing down a walnut orchard. When one family decided to go to a free beach, we went, and Joy (then two years old) joined their children and others romping confidently naked through waves of water and good vibrations. Larry chaperoned a van-load of kids through *Willard* and *The House That Dripped Blood*, enjoying himself despite some doubts about the filmic fare, but finding the kids delightful company.

In small parcels we learned through participation and observation what it was like in each family, how they communicated, how children and adults related, how conflicts were resolved and decisions made. The duration and timing of the observations was determined almost entirely by nonresearch restrictions. While Larry's consulting commitments permitted some flexibility, seven or eight weeks of field research was the most we could do at a shot. A typical stay with a family would last two and a half days, and we averaged three such visits spread out over an eighteen-month to two-year period.

SUBSTUDIES. Over the course of three years of research, eight separate substudies of respondents in the base study and others in multilateral marriage were designed and executed. These studies included a total of twenty-five pages of questionnaires and two standard personality inventories (totaling 375 pairs of items) for adults plus a complete battery of techniques for the children.

The *family background* substudy deals with facts of personal history in the families in which respondents were raised. Their religious and political orientation as children and at present are also explored. A substudy on *attitudes* conducted at the same time explores opinions on sex, love, marriage, and the law in such a way as to permit some comparisons with Athanasiou and Shaver's survey of readers of the magazine *Psychology Today*.[4]

To our own observations on the quality of the two-person marriages which respondents had when they entered the group-marriage relationship, we added a substudy of *marital adjustment and satisfaction*. Besides asking for self-evaluations of how happy they were with their marriages, we used a standard inventory to assess their present relationship and their retrospective evaluation of their relationship just prior to the group's formation. Included were further questions on the impact of the multilateral marriage on their sex lives.

Personality and interpersonal perception were investigated in an elaborate substudy employing a widely used personality "test" in a novel way. The instrument we used assesses the amount of a person's need for various things, such as the need for achievement and accomplishment or the need to have things orderly. But we were also interested in how aware respondents were of their own and each other's needs, in the hope of relating this to how well a given group functioned. At the same time, of course, a composite picture of personality was being developed which could be interpreted as part of the answer to the question of personal (internal) motivation for trying a multilateral marriage.

Another standard personality instrument was used in a substudy on *psychological health*. More than any other substudy, this one was a response to outside pressure. The general belief was that people must be "sick" to enter anything so "deviant" as multilateral marriage. This did not square with our observations, but our observations were challenged by professionals on the grounds that we were unqualified to make such evaluations. A standard inventory dealing with psychological health was utilized in this substudy.

The most ambitious of the substudies was not done alone. We worked with Angela Hunt of Iowa State University in an exploration of the self-concept of children whose parents had participated in a multilateral marriage. We wanted to learn how children saw their multilateral family and how, if at all, their self-concept, their family relationships, and their relationships with peers were affected by their parents' unusual marriage. Angela developed interviews and observation techniques especially for the study, and these were supplemented with a standard measure of development for preschoolers and a standard measure of personal adjustment for school-age youngsters. Rating scales were devised to permit all three of us to contribute to evaluation of the child-rearing styles and the role of the children in the various families.

Two substudies which deal with nonrespondents are not reported in detail in this book. The first is a brief survey of some sixty-odd reported group marriages which for various reasons could not be included in the base study. The purpose of this survey was to provide comparative data and the basis for more reliable generalizations from data in the base study. Where comparisons are drawn, this substudy data is referred to as the *nonrespondent survey*. The last substudy is not reported in this book. It also was undertaken for comparative purposes but surveyed members of a West Coast organization interested in group marriage. Its members were potential future participants in group marriages. Both surveys used short (two-page) questionnaires and included items from the Athanasiou survey mentioned earlier.

Details of the methodology employed in each of the substudies are explained in the appropriate chapters.

PARTICULARS. The study is broad in its attempt to include sociological and psychological, systems and personal perspectives. We view it as preliminary to what we hope will be a growing stream of research on specific hypotheses suggested by our findings. For the most part, the study is exploratory and descriptive rather than dealing with the testing of theories or hypotheses.

An important function we hoped to fulfill in the study was to investigate ways in which participants in multilateral marriages might be different—in family background, in personal attitudes, in personality, for example—from others who are not so involved. The use of a control or comparison population, ideally from the same neighborhoods, was precluded by financial, time, and even ethical constraints. This left us with the scientifically less valuable option of gathering information for which norms or standards had been established using other populations. Though this is a widely used research technique, it raises some messy issues. Norms are not always established with randomly chosen or even well-chosen populations. The passage of time since the establishment of norms may render a comparison meaningless. This generation may show significantly different personality patterns than the last, independent of whether they opt for group marriage.

Finally, weighing all the objections and gains, we noted that family professionals and ordinary people were making comparisons of those in alternative and conventional lifestyles even without data. So we chose to use techniques based on established norms, however inadequate. The measures of marital adjustment, personality needs, psychological health, development and adjustment for children, and items from the Athanasiou and Shaver survey were selected in part because they did provide some limited control in the form of results reported for other groups of people.

THE STUDY ISN'T . . . We are very aware of what our study is not. It is not definitive; it is merely a first attempt to develop valid descriptive data in this particular area. By the standards which are appropriate for this type of study we feel that what we have done is, if anything, more refined and more controlled than most initial studies which enter the literature.

We would not be publishing were we not personally convinced that the limitations in our study do not significantly compromise the results. As we expect the most rigorous standards of criticism to be applied to so controversial a study, we would rather anticipate objections, and by carefully qualifying the data increase their worth.

None of our findings is to be construed in any way as applying to multilateral marriages other than those participating in the study except as we explicitly identify legitimate generalizations or extensions. We have reason to believe some findings can be generalized, and we have not altogether avoided conjecture, but in every case we have identified speculation as such or have stated the evidence supporting the generalization. In the interest of linguistic simplicity we have not so elaborately qualified every statement throughout this book, but the qualification is to be read implicitly into every report not explicitly identified otherwise.

THE MISSING LINKS. In most cases we do not have all the data from all members of a group, consequently the composition of the substudies differs somewhat. Our initial hope of being able to cross-reference and cross-correlate all the data cannot be realized. It is always possible that such missing data would have significantly altered results had they been available.

A number of groups dissolved before all data could be obtained. Certain of the measures required group consensus or were based on the assumption that the respondent was in the multilateral situation when he was reporting. Others yielded meaningful individual measures even after a group had dissolved. The entire battery of tests and questionnaires represents a considerable investment of time and energy to complete, and enthusiasm often flagged. Some respondents specifically regarded written or discrete responses as inadequately representing their experience, which could only be truly appreciated by being with them. Members of dissolved groups would sometimes scatter geographically. Twice, one departing couple were sufficiently embittered or disillusioned by their experience not to want to talk about it or to facilitate its study. When groups dissolve there cease to be the incentives for working with us. We spent nearly two years pursuing the couple who were undoubtedly the most negative of any people in evaluating their multilateral experience. Finally we were able to take them to dinner and they were willing to discuss their feelings. As a result of the evening, they decided to fill out the forms and take some tests, completing our data on that group. Without our continued presence and any real incentive, they failed to keep their promise. Yet the talk did give us the missing perspectives on the breakup itself and enough information to justify the feeling that what they could offer on that group was not unexpected.

The completed questionnaires of one group were garnered by one of the men in it. With various excuses he withheld them from us and the others for a year. Finally, after an emotional face-to-face confrontation which convinced him of our integrity, he handed them over to us. Our hearts jumped; our data base jumped! Our pleading had paid off. But the next day the folder had disappeared from the end table where we had laid it down —he had reconfiscated the questionnaires and taken them with him on an extended trip.

In other cases mechanical snafus of various sorts, such as bad timing of a trip or insufficient time, were responsible for our being unable to complete data-gathering on a base study group. Other data reached us too late for inclusion in the analyses.

The significant effects of these missing links, if any, are on the quantitative analyses. Through diligent pursuit we have some inputs from every member of every group and can incorporate perceptions of dissident members with our own observations and with the perspectives of others in the same groups who have been more actively involved in the study. Thus our qualitative results include the entire forty-four members and eleven groups in the base study.

If a bias would be introduced by the absence of certain returns it would be because those whose returns are least adequate are somewhat more alienated, less likely to view their experience positively, and more likely to have some stake in silence. There are only five individual respondents who are not represented in any of the quantitative substudies, however. We did not find that the returns we received after the longest delays were any different from those received without repeated requests. We thus doubt that the total effect of the individual missing data elements can be significant.

The number of elements in each of the parts of the study are presented in Table 5-1 (below). Compared to many studies of less exceptional family patterns, the number of individuals and groups comprising the "sample" may appear miniscule. Nevertheless, this is the largest data base yet amassed on multilateral marriage. The difficulty in locating participants in the leading edge of a phenomenon is the principal limitation. "Sampling" issues are further discussed in Appendix II.

THE OTHER GROUPS. There remains the question, "What about the other groups?" What might be the effects on the study findings of groups that did not participate in the study? It is conceivable that only certain kinds of groups came to our attention and that only certain kinds consented to being in the study. These effects are, respectively, "sampling" bias and volunteer bias. (We use the quotes because our means of identifying groups in no way constitute a sampling procedure.)

Our very commitment to sharing and mutuality can work against

Table 5–1.   Data Obtained in Base Study and Substudy.

Study/Substudy	Number of Items (usable)	*From* Number of Individuals	*In* Number of Groups
Base Study			
Family Summary	9(9)	n.a.	9
Individual Summary	33(33)	33	11
Taped Interviews	38(36)	36	10
Direct Observation	n.a.	44	11
Background/Attitude			
Background/Attitude Inventory	31(29)	29	11
Marital Adjustment			
Burgess-Cottrell Scale	28(25)	25	11
Satisfaction Questionnaire	29(29)	29	11
Personality and Perception			
Edwards Personal Preference Schedule	42(42)	42	14
Drewery/Constantine Form	33(0)*	33	11
Psychological Health			
Shostrum's Personal Orientation Inventory	44(42)	42	15
Comparison			
Nonrespondent Survey	24(18)	27	15
Children			
Parent Rating Scales	40(39)	n.a.	13
Rogers' Personal Adjustment Inventory	20(17)	17	11
Denver Developmental Screening Scales	9(9)	9	8
Taped Interviews	31(31)	31	12

* Not analyzed for this study.

us. Shortly after our arrival in a distant area where we had several responding groups, we called one that had agreed during a previous visit to join the Study Project as respondents. Since there had been no opportunity to get any data at that time, they were a major reason for us to visit the area. When we called to confirm the meeting which we had tried to establish by mail, we were told that the group was reneging on their commitment principally because of one woman. The other woman was in favor of participation, the two men more or less neutral. A long, tense phone conversation yielded an agreement to meet for a few minutes to discuss the reasons for their dropping out. We felt that every responding group was important, not only because of the small number of groups, but because anyone wishing to drop out becomes significant for that very fact and a potential hole in the data.

This group consisted of two couples who had opted for monogamous sexual relations with their cospouses rather than legal partners shortly after initiating cross-marital sexual involvement. This was seen by them as a temporary adaptation to particular problems at the time of our initial contact. But why didn't they want to remain in the project? Principally, we concluded after the few minutes stretched into hours, because they did not want any feedback on their situation. What we found was the reluctant woman, having "lost" one husband, clinging to her new one and exercising pervasive passive-aggressive control over the group in order to maintain the status quo. The group had developed an increasing number of subjects which were excluded from examination. Later this impression was confirmed by others who knew the group and remained in contact with them. While it is a matter of indirect inference, we feel that this group did not want to face realistically what was happening in their family. Feedback from us (for example on their different expectations or on the patterns of control in the group) would have threatened a status quo which could only be maintained by not dealing with certain areas. But then, we cannot *know*, for we accepted their "resignation." Even so, not all information was lost, for prior to their leaving the study we were lent their personal journal recounting their first six months together. Later this group concluded they no longer had a multilateral marriage.

REALITY. Our vision of methodologically sound but humanistic research has been marred in various ways; yet for the most part we believe we have been successful in uncovering the real nature of multilateral-marriage participation while remaining involved human beings. We have given much attention to potential sources of bias and distortion in the study. We do not believe that the cumulative effect is substantial. Further discussion on this is found in Appendix II.

We have had our findings verified in several ways. First, of course, our own respondents are a source of validation. We learn from them exceptions to our summarizations, and we get frequent assent even where the truth we return is hard to take or differs from the way in which participants see their own relationship. We also get feedback from other group-marriage participants who were not in the study. Almost universally we have been told, "Yes, that's how it was! Somehow you have really captured our own experience even though we weren't in your study." While this input may have limited scientific value, it has certainly helped our own sense of moving in the right direction.

On two occasions we have had a chance to compare notes with therapists or counselors working with respondent families in facilitating their experience. Naturally, this was done with the clients' full knowledge and in a way involving no violations of confidence. To our delight, we found that we had discerned many of the most important, even hidden, dynamics of the family in a remarkably economical way. This is not to say we had the depth of insight that these professionals who had worked extensively with one family had of that family, but for the most part the information we did have was confirmed and acknowledged to be important to understanding the family.

Usually, of course, our respondents do not see themselves directly in our papers because of our decision not to present comprehensive case material. On one occasion[5] a case-study format was clearly indicated. Keeping strictly to material relevant to the process of group breakup, we presented one typical case and another case, atypical but not singular. Each discussion was approximately six hundred words and disguised all possible identifying details. Nevertheless, these discussions were recognizable to the respondents involved, as indeed anything short of distortion would be. While we made no value judgments, we did report observed behavior relevant to the specific cases and the more general context. In some places these reports might be judged by others as reflecting unfavorably on the participants. Additionally, some issues which the participants had originally avoided or denied were discussed openly.

One couple who might have felt they had been presented somewhat harshly wrote: "Well. Read your paper. Note we were included. Think your write up was relatively (in fact, *very*) accurate."

On the other hand, to quote from a letter we received from a couple in the other group:

> As you probably anticipated, neither [J.] or I agreed with your interpretations. Other intelligent observers of the experiment (for examples, the [Adlers], friends of all the participants) which while including most of your facts, would give a whole different tone to the year's events. Your choice of words, and of wording, even more than the ideas expressed seem to indicate a strong emotional bias.

To us it seemed that part of the difference could be accounted for by another of those involved human slips in which we had neglected to send this couple a copy of the paper until nearly a year after it was written. Even after a long second inquiry from us, they presented no substantive criticism on specific points. We were able to modify the paper productively before final publication. The results are now a matter of record.[6]

In the end, consistently pursuing our aims of an open, honest, mutual process seemed to pay off. Relations with the B———s, the group with whom we weren't able to establish a trusting relationship first, continued to be somewhat strained. The differences in viewpoint have not changed, though they are at least open and acknowledged. Their last letter told of their successful relocation to a new state. They expressed their continued interest in and support of what we are doing. Where once they were very fearful of outside knowledge, even ours, they now suggest that our publicizing of group marriage through national media is indicated. They asked for our help on some personal matters and offered theirs to us.

We close as they did, hoping everything is well and happy with all of them.

REFERENCES

1. A sizable body of research on self-disclosure and its effects is accumulating, largely under Sydney M. Jourard of Florida State University. His book *The Transparent Self* (New York: Van Nostrand Reinhold, 1964) is an excellent introduction to the concept of self-disclosure and its effect on growth. Relevant research includes Jourard and Leo A. Kormann, "Getting to Know the Experimenter and Its Effect on Psychological Test Performance," *Journal of Humanistic Psychology*, 8, 2 (Fall 1968) and Jourard and Jaquelyn L. Resnick, "Some Effects of Self-disclosure among College Women," *Journal of Humanistic Psychology*, 10, 1 (Spring 1970).

2. Popular accounts which confuse group marriage and communes have presented misleading and deficient pictures regarding both phenomena. Among these are Morton Hunt, "The Future of Marriage," *Playboy* (August 1971). [*Cf.* our commentary in "The Forum," *Playboy* (March 1972)]; Dr. Reuben's column in *McCall's* (March 1972); and Reese D. Kilgo, "Can Group Marriage Work?" *Sexual Behavior* 2, 3 (March 1972).

3. Cuber and Harroff describe their interview approach in their book *Sex and the Significant Americans* (Baltimore: Penguin Books, 1965) and Hendin, *et al.* in their book, *Psychoanalysis and Social Research* (Garden City, N.Y.: Doubleday/Anchor, 1966).

4. Robert Athanasiou, Philip Shaver, and Carol Tavris, "Sex: A *Psychology Today* Report," *Psychology Today*, 4, 2 (July 1970). The survey data and questionnaire items have been used in other studies including Athanasiou and Shaver, "Correlates of Heterosexuals' Reactions to Pornography," *The Journal of Sex Research*, 7, 4 (November 1971).

5. An address delivered at the American Association of Marriage and Family Counselors, "Conference on Divorce and Divorce Counseling," Washington, D. C., March 20, 1971.

6. "Dissolution of Marriage in a Non-conventional Context," *The Family Coordinator* 21, 4 (October 1972).

6

Who and What

SCHEDULING A RESEARCH TRIP to visit twelve widely scattered families in forty-nine days leads to some jarring juxtapositions. In three grueling days we might have 1,200 miles to drive, and then, after a few days' visit with one group, find ourselves with two days to cover a mere two hundred miles. Sometimes the contrasts in lifestyle of the families we were visiting were no less dramatic.

In Faircrest Hills, the landscapes of automatically sprinkled foliage are like bright green enclaves, besieged by the golden natural brush of the surrounding hills. There, in a $40,000 ranch-style home, four people had tried to make a success of a multilateral marriage. Two of the former participants still live there, but on the occasion of our visit all four partners are having a reunion. Still friends, they get together occasionally. The house is kept immaculate and the kids are kept in line, both with the aid of a fulltime housekeeper/baby-sitter. The three preschoolers, though more controlled by their parents than many of those we had seen on this trip, were no better behaved. The children seem to be the nexus of unarticulated tension. They are told repeatedly not to interrupt as we adults try to talk shop, but they do, repeatedly, and somehow to us it seems we might as well invite them in. But we don't.

An entrepreneur, Harold enthusiastically fills us in on his latest venture. Alicia, who lives with him, is a career professional, competent and confident. They have tried forming a multilateral marriage more than once—a threesome, a foursome, once by correspondence and weekend exchange visits with a couple living three hundred miles away.

Angela Hunt, working on a substudy of the children, was traveling with us this time. She and Larry, carrying tensions from six weeks of cramped travel and accumulated misunderstandings, begin to argue. At first Harold, devout follower of his own "scientific religion," tries to facilitate by interpreting what is going on. Larry jumps on him for interfering, then resumes with Angela until it is clear that neither is reaching the other. Stalemate. Again.

"You know, I like you better," Alicia says. "You seem more human now. I don't think you were really that real to us before." She says it warmly and sincerely. Soon, though, the discussion is again intellectual. Emotions are real here, but "sane," "rational," "responsible" are words that somehow keep appearing in conversations with Harold and Alicia.

The days warm early and though the sun is low when we leave the next morning, it is a long hot day of driving. By supper we arrive in Hinsville. A few blocks off Main Street we have a choice, whether to stop first at the T——s or at the M——s. The two modest homes are a block apart but they house a single family. We flip a mental coin and pull up at the T——s. Ann M—— opens the door to come out and greet us, but little Jack T—— squeezes past and outruns her. The T—— house, like Ann and Steve's, is neat but more clearly lived-in than the suburban ranch we left that morning.

Jim arrives home from the shop where he repairs heavy machinery, and Steve, a surveyor, surprises everyone by returning a day early from a work trip. Jim and Steve dig cars and it takes little to induce them to give us a hand repairing our cracked rear bumper. Then we drive over to the other house.

Ann, Steve, Jim, and Carol have been group-married for nearly five years and have developed good communication and problem-solving skills. They are conservative in many respects (Steve once remarked, "Dissent is one thing, but boy, when somebody hassles my country's flag, that really burns me"), but theirs is a libertarian tradition. They are group-married yet are sensitive enough to spare Carol's mother having to face that fact unwillingly. They avoid hassles by keeping separate houses in their small town, but look forward to living together again, perhaps in a farmhouse at the edge of town.*

Next week Jim and Steve will go hunting together as they have often done for years. There is an easy comradeship between them, as between Carol and Ann. Yet despite their comfort, their closeness, their communicativeness as a group, disappointment, doubt, or anger has a few times festered for an extended period before the group could or would deal with it. They are contradictions—conservative yet liberal, open yet reserved. Not the least contradiction is that they seem to like us, care about us, and it's mutual. They are clearly committed to their lifestyle, no less than those whose choices have been more antiestablishment.

We want to stay and we want to go; our ambivalence in moving on to the next group is considerable. Another day's drive through verdant forest country brings us to an even tinier town and "The Fellowship," a rural commune whose membership varies somewhat with the season, but includes seven adults and two children at this visit. We leave the trailer at a vestpocket park down the road, then head up to the main house by a driveway that is more alpine ski trail than driveway. Twice on earlier visits we had assaulted that driveway with our trailer in tow. Twice Bill had to hike to a neighboring farm to borrow a tractor and pull us out. The second time the cost to us was a transmission overhaul.

Bill, Cindy, and Judy are a triad who form the core of the community. They have been "married" five years. Others who have lived in the community have had conventional marriages or been single, but close ties hold Bill, Cindy, and Judy in an intimate network that includes some former community members and some who one day hope to settle down here. A sense of "community," if not actually of "family," extends to these people.

The main house, Bill says, was probably erected in a day or two by a farmer and his neighbors. Consequently it is solid, with over-

---

* And they asked us to note that they have now moved in together.

size framing members, but small and somewhat irregular. One very tiny bathroom serves everyone. People remove their shoes for the sake of the beautifully braided rug which dominates the living room, but the general feeling is more of disorder, old paint, and dull linoleum.

Outside, goats so homely they are beautiful wander amid geese, ducks, and chickens. An orchard yields enough nuts to sell. Their organic garden is a thing of beauty, a delight to the eye with its rhubarb, spinach, purple beans and cabbage, tall corn and sunflowers waving over vines ripe with ground cherries. The garden is the source of a good portion of the community's varied, near-vegetarian diet.

The diet is being broken for a party, a feast that will last from supper to midnight, crowned by succulent slabs of roast pork cut from the sides of a whole hog which has spent the day underground, slowly roasting in a bed of hot stones. The occasion is the pooling of several birthdays, an opportunity for extravagance, an excuse for generosity which is more Christmas than August birthday party. Neighboring communes and distant "family" members have been invited. There are small presents for everyone who shows up, even a *piñata* for the children.

In contrast to the nonreligious humanism of the last two groups we visited, the tenor here is more mystical. The ubiquitous astrology is present, of course, along with occasional references to the occult. It was hard to tell how much was serious, how much put-on when Bill told about the stray cat which he believed was once a witch, unable to change back to human form but still capable of entering locked cars. Others, though, clearly took the tale seriously.

These, then, are some of the groups, some of the people who have tried multilateral marriage. They are affluent; they are trying to make ends meet. They are well-educated and schooled in life. They blend into a small-town neighborhood, and they have built a radical lifestyle. There are twenty-three other groups comprising 104 marital partners in total on whom we have information. Eleven groups, including the three very different ones we have just described, have been the focus of the intensive study outlined in the preceding chapter. From the study and the survey of nonrespondent groups, we can describe in some detail who is trying multilateral marriage and what the groups are like.

CHARACTERISTICS. Who are the people? Many of them are young —half are in their twenties—but that also means that half are thirty and over. The youngest participant we have ever encountered was an eighteen-year-old woman who was in a triad for a short period of time with an older couple; the oldest was a lifelong communitarian devotee, fifty-nine when he entered a multilateral marriage. Young couples in their late twenties, who have been married for six to eight years and have two or three children are the most likely to attempt a multilateral marriage. The range, though, is substantial, for just over 10 percent are in their forties, and several couples had been conventionally married more than fifteen years when they started their attempt at multilateral marriage.

Usually, couples already married come together in a multilateral marriage, single people were in the minority (twenty-eight of 104 participants), and among them were three couples with common-law relationships. This is manifest in the predominance (63 percent) of tetrads among the group marriages which have been located. Triads, 22 percent, were next most common. Of these six, only one involved two men and a woman, but our knowledge of other groups suggests this understates the proportion. Larger groups actually constituting multilateral marriages are rare; only two pentads (five partners) and two hexads (six partners) have been located. We have good reason to feel that still larger groups with a genuine marital relationship are extremely unlikely. We have heard of groups of eight and twelve, but in all cases, personally checking those leads disconfirmed such a group.

Better than four out of five of the multilateral-marriage families included children, typically two or three children in the whole group. Of the sixty-nine children, sixty-seven were children of the existing or previous dyadic marriages of the marital partners. We have included in this group three children for whom a single woman is legal guardian. Four of the eight divorced or separated people who entered as singles brought children with them.

Multilateral marriages are everywhere—in major cities, small towns, and rural America. Dividing the country into six regions, the Northeast accounts for about 25 percent of groups and the Southwest for another 30 percent. The rest are more or less evenly divided among the remaining regions, with the Southeast getting less than its share. More precise subdivision would violate our commitment to geographic anonymity. The range of living conditions and lifestyles is fairly represented by the three groups described earlier. Of informants in the nonrespondent survey, 35 percent said they lived in a major city, the same proportion were suburban, and another 12 percent indicated they were urbanly located in other than a major city. The remainder were rural or located in small towns.

If our "sampling" methods are not hopelessly biased, then communes are a much less common habitat for multilateral marriages than the media would have us believe. Only two of the twenty-six groups in the combined base study and nonrespondent survey were in intentional communities. Two more also described themselves as intentional communities, with the multilateral family constituting the entire community. One base study group was in the rural commune setting described earlier in this chapter, the other comprised a foursome which was part of a social-change community. This intentional community drew its economic base from a fairly large nonresident membership which used the community property for recreational purposes. An inner circle of less than a dozen members, including the tetrad, resided in the community and managed it.

The "Monday Night Class," the mobile commune of cross-country bus-caravan fame, was reputed to have a number of tetrads within it.[1] We have fewer than a dozen reasonably reliable reports of multilateral marriages in communes that we were unable to follow up on. It appears that most multilateral marriages are in more or less conventional communities.

There are a number of counties around the country which are commonly cited as archetypally representative of conservative strongholds. One of these is the locale of no fewer than four multilateral marriages. In short, multilateral marriages are far more common on tree-lined suburban streets than in agrarian subsistence communes.

Though multilateral marriages and communes do not appear to be commonly found together, some of the same people are interested in multilateral marriage and in community. And twenty-three of twenty-seven informants in the nonrespondent survey indicated that a sense of community was among the reasons for being interested in expanded family relations; fifteen felt it was a strong reason.

TIME. More than almost anything else except sexual details, people want to know how long the marriages last. Averages are meaningful only for groups which have broken up already, yet clearly that understates by the contribution of those still together. Since they *are* still intact, they will ultimately last longer than their current duration. The details are to be found among the basic data in Appendix III. The durations can be summarized in several ways. By the end of three months, at least 93 percent are still surviving. By the end of a year at least 44 percent of those who tried a multilateral marriage were still together. Seventeen percent are together at the end of three. After five years, at least 7 percent are still hanging in there. These figures are qualified with "at least" because of the inclusion of the duration of still intact groups as of the analysis date. The mean duration of the seven intact groups on which we have data is thirty-seven months as of the date of analysis.

Respondent groups in the main study differ from those in the nonrespondent survey. Since it takes time to locate a group and to gather data on it, this biases against inclusion of short-lived groups in the main study. Respondent groups are typically longer lived, and the difference in durations compared with nonrespondents is *statistically significant.**

One interpretation which will almost certainly be put on these data is that multilateral marriages don't last, that they are failures, and consequently should not be tried in the first place. To put these figures in perspective, however, we should note comparisons and contrasts with conventional marriages. The median duration of ordinary marriages in 1967 was only 7.1 years and falling.[2]

* See Preface.

The one-in-three divorce rate is seldom used to argue that people should not get married, but rather, that partners should try harder, endure more, improve their relationships, or be better prepared when they enter. Conventional marriages are most vulnerable to divorce in the first year, and one wonders what the early separation rate would be if there were no barriers to it. Multilateral marriage is acknowledged to be more difficult than two-person marriage, despite some advantages. These figures show that multilateral marriage is a form of marriage which, even without prescribed roles or behavior and without social approval, is at least viable in today's world over the short to intermediate term. We will have more to say on this in later chapters.

JUST WHO. We know quite a bit about the personal attitudes and family backgrounds of respondents. In interviews, most described quite unextraordinary childhoods. The substudy on backgrounds and attitudes (details of which are reported in Appendices V and VI) included twenty-nine respondents.

Most of the respondents' parents are still living. About 20 percent, approximately the expected number, had parents who divorced or separated during their childhood. Three were adopted children. They had the usual number of brothers and sisters, though 56 percent of the women had no brothers. Many did report that friends, boarders, or relatives lived with their families when they were children.

In describing the kind of discipline they felt they had as children many more checked "strict" or "authoritarian" as characteristic than "lax," "permissive," or "free." But discipline was variable and described in terms of "inconsistent," "flexible," and "informal."

More than half said they were brought up in an orientation that was religious or strongly religious, yet a surprising 38 percent said they were raised in a nonreligious atmosphere. More than three-quarters now put themselves in this category. As children, the religious orientation spanned the spectrum from orthodox to liberal, but almost all who responded on that item said they were now liberal. As adults, one in three considers himself to be a humanist or ethical humanist and one in four is agnostic. Five said their religion was their own, unique private version, and a few favored mysticism and metaphysics.

Politically, too, they span a considerable spectrum but tend toward the radical end. Nine of twenty-nine said they were radical and five checked revolutionary; only two considered themselves conservative, none strongly conservative or reactionary. When they are not completely apolitical, as are one in five, they are at least not oriented to party politics (62 percent). Those who did indicate party orientation were split—Democrats three, Republicans three, Peace and Freedom three. Nearly one in three felt they were antiestablishment, none pro-establishment. Both religiously and politically the participants in multilateral marriages are much more liberal than their counterparts in swinging.[3]

We sampled their opinions on sex, love, marriage, and the law. The findings are detailed numerically in Appendix VI. We compared them on some items to a sample from a large-scale survey on sex conducted by Athanasiou *et al.* among readers of *Psychology Today*.[4] Though that survey revealed a sexually liberal readership, respondents proved to be more liberal, agreeing more strongly or more often with such statements as "Religious groups should not attempt to impose their standards of sexual behavior on others," and "Women should be free to initiate sexual activity," while disagreeing more forcefully with statements like "Easy access to birth-control information and devices increases promiscuity." All these differences were *statistically significant*. While espousing liberal sexual attitudes respondents *were* somewhat romantic. They disagreed that "Lovers ought to expect a certain amount of disillusionment after they marry." They disagreed somewhat more that true love seldom lasts forever, but this difference was *not significant*. Their high marital expectations take them into multilateral marriage and are reflected in their feeling that true love can last and that one need not accept disillusionment. They agreed only just barely (and *not significantly* more than the readership informants) that love is more important than practical matters, which is still suggestive of high expectations.

As we expected, respondents strongly agreed that most of us can sincerely love any one of several people equally well, an antiromantic but very multilateral attitude.

Some of the dissenting commentary added by respondents is as revealing as their ratings on attitudes. One respondent who disagreed that sexual behavior should be judged on the quality of relationship rather than legal status said, "Sexual behavior should not be 'judged' at all." A couple of respondents felt birth control did increase promiscuity but added they thought that might be okay. One who disagreed strongly that love is more important than practical things added, "Love is very practical." On the next item, about "true" love, he asked, "Is there such a thing as untrue love?" And one respondent, who agreed that homosexuals should be considered no better than criminals, explained, "and criminals should be considered no worse than homosexuals or successful businessmen, for that matter."

The attitude substudy included nearly two dozen additional items of special interest to us rather than for comparison with Athanasiou's study. Earlier, we had noticed that fiction on group marriage often transliterated traditional values into multilateral terms. In Rimmer's *Proposition 31*, for example, the protagonists form a tetrad with a strong sexual fidelity ethic and deny that they will become interested in others beyond their expanded marriage. To see to what extent real people felt this way, we took a number of statements expressing traditional attitudes about marriage and recast them into a form applying to group or multilateral marriage. For example, "For the sake of the children, partners should strive to keep a group marriage together." Respondents definitely disagreed with that statement and disagreed or disagreed somewhat with five of seven such statements. Thus they had not simply transposed traditional morality. Detailed findings from this substudy are reported elsewhere.

CLASS. For some strange reason, the socioeconomic background of participants in various lifestyles is of wide interest. Perhaps people are wondering whether it's their kind of people getting involved or not. Not surprisingly, whatever the new lifestyle, one is apt to find a preponderance of people from middle-class backgrounds; most people are, after all, middle class.

In casual conversation, "middle class" is an amorphous aggregate, but to sociologists, class is a precisely defined variable which requires several properly obtained indices to evaluate. Frankly, we weren't very interested in socioeconomic status (SES) and consequently did not design our data-gathering to permit ready identification of SES.

Both respondents and nonrespondents are well educated, and among those without college degrees are several self-educated individuals who are extremely well read. Informants in the nonrespondent survey reported *significantly* more education than respondents. Less than 5 percent did not have some college. Thirty-six percent had received bachelor's degrees; 13 percent had reached the master's level and an equal number had Ph.Ds.

It is difficult to summarize their income level. Nonrespondents, almost all of whom had returned to conventional marriages when they answered, reported total family income. Group income and in some cases individual incomes are available for respondents, but these are not comparable with incomes by nuclear families and include several sources of temporary distortion. We believe the figures for nonrespondents are more representative of class membership for purposes of comparing participants to people in conventional marriages, but the difference in educational level between respondents and nonrespondents would suggest some differences in economic level, too. The median income for families of nonrespondent informants was $10,000 per year, the middle 50 percent fell between $6,500 and $15,500 per year. We shall have more to say on money in Chapter 12.

Occupationally, participants were as varied as one might expect. They were college students and college professors, sales people and managers, farmers, mechanics, and carpenters. Among the professionals were engineers, psychologists, social workers, nurses, and one physician. Some were in the theater and commercial arts. Even the clergy were represented—by a minister and a theologian. In keeping with their educational achievement, more tend to be employed in the professions than would be in the general population. Among respondents we noticed a number of cases of what society would label as "downward mobility" when prior occupations were compared with present employment. These were people who had put lifestyle over career, such as the engineer turned to ranch maintenance and the social worker employed as a courier.

Ramey's analysis of questionnaires from a New York-based

organization of people interested in expanded families provides some comparison data.[5] Only one group marriage was represented in that population, but many members were interested in group marriage. By collapsing standard U.S. Census Bureau Occupational Classification categories in the same manner as Ramey, we found that respondents and survey informants differed from both the United States population (which we expected) and Ramey's group *significantly*. Both the "interesteds" in Ramey's study and the "doers" in ours were predominantly from higher occupational categories, but those in our study are more varied and more representative of the total population. Ramey did not have exact information on education, but reported over 90 percent had completed four years of college, much higher than among either respondents or survey informants. (Ramey's informants did not differ *significantly* in age from ours.)

We will yield to the temptation to add some interpretation to the distribution of occupations. For men in our study, professions are overrepresented and skilled trades normally represented. These are the occupational endeavors which afford maximal flexibility in work commitments and are more likely to leave free the energy required to form and maintain an expanded family. Sales and managerial positions are more likely to require an open-ended job commitment, and these are under-represented. We will deal with the data on women in the next chapter.

REFERENCES

1. W. L. Claiborne, "Monday Night Class," *Washington Post*, December 24, 1970, pp. 131–132.
2. U.S. Public Health Service, "Increase in Divorce, United States, 1967," PHS publication No. 1000, series 21, no. 20. (Washington, D.C.: Government Printing Office, 1970).
3. Gilbert D. Bartell, "Group Sex among the Mid-Americans," *Journal of Sex Research 6*, 2 (May 1970).
4. Robert Athanasiou, *et al.*, "Sex," *Psychology Today 4*, 2 (July 1970).
5. James Ramey, "Communes, Group Marriage, and the Upper-Middle Class," *Journal of Marriage and the Family 34*, 4 (November 1972).

7

Cowives and Cohusbands

INTRODUCTIONS CAN BE HARD for someone in a multilateral marriage. One of our respondents supplied the missing noun when she wrote us of her "cowife." The word fitted, we adopted it, and soon both "cowife" and "cohusband" became part of the vocabulary to express that relationship which is possible only in a multilateral marriage.

One most important word for the relationships in a multilateral marriage is not often spoken—love. It is much less observable than patterns of child-rearing, much less conceptually elegant than the need for sex. Yet love and loving, for more than one person, is an essential element of the experience of cowives and cohusbands. Of the major or strong reasons for involvement, love was second only to companionship. Without understanding the deep, committed love that partners often feel for each other, one cannot understand multilateral marriage. In a quiet moment, Herman reflects: "Of course I'd like to see them all together again, maybe someday, slowly, we can all move up to the farm. I love them, don't you see? I love them all, still, very deeply." In a way, though, love can cloud rather than clarify, and consequently we have chosen to defer a discussion of it until we have laid the groundwork.

ONE, TWO, THREE . . . INFINITY. Another, less escapable, word to characterize multilateral relationships is "complexity." Nearly half the respondents considered this one of the problems of multilateral marriage. When two people become three, they triple the number of interpersonal relationships in the group. Among four partners, there are twelve relationships which must be built and maintained. Together they form a single interrelationship, but Sue's relationship to Charlie is different and separate from Charlie's relationship to her. Love, trust, even talking, are not always reciprocal. Each of these distinct, one-way relationships, whatever it may be, becomes part of what a group is, part of the total complexity. Complexity in this sense grows rapidly with increasing size of the group. Within a group of six there are thirty separate relationships; with ten members there are ninety.

In less cohesive and involved groups than multilateral marriages, not everyone is strongly affected by all the relationships. For instance, Sally in a four-person marriage is herself involved in only three relationships. But those other nine relationships also affect her and contribute to the complexity of the situation confronting her. Charlie's quarrel with Sam makes Sam impatient with her. She may even be called on to mediate or be asked to take sides. Ennui in Sam and Sue's interrelationship may infuse and depress the entire group. The more active and caring the relationships, the greater will be the effect of an individual or individual relationship on the group as a whole. Swings in mood are sometimes amplified; downs are felt as the end of the world, excitement as a peak experience.

The complexity of the multilateral-marriage experience comes up against fundamental human limitations. With only twenty-four hours in a day, dividing one's time between group activities and relating separately with individuals is problematical. Inevitably, with larger and larger groups, the period between contacts grows, or the contact shortens and relationships become more diffuse.

AT, WITH, AMONG. Playing with the mathematics of multilateral marriage may facilitate understanding what complexity really means. Relationships can develop only through interaction—talking, touching, making love, working together on a common task. At times, building individual relationships may be in competition with formation of a group relationship or identity. Normal married couples have no such problem. There is only one way a couple can group itself to talk or to go bowling together. But in a hexad, with six partners, there are fifteen different pairings, twenty distinct trios, fifteen different subgroups of four people, and six ways of leaving one person out. Jumping to a twelve-person marriage, there would be a staggering total of 1,012 such subgroupings.

These numbers are important because the patterns of communication change according to the number of people in a group. A dyad may seem easy to understand, but even there the dynamics of communication may be quite intricate. What Sue will disclose of herself to Charlie depends on all the unique, idiosyncratic details of their interrelationship, on his disclosures to her, and on his reactions to her disclosures. In every human interrelationship, there will be things withheld and things disclosed, things tempered and things communicated unmodified.

Communication was the number-one-ranked problem for participants in multilateral marriages making them little different from conventionally married couples. But dyadic communication and communication in larger groups of unspecified number differ in several dimensions, with no clear overall advantage for any particular size. The larger the group, the less the available "air time" for each individual to talk, and the more it is likely that some individuals will be short-changed on air time. On the other hand, the process of the group itself may facilitate effective communication and authentic self-disclosure, perhaps offsetting the more divided air time. Encounter groups have demonstrated the power of small groups to facilitate communication. Yet, where some things may only be disclosed selectively, group communication may represent the lowest common denominator of what is taboo to no one.

Triadic communication is unique in many respects. Three people frequently find themselves in a configuration in which one person acts as a facilitator for communication which is primarily between the other two. Married couples can appreciate the contrast with dyadic communication, which can so readily reach a dead end or endlessly cycle, with neither party understanding quite what the other is saying. The triad also readily becomes "two-on-one," an alliance which can be destructive but more often very effective. When one person tells you she sees reality differently from your cherished view of yourself, you can easily dismiss it as her opinion versus yours. When *two* people you love and trust tell you at once that you are all wet, you are more apt to listen.

Tetrads must cope with an almost irresistible tendency to become two parallel dyads. Every couple which has visited another couple knows how easily discussions split into two pairs, usually with the women forming one and the men forming the other.

Offsetting the costs of complexity, multilateral marriages enjoy a richness of options. When communication temporarily or partially breaks down between two people, there are alternate paths, a third person may facilitate for them, or the group as a whole may work on the issue. Contact can be maintained in a multitude of intimate pairs and through group process. Yet there are trade-offs. Groups which try to keep everything in group space, favoring total group cohesiveness through sharing everything as a complete family, may find they have sacrificed something in the way of deep personal relationships and variety through differentiation of the relationships in which each partner participates. But without at least some interaction as a complete group, there may be only a loose collection of individual interrelationships rather than a family identity.

Family meetings are common means of assuring a certain amount of frequent contact with the entire group. For many multilateral marriages, these meetings are regular, usually once a week. The entire group, frequently kids included, get together to discuss current family issues, resolve conflicts, air beefs, and make decisions. For a time one family found their needs so complex that they set up three different meetings a week.

Needless to say, decision-making can be much more complex in groups, especially multilateral marriages, than in pairs—so much so that we will save that for another chapter.

PROCESS AND PAPERS. Typically, we have found that participants in multilateral marriages work for a level of communication probably not common in conventional marriages. They seem to be seeking to know each other totally as people, which may mean delving into areas most Americans share with no one—their private dreams and secret fears, their real, spontaneous, and undiluted feelings. In this sense, their communication goals seem to be closely related to the efforts of encounter and sensitivity-training groups in fostering complete, authentic self-disclosure and effective listening. As in encounter groups, the communication in many multilateral marriages often gets into the area of *process* or meta-communication, talking about the talking itself. Communication itself is examined and discussed as the partners explore what went wrong with an exchange or what their feelings were about something that was said.

Of course, not all communication is at this high personal plane nor as involved in process. Like the rest of us, the papers, politics, hobbies, food, and trivia of daily life are uncomplicated subject matter for conversations. And even the array of communication options of the multilateral marriage cannot ensure against a complete breakdown in communication. What more need be said when one man spends hours drafting a long written message to his cohusband who is seated at an adjacent desk, doggedly turning out his own end of the paper dialogue. But then, the "silent treatment" is not new to most American couples.

BONDED. Even after years of the most intense, involuted communication between cospouses and within the group as a group, we notice an interesting phenomenon in the relationships between partners. The vast majority of respondents entered into the multilateral marriage as established couples, most of them with years of marriage behind them. We call these previously established pairs relationships "primary bonds," because they continue to hold some differential precedence even after years of multilateral marriage. Borrowing from ethology, the study of animal behavior, some respondents have referred to this relationship as a "pair bond."

There is reason to believe that pair-bonding is an innate human propensity.[1] From our research we can only assert that over the short run, up to five years, a primary bond continues to be differentiated by most participants, either in their stated perceptions of their relationship or in their behavior. This does not mean that very deep secondary relationships are not possible; in some cases, a primary bond is almost indistinguishable. The evidence for the primary bond comes from interviews, from questions on preferences among group members, and from what happens when the multilateral marriages break up. Out of sixteen group dissolutions involving twenty-five established couples, only five couples separated or divorced in the process of group dissolution. Within a group, a change of primary bond has occurred only once.

At first, the existence of a primary-bond relationship would appear to be the antithesis of multilateral marriage. Among some respondents (two groups) there has even been an ethos which includes an emphasis on equal love. Collectively, respondents agree somewhat that partners ought to strive to love all their partners equally. This contradicts the concept of a primary bond, observable even in those groups seeking to love equally. Our data are insufficient to say whether this equal-love ethic is practicable, much less whether it is more or less effective in a multilateral marriage than openly acknowledged primary bonds. We do know that the equal-love ethic is exceptionally hard to live up to, that human beings do evaluate and rank their relationships with others. And despite the nearly universal presence of primary bonding, "existing marriage" ranked low in respondents' reports of problems. A parallel can be drawn with parent-child relationships. Children know that parents have preferences, however hard the parents may try to erase or deny them. Rather than trying hopelessly to equalize relationships, it may be better simply to acknowledge them, thus freeing energy to make the most out of the unique relationship with each child.[2]

Our observations suggest that emotional energy is wasted in trying to love every marriage partner equally or in maintaining the group myth that preferences do not exist. In one tetrad, for example, the group argued that they all loved each other equally, and they protested being asked to answer questions which explored their rankings of other members in terms of love, preferences as sexual partner, etc. Yet in private interviews, three of the four expressed definite preferences for particular sexual partners.

HOMO SAPIENS. It may seem easy enough to see how a man could love and live with two women, but how can any woman get along with another woman? Or a man with another man? Can a woman really share a kitchen with another woman? For that matter can a man?

We found that formation of good relationships between members of the same sex was essential for good group functioning. It is unlikely that any multilateral marriage can survive indefinitely with inadequate same-sex relationships, regardless of the intensity and quality of the cross-sex ones.

Men had quite different experiences from women in forming same-sex bonds. There were practical matters. Women were more likely to be at home or have flexible work schedules giving them time alone in same-sex dyads. Social conditioning was a much stronger influence. Most women have been socialized to be more flexible and accommodating in interpersonal relationships with men, and this adaptability seems to facilitate relationships with other women.

The biggest difference is in communication of feelings. It is acceptable in this society for men to express negative affect, to insult, attack, or put down each other. It is much less acceptable for them to express positive feelings like warmth, admiration, or affection. It is especially unacceptable for two men to communicate affection nonverbally or physically, yet this is the stuff of which strong bonds are created. For women, on the other hand, expressiveness regarding feelings is part of the cultural stereotype, and embraces or even kisses between women are accepted and commonplace. We suspect that the men in multilateral marriages will at least have to reach the point where the expression of affect is more balanced and where they can be comfortable with simple physical expression with each other. This is very much a culturally defined matter. One need only go to Europe to find grown men embracing and fathers lip-kissing their sons.

The same-sex bonds ramify in cross-sex relationships. Sue's love for her cowife Sally reduces her perception of Sally as a competitor or as a threat to her primary-bond relationship. The unseen ghostly opponent is usually much more threatening than a flesh-and-blood person whose feelings and foibles are familiar.

Good, openly communicative same-sex relationships are 60 percent of good multilateral relations.

EQUALIZATION. There is a certain amount of intrinsic equalitarianism in multilateral marriages which is a function of both structure and possible practical advantages. The Women's Liberation movement has begun to see group living and group marriage as possible means to facilitate role freedom. With more people around, so the argument goes, no one person need get stuck in one job. Often we found the thinking among liberationists really ran more to, "If I were in a group marriage then I could pursue a full-time career or do what I want while the *other* woman or the *men* did the housework and took care of the kids." Needless to say, there is a fallacy in this reasoning.

Some tasks grow as fast as the size of a family grows, but some tasks don't. One person can babysit for two kids or one person can babysit five. A house for eight is not twice as large as a house for four. Thus there *should* be fewer responsibilities per adult in an expanded family.

On the other hand, some things take more time and energy in groups (decision-making, for example). The determining factor may not be the flexibility of roles and working arrangements within the family, but the rigidity of responsibilities outside. Shared jobs and interesting, well-paying part-time employment are available, but only within reach of a few. We shall look at economic factors in more detail in Chapter 12.

The general and sexual liberalism required for participation in a multilateral marriage would be expected to be accompanied by an equalitarian ethic. We found that respondents were very equalitarian in attitudes. They agreed very strongly that men and women should have completely equal rights and responsibilities, that most roles were artificial and arbitrary, and that men should be free to do housework and raise children and women to pursue careers if they so desire. Males expressed more equalitarian attitudes than females on these items, but the differences were not significant. Both men and women also agreed, but less strongly, that group marriage allowed more sex-role freedom than conventional marriage.

What have been the *real* advantages to men? to women? Our own observations and informal conversations suggest that the lower degree of certainty on the last item is meaningful. We found that people were working for role flexibility and sexual equality within multilateral marriages, but many were somewhat dissatisfied with the actual progress. Most of the women who were not students were employed. Four out of five were in professions and 12.5 percent were in management, nearly three times the national average. And male and female respondents were more equally distributed occupationally than either men and women in general or than people merely interested in group marriage.[3]

In the homes, most tasks were shared or rotated in some way. There were some families in which male/female roles were substantially reversed, others with substantial equality and still others with more or less traditional roles. *But,* overall the *actual* distribution of tasks was not equal and leaned slightly in the direction of traditional male-female role distinctions. Even so "housekeeping" and "work sharing" were among the lowest-ranked problems for both men and women.

We observed one pattern in several groups. Even where schedules and sign-up sheets are used to assign tasks, there will always be some disparity between the program and the performance, leaving some residue of unfinished or sloppily done work. This residual shitwork is even more likely to pile up when task sharing is less structured. It accumulates until someone can no longer stand it or is simply in the mood to clean latrines, or seeing that it won't get done otherwise, tackles the job in resignation. The person who does this is likely to be the person with the highest need for order, the greatest prior experience in the task, or the one least assertive of personal rights. In high probability that spells "woman," due to the way men and women have been differentially socialized.

Whether or not a family had children was highly relevant. Obviously, with no children, no one need be at home. Often in families with children only one person would stay home, and this person was most commonly a woman. Whoever it was obviously could end up with more responsibilities than in a conventional household. Both "housekeeping" and "work scheduling" were much more often cited as problems by members of families with children.

We have finally concluded that there is a latent potential for true equality in multilateral marriages, but that potential has been far from fully realized in most groups. Liberation, role freedom, and equality for men and women simply require a great deal of hard work to achieve, whether one is in a two-person or a six-person relationship. Multilateral marriage in itself has little effect compared to attitudes and willingness to strive for equalitarian relationships.

We can expect the latent potential of multilateral marriage to continue to attract participants with highly equalitarian attitudes as Ramey observed in members of an expanded-family interest group.[4]

REFERENCES

1. The writings of Desmond Morris, *The Naked Ape* (New York: Dell, 1969), and *Intimate Behavior* (New York: Random House, 1972), are relevant to "pair bonding" in humans. Psychoanalyst François Duyckaerts details the development of relationships in *The Sexual Bond* (New York: Delacorte Press, 1970).
2. Hiam Ginott contrasts uniform and unique love, quality and equality in *Between Parent and Child* (New York: Macmillan, 1965).
3. James Ramey, "Communes, Group Marriage, and the Upper-Middle Class," *Journal of Marriage and the Family* 34, 4 (November 1972).
4. *Ibid.* See also Appendix III.

PART III
OUTCOME

8

Beginnings

Joe and Mark had gone to the same high school and became good friends through work. By that time, both had been married a couple of years. Joe and Jessica had dated a few times, but Jessica ended up marrying Mark; and Joe married Bev. The two men shared many interests. All four became fast friends, and did many things together. When Mark and Jessica moved into a new place, naturally Joe and Bev joined in the work. They didn't finish until late and decided it would be a good idea to get some sleep before morning. Since all four climbed into the only bed, it was a giggly night, and later Jessica said, "That was the first night we really were close." Not much later, Mark asked his wife, Jessica, what she would do if Joe ever asked her to go to bed and he (Mark) didn't mind. Her immediate reaction was that of course she would say No, because she was married to Mark and loved him. But as she thought further, she eventually decided that the idea was not so bad after all.

Then Bev picked up a copy of *The Harrad Experiment* and passed it on to her husband. And she suggested that Mark and Jessica read it, too. There followed visits, phone calls, and letters on the subject. After months of talking up their enthusiasm for trying it, they finally decided to live together.

There are other groups like Joe, Bev, Mark, and Jessica who began as friends and whose relationship slowly evolved into a multilateral marriage. We might call these the "serendipitous" relationships in that the original intentions were not the formation of a multilateral marriage. We would put three of the base study groups in this category. Two more are borderline cases which have some of the serendipitous characteristics but also share aspects of their beginnings with the other, larger category which we will call "pursued" relationships.

Rachel and Steve happened onto *The Harrad Experiment*, and as they read it together became increasingly excited by Rimmer's ideas. They started thinking of friends as potential partners. With malicious forethought they invited Harry and Jill B———, their number-one draft choice, over for dinner. A copy of *Proposition 31* had been carefully left on the coffee table where they hoped their friends would see it. Jill opened the subject with, "I see you have a copy of *Proposition 31*. I read a review of it. The idea sounds thoroughly disgusting—sleeping around and all. I devote my life to Harry. One man is all I need." Harry looked pained but chimed in. The dinner conversation was somewhat strained as Rachel and Steve realized that the B———s were not likely prospects. Some friends snubbed them for their "perverted" leanings, and soon Rachel wondered if they might be alone in their interest in group marriage.

Spring became summer and while camping at Miswanatchuk State Park, Rachel and Steve met the P———s. The P———s' campsite was next to theirs, and somehow in the lazy evening of chatting by Coleman light, "the subject" came up. Joy, ecstasy! The P———s shared their interest. Suddenly Laura P——— seemed awfully attractive to Steve, and Rachel began to think that Marty was okay after all. But the P———s were from upstate, so the best that could be done was to correspond. In the letters, ideology gave way to feelings and to plans for a weekend together to see how things would go. After another weekend in which they became sexually involved, they all decided to live together in a group marriage. Steve and Rachel's house was the bigger, so the P———s moved in with them. . . .

Laura, Marty, Steve, and Rachel pursued group marriage

and each other. Pursuers have problems that "innocents" who stumble into serendipitous relationships do not have. Few people are interested in group marriage, and meeting them is problematical. To raise the prospect of multilateral involvement, even with people who might potentially accept it, may ensure only a fast exit. Yet it would be dishonest for pursuers to pretend naïveté to the ramifications of a deepening friendship. When pursuers finally meet, they may seize upon each other out of fear of blowing what they suspect could be their only chance. There is too little time for them to get to know each other, much less understand subtle differences in basic personality which could be telling in a multilateral marriage.

We once quipped that couples interested in multilateral marriage ought to marry only neighbors who had been good friends for several years. We meant only that prolonged proximity and frequent interactions in a variety of contexts are required to know people well enough to marry them. We believe that longer "courtships" are conducive to longer marriages. In fact, the longest-lived base study group is a serendipitous group of long-term friends. Even this formula is no guarantee, for we recently heard from a group formed under very similar circumstances whose life together lasted only months. Years of friendship was not preparation for the reality of group living.

The problems of self-conscious courtship will probably affect many more people in the future as knowledge of alternatives removes the chance for innocent development of intimacy. This is the college coed's dilemma. To be prepared with contraceptives is to acknowledge the potential for sexual intimacy; to fail to prepare is irresponsible and risky. This is not an exclusively feminine quandary. A man may carry a condom with him because he is responsible, yet should it fall from his wallet while paying the bill on his first date, that may be his last with that woman—even though she might have potentially become sexually intimate if it developed "naturally," without "premeditation." This loss of innocence need not be mourned, but the transition, until new social norms are fully established, will pose many complications.

There do seem to be distinct steps involved in how respondents became interested in multilateral marriage, although they are not always ordered the same way. One step involves intellectualizing such concepts as the ability to love more than one, group living, personal growth, shared child-rearing, etc. For many, the crucial step is growing to love more than one person intimately and wanting an acceptable way of expressing all love openly.

COURTSHIP. It is surprising to many people who are curious about group and multilateral marriage that couples frequently date and court much like individuals interested in a conventional two-person marriage. Only the courting may be between two couples or one couple and a single man, for example. We have observed most of the paradigms from conventional courtship carried over into group courtship. Two couples may insist on a form of anticipated commitment—an "engagement"—before permitting sexual intimacy. They spend long hours on the telephone, have lovers' quarrels, break engagements, exchange love letters—in short do what people are generally expected to do when moving into marriage.

Casual inquirers have often assumed that the men are forcing their wives into a lifestyle that the women only reluctantly agree to live. It happens, but rarely. From our interview data, women were prime initiators or advocates as often as were men. But we did notice one sex difference: in general the men are better described as talkers and the women as doers. Women, once they made up their minds, tended to put the talk into action. This scene was reenacted in the beginnings of many groups: two men, talking on about theoretical and ideological issues while two women are busy doing something together, developing a real, multifaceted relationship.

The initiator or catalyst of involvement in a multilateral relationship, often became the first to retreat as the marriage evolved into reality.

There must, of course, be some one person whose commitment or enthusiasm is lowest, and some relationship has to be the weakest at any one time. During courtship, participants are usually well aware of the identity of the laggard or weak link. The laggard's heel-dragging will be tolerated by the others only within limits. If the contrast in enthusiasm is too great, the laggard can be the target of considerable pressure from the other three, four, or five people who feel they have met their mates and stand on the threshold of Eden. This pressure may work at the expense of ongoing tensions or it may backfire. Whenever one person opted out of a forming relationship among couples, the whole deal was off. We do not know of couples separating so that one could enter a group relationship.

Pressure on lagging relationships can be dysfunctional, too. Relationships will, of course, develop or not at their own unique pace. Generally, people cannot be forced to relate or to develop friendship, love, or intimacy. A most common problem occurs when one cross-marital pair is ready for sexual intimacy and the other is not. The situation itself tends to pressure the less-ready pair into sexual relations almost independent of the actions of the other pair. If the sexually ready pair have intercourse, that dramatizes the differences in level of intimacy and places expectations on the other couple. That couple could act out jealous behavior by "retaliating" sexually, or with their security shaken, have intercourse in a quest for warmth. If the more advanced pair staves off sexual actualization, tension and resentment of what the slower pair has "put on them" may build.

It should be apparent that great delicacy is required for smooth negotiation of the tortuous path to a multilateral wedding.

WEDDINGS AND HONEYMOONS. American husbands are notorious for forgetting wedding anniversaries, but at least they can look them up (or consult the wife's calendar) if they really need to know. Not so for the multilaterally married. Some "group weddings" have been publicized, but our respondents are not long on ceremony. A few groups had matching rings or pendants made. Some who maintain journals state within them the date of "marriage." One group made a verbal contract to remain together for a year and then reevaluate their commitment. But sometimes respondents had to pause and think before coming up with a date for when their marriage started. One group dated their marriage from their first sexual involvement. Another identified it with when they first felt really committed to each other and to the idea of a group marriage. Many groups chose the date they moved in together.

The honeymoon period of multilateral marriages often finds the partners totally absorbed in their new relationships. A consuming flush of excitement seems to be almost a property of developing intimacy; it is experienced even after many such encounters. Cross-marital pairs can become preoccupied with each other to the exclusion of their original spouses and their children, unless they are conscious of the temporary effects of novelty. This initial honeymoon period is not a good time to make decisions. We are suggesting that it ought to precede the wedding (commitment), and indeed it often does. Not a few people whose groups dissolved have felt that they became sexually involved too soon. Yet as a group, respondents rejected the statement, "Early sexual involvement among potential partners in a group marriage creates problems."

The honeymoon is followed by a period of integration when partners try to work out the nitty-gritty of a joint lifestyle. The ideal has to give way to the disconcerting necessities of settling on finances, getting enough sleep, catching up on housework, and other functions which have been neglected in the earlier excitement.

Thus end the beginnings.

9

Health and Happiness

"My question," the speaker at the back of the room begins, "is this: What is wrong with these people or their marriages that drives them into group marriage?" We pause a moment before replying, though we have heard this question numerous times before. Queries are stated in this form most often when the subject is exceptional and disapproved. People ask what "drives" homosexuals to prefer relations with their own sex; they do not ask what "drives" heterosexuals to prefer the opposite sex. The intrinsic bias in this formulation is best revealed by reversing the question, as we have many times been tempted to do, and asking the speaker, "What is wrong with *you* or with *your* marriage that *drives* you to stay monogamous?"

People do make value judgments, even bury them in the formulation of their questions. "Valuing" is a normal human activity which in normal discourse may not present problems. In any attempt at scientific inquiry, however, the form of the question is very important. How you ask the question determines what kind of answers you will be able to find; ask the wrong question and you may guarantee you will get the wrong answers.

Among even the most careful professionals, we have found a tendency to assume that participants in multilateral marriages must be sick, emotionally or psychologically ill or imbalanced; the only remaining question is in what way. It seems to us to be important to isolate the separate elements of such a question. A legitimate social and scientific inquiry is imbedded therein. And, as noted before, there is a value judgment which reflects on the inquirer and his value framework. There is also the inquirer's intended or potential use of the answer, and the interpretation which he might add.

The question may be strictly answered by stating the observed problems of individuals entering multilateral marriages. Even if these are in fact isolated within a total clinical picture that is normal, people have a tendency to recall only the sickness. What we have cited as a lone instance of difficulty has sometimes been quoted later as applying to all or most or many participants.

There remains the issue of motivation for the inquiry. The questioner may be concerned about what aid might be offered to participants. More often we have found that emotional pathology is the modern-day substitute for religious or moral condemnation. Actions which were really based on religious thinking have been justified in twentieth-century America, in part, in mental-health terms. Among numerous examples are discrimination and harassment of homosexuals, discouragement of premarital intercourse, and the like.

OBSERVATIONS. We, too, were interested in the relationship, if any, between emotional health or marital happiness and adjustment, on the one hand, and participation in multilateral marriage, on the other. In our observations, we attended to the nature and quality of interactions between individuals, how they seemed to function in various roles, and what they themselves said of their sense of strength or weakness, ability to cope or inability, growth and regression, and the problems and strong points in their marriages. Out of these observations, the interviews, and our participation in the family process, we formed some distinct impressions of the health and happiness of individual participants and respondents as a group.

We found most of them to be normally healthy people. Among those who valued careers and related aspects of achievement were some highly successful individuals; a theatrical producer who had achieved national recognition, a talented commercial artist, a competent and effective sociologist and counselor, to select a few examples. Several students completed graduate school during the period of our study. Even those who rejected the traditional work ethic or usual vocational alternatives were often highly successful at their chosen orientations or endeavors, not just growing vegetables, for example, but mastering the intricacies of organic gardening to produce the best vegetables in seven counties in a garden that was an aesthetic experience.

We do not feel that material accomplishment correlates very well with real emotional health, but *at least* most of these individuals can function well in a task sense, many at a high level.

Compared to many people of our acquaintance and certainly to societal norms, participants come across as significantly more open and communicative. They seem to be in touch with their feelings and motivations and prepared to share those directly with us and with each other. In the argot of the counterculture, they are "up front." This is, of course, part of the ethic associated with multilateral marriage and an essential value in a high "growth orientation," but it is also something that most participants seem to be able to actualize.

In this general picture of healthy functioning are some exceptions. One woman had been in long-term individual psychotherapy. She often had great difficulty coping with not only the multilateral marriage itself but more mundane matters, such as holding a job. Eventually she committed suicide. In contrast to the general case of communicativeness is one man who was financially very successful and a charismatic leader in the intentional community which accreted around him. He had a lukewarm style of expression which communicated little feeling or emotion. Seeming to have little awareness of the real feelings of the people around him, his description of his situation was often totally disconnected from their perceptions of real events. Otherwise functional groups would sometimes go through periods of considerable stress, triggering unusual and dysfunctional behavior by some or all of the members. Nevertheless, from our knowledge of all our respondents we would have to characterize them as a whole as unexceptional in terms of individual emotional problems and marital difficulties.

REALLY? Having conveyed our clinical impressions, the dialogue which opened this chapter might continue with another question. "Yes, but who are you to say that these people are not sick or that they have no more than average marital difficulty? How can you substantiate your impressions?" How *do* we substantiate such findings, when in many cases only we can have access to a group?

Fortunately there are psychological "tests" (more correctly called "inventories") which attempt to measure the factors of interest to us and our questioners. One of the best known and most widely used of these is the *Minnesota Multiphasic Personality Inventory* (MMPI), a long test as formidable as its name. The MMPI develops a picture or profile of the extent of various kinds of problems in a person's makeup based on his answers to a large number of questions. There are many issues about the validity, potential uses and misuses, and meaning of psychological instruments of this type based on pencil-and-paper replies. Suffice here to say that, while there are dissenting voices, psychologists, psychiatrists, and others who deal with personality and mental health rely heavily on such measures.

The MMPI purports to measure elements of pathology, of psychological difficulty according to standard categories by which these may be diagnosed. In a sense, it asks the question, "What's wrong with this person?" For those questioning us, the first choice of a check on our observations about individual psychological health was usually the MMPI. We felt its emphasis on "pathology hunting" was inconsistent with the philosophy of our project, and its use of diagnostic categories would make sharing information with respondents very difficult.

We chose to ask the question more directly with an instrument which measures positive elements of psychological health. The *Personal Orientation Inventory* (POI) was created by psychologist Everett Shostrom[1] to deal directly with the concept of self-actualization as developed by the late Abraham Maslow and others.[2] It has not been used as extensively as the MMPI (very few personality instruments have), but respect for the POI has grown as the number of studies using or testing it has grown.[3] The POI has obvious advantages within our study, especially the fact that the results are easily shared with whoever takes it and are useful to the individual in suggesting areas of strength and areas for further growth. In fact, the POI has been widely used in personal counseling.

In the POI, responses to 150 pairs of statements are used to develop scores on two major scales and ten subscales. Each scale purportedly measures some factor known or believed to be part of self-actualization, that is, of personal functioning at a high level. In general, higher scores mean a higher level of psychological functioning or health, although extremes on any scale may be suspect or may suggest less than optimal balance. Scores for any individual can be compared against standard scores for a "normal" group of people.

The results of our substudy using the POI corroborate our previous conclusions.[4] As measured objectively by this test, respondents proved to be psychologically healthy individuals, in some ways significantly above average. As could be expected, the range of scores was substantial, representing the range from those few with significant impairment of personality growth to those few with very high, even suspect, levels of self-reported functioning. But the median, the middle score, fell somewhat above average on all but one scale (which was only marginally below average). A profile of these scores is shown in Fig. 9–1.

Those scales on which respondents showed up as being *significantly** above average reveal an interesting composite picture of personality.

The typical participant in a group marriage was found to be substantially *inner-directed*. Such a person is autonomous and self-supportive, not dependent on others for support, for a sense of self-worth, or for direction and purpose. His values and support are "built-in." It is possible to be excessively inner-directed, but generally inner-directedness is associated with emotional health. We would expect individuals in a form of marriage running counter to prevailing values to be inner-directed.

While their sense of values was internally derived, respondents were also found to be flexible in the application of those values in real-life situations. This quality, called *existentiality*, is also a healthy attribute one might expect to find among participants in a form of marriage which almost certainly would have been unac-

* See Preface.

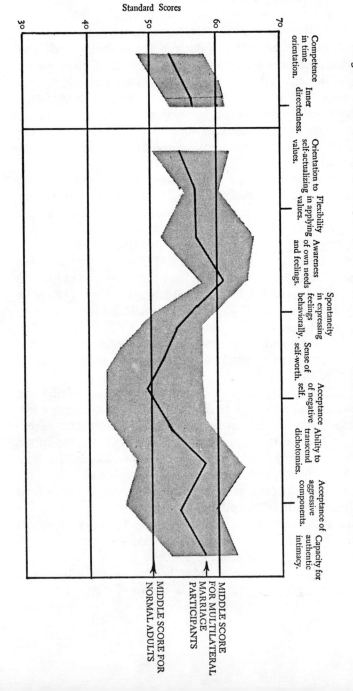

Fig. 9–1 Profile of POI scores of 40 participants in multilateral marriage. Shaded area represents 50 percent of scores.

ceptable within the value system in which they were raised. Existentiality is a measure of one's ability to use good judgment rather than be rigid and dogmatic.

Participants also scored above average in *feeling reactivity*, which means they are aware of their real feelings and needs. They are "in touch with themselves." More than that, they are highly spontaneous, able to communicate their needs and feelings freely in behavior. They are expressive of what they really feel. Scores on *spontaneity* were higher and the range narrower than on other scales. These results, too, make sense. Being aware of one's inner needs and desires and being able to take action on them would relate to their actually participating in what many only fantasize and then discard.

Second only to spontaneity, participants were highest in their *capacity for intimate contact*. They had exceptional abilities to form warm, meaningful interpersonal relationships. This capacity includes the ability to form authentic "I-thou" relationships based on individual uniqueness and expression of real feelings, unencumbered by excessive obligations and expectations.

This composite is hardly the profile of a sick or socially undesirable person. The notion that participants in multilateral marriages must show some pattern of real psychological problems must be firmly rejected. Caution is indicated in generalizing the observational and test results to any other group of participants in this or any other nonconventional marital form, but at least we can strongly assert that such people are not *necessarily* sick, simply because they violate community standards of morality.

We are making no assertion beyond the fact that respondents as a group appear through testing and observation to be psychologically healthy. No cause-and-effect relationship can be inferred. We believe that multilateral marriage does facilitate personal growth and shall go into that question in Chapter 11, but without controlled before-and-after measures we cannot support that contention with hard data.

BLISS. Even if as a group respondents did not have significant personal problems, they may have had difficulties in their marriages or other relationships which played a role in leading them into multilateral marriage. We were handicapped by the fact that we had no access to respondents until *after* they entered a multilateral marriage. Any assessment of their dyadic marital relationships had to deal with the dyads within or after the dissolution of the multilateral marriage. Otherwise the assessment would have to be retrospective.

Observations and interviews revealed both stable, highly functional, happy dyads and rocky ones. In a few cases, openly or unconsciously, the multilateral marriage was attempted to compensate for deficiencies in existing dyadic marriages. Nevertheless, we found the dyadic marriages to be fairly normal on the average. If anything, most of the couples seemed to have an above-average commitment to working through problems and to maintaining open, authentic communication. Of course informal comparisons to such a hypothetical average are highly subjective.

When we asked them to rate how happy they thought their dyadic marriages were just prior to their entry into the multilateral marriage relationship, the majority reported that they were happy, averaging 3.7 on a five-point scale. Of course, such self-ratings are difficult to make and interpret, as well as being grossly oversimplified. Like most couples, they feel they had been happily married. Then we asked them to assess their present primary relationship, whether they were still in a multilateral marriage or had returned to conventional marriage. Their averaging rating of their present relationship was 4.4 on the five-point scale. Having gone through the group-marriage experience, they saw themselves to be *significantly* happier.

When asked to rate their *total* group experience, they rated it as somewhat happy (mean of 3.4 on a scale of five) and reported that they felt their partners were about as happy.

ADJUSTMENT. Our criteria for selecting an instrument by which to measure marital adjustment were that the chosen method had to (1) have established norms for "ordinary" couples to serve as a comparison, (2) be widely used and recognized, (3) be brief and (4) be based on conventional concepts of marital adjustment but not on *a priori* assumptions that sexual involvement outside the dyad was in itself an indication of maladjustment. Finding a suitable measure proved to be an arduous undertaking.[5] Many inventories assumed that mere *fantasies* of alternate sexual involvement were indicative of marital discord. Others were too long, too difficult to obtain, or too experimental.

We reviewed a large number of measures before selecting the *Burgess-Cottrell Marital Adjustment Form* (B-C Form),[6] one of the older of several widely used, closely related tests of marital adjustment.* These measures are useful research tools but are open to justifiable criticism.[8] They are composites of many items, hence they lose some of the differential significance of the many aspects of a relationship. As pencil-and-paper instruments, they depend on the respondents' ability to perceive *and* relate their actual marital experience within the test framework.

Two of the strongest criticisms of this type of test were acceptable or advantageous in our use. The Burgess-Cottrell Form and others of its ilk really measure more an individual attitude or perception than a property of the marital relationship. This fits precisely with our methodological stance on relationships. Each independent perception is valid and valuable in itself. It is no contradiction that a marriage might be good as reported by one spouse and bad to the other. The B-C Form also appears to measure "conventionality" as much as it measures any aspect of marriage. Repeated studies have found that subjects with traditional, conventional attitudes tend to score higher in marital adjustment than less conventional subjects. Despite these and other limitations, the B-C Form has been found to be of some value in predicting the degree of success of different groups of couples.

If anything, the B-C Form is extremely conservative in its assumptions about the well-adjusted married couple. The score is

---

* Of the related tests, Locke and Williamson's more recent multiple-index test of marital adjustment is probably the most carefully constructed. Their test is derived from Peterson and Williamson's test which included nineteen of the items on the Burgess-Cottrell Form.[7] None of these more recent tests, however, have usable established norms, an important selection criterion for our purposes. A comparison reveals the Locke and Williamson test to resemble very closely the B-C Form, with improvements in wording, scoring, and division of adjustment into independent factors. Though the norms for the B-C Form are dated, their availability was the deciding factor in our selection.

based on such things as the extent a couple agrees on issues such as money, in-laws, religion, and sex; on how often they kiss; and on whether they have ever wished they hadn't married. This conventional orientation suited our purposes, precisely because group-married participants were *not* conventional and did not hold traditional views on marriage. It was thus a stronger test of our hypothesis that even in conventional terms participating couples had normal marriages.

As with marital satisfaction, we could not go back and measure the marital adjustment before couples entered into multilateral marriage. We modified the B-C Form to permit its dual use in the present relationship and in a retrospective evaluation of what respondents remembered to be the situation just prior to trying the multilateral marriage.[9] To our knowledge this technique has not been tried for assessment of earlier marital adjustment. In the absence of a separate study to validate the technique, we cannot say what effects its use has on scores. Perfectly reasonable but conflicting arguments can be constructed to predict that retrospective scores would be either inflated or diminished. Having no alternative, we have chosen to accept results at face value.

The present scores of respondents did not differ *significantly* from the norms. They did tend to include fewer respondents with very low marital-adjustment scores and fewer with very high scores; that is, respondents tended to be more "average" than average. For the retrospective reports on their prior relationships, this tendency was *statistically significant*. Nearly half of the prior scores fell in the three middle scoring ranges as opposed to less than one-quarter in the normative population.

Comparing before and after scores for the twenty of the twenty-five respondents who reported on the same dyadic relationship for both prior and present tests, we found a *statistically significant* increase.

Our own guess is that a couple with very poor marital adjustment is unlikely to enter into a multilateral marriage, because the extent of their problems is unlikely to leave enough energy to form the requisite new relationships and because they are less likely to be able to agree on the radical and very threatening action of opening up their relationship to others. The relative absence of very high scores could mean that highly adjusted couples would not likely be motivated into a new and highly risky form of marriage, but another explanation seems more likely. Very high scores are possible only if a couple agree (or believe themselves to agree) on virtually everything, have never had doubts about their relationship, find nothing in the relationship annoying, and find nothing to dislike in the spouse. In contrast to more traditional couples, respondents were openly accepting of differences and did not see them as negative. In a sense, then, there is a lower ceiling on scores for nontraditional couples.

In an early paper,[10] we noted that the multilateral-marriage environment often operated to expose habituated, unproductive behavior in dyadic relationships and to provide support for improvement in these relationships. We interpret the *significant* change in B-C scores as additional evidence that this is indeed the case.

CONFORMING. As noted earlier, numerous studies have found a relationship between conventionality and marital adjustment. More conforming or traditional couples tend to show up with higher marital adjustment. This has often been used to support such apple-pie wisdom as "The family that prays together stays together" or "Chastity leads to marital bliss." Recent research, however, suggests that the only real difference is that traditionally moral, religious, conservative people are simply more prone to distort the description of their marriage in the direction of social desirability.[11] To state that in reverse, less conservative and unconforming people are more apt to present an undistorted appraisal.

It is thus with some confidence that we assert, based on both observation and measurement, that people who have entered multilateral marriages, to the extent that respondents are representative, tend to be typically happily married. We can definitely rule out significant marital problems as a motivation in the vast majority of cases.

REFERENCES

1. Everett Shostrom, *Manual for the Personal Orientation Inventory* (San Diego: Educational and Industrial Testing Service, 1966).
2. Three of Maslow's important books discussing self-actualization and

his theory of a hierarchy of human needs are available in paperback: *Motivation and Personality* (New York: Harper & Row, 1970; 2nd edn.); *Toward a Psychology of Being* (New York: Van Nostrand, 1962); and *Eupsychian Management: A Journal* (Homewood, Ill.: Irwin and Dorsey Press, 1965).

3. An extensive bibliography on the results of use of the POI has been collected by Robert R. Knapp, "The Measurement of Self-actualization and Its Theoretical Implications," a report (San Diego: Educational and Industrial Testing Service, 1971).

4. Several of our earlier papers described participants as normally healthy in a psychological sense. The complete POI substudy is reported in Larry Constantine, "Emotional Health of Participants in a 'Deviant' Family Form" (unpublished). A related paper is Larry Constantine, "Personal Growth in Multiperson Marriages," *The Radical Therapist 2*, 1 (April-May 1971).

5. We were abetted in this search by the excellent book by Murray Strauss, *Family Measurement Techniques* (Minneapolis: University of Minnesota Press, 1969).

6. E. W. Burgess and P. Wallin, *Engagement and Marriage* (Philadelphia: Lippincott, 1953). Norms in Burgess and Cottrell, *Predicting Success or Failure in Marriage* (Englewood Cliffs, N.J.: Prentice-Hall, 1939).

7. See entries in Strauss' *Family Measurement Techniques*, pp. 57–58, 181, 182, 183, 271.

8. An excellent discussion of the pros and cons, as well as a copy of the Locke and Williamson test, can be found in J. Richard Udry, *The Social Context of Marriage* (Philadelphia: Lippincott, 1971; 2nd edn.).

9. With the kind permission of the publishers, Family Life Publications of Durham, N.C.

10. "The Pragmatics of Group Marriage," *The Modern Utopian 4*, 3–4.

11. Vernon H. Edmonds, Glenne Whithers and Beverly DiBatista, "Adjustment, Conservatism, and Marital Conventionalization," *Journal of Marriage and the Family 34*, 1 (February 1972).

10

Reasons and Unreasons

W**HY** *do* PEOPLE get married?

The answers are never simple or singular, and the ready ones may be suspect. Sex is very likely to be among the important reasons for the sexually conservative to marry, since the alternatives are few and restrictive. Yet the conservative is unlikely to admit that sex was a reason. In the deepest psychological recesses, everyone's reasons for marrying are manifold and subtle.

The direct approach is simply to ask a person why he married as he did. The result is what we described in Chapter 5 as the "public level." At the public level one hears the somewhat rehearsed, socially acceptable answers. The outsider would hear no more if he were to ask any married couple why they got married. Public-level reasons are real reasons, but they are never the only ones and may not be the most important.

At the public level, the multilaterally married tend to speak in family terms—expanded family, a sense of family, advantages for children. Children, economic and other practical potentials of the multilateral marriage, and freedom from rigid sex roles figure very high. Sex, if it enters the conversation at all, is likely to be downplayed. Sex is usually the first interest of outsiders. Some visitors have even assumed that they will be invited to indulge in an orgy.

We are not the only ones to see the deemphasis of sex by participants in multilateral marriages as a protective reaction to the
overemphasis of sex by outsiders.[1]

In the previous chapter we eliminated serious personal or marital pathology as a factor in most cases, so the question remains:
Why really do they marry multilaterally?

PRIVATELY. With an established relationship of trust, we felt that
questionnaires gave us access to respondents' private level of
motivations. The Individual Summary of the base study included a
checklist of fifty-six specific reasons why people might want to
undertake a multilateral marriage. The list was compiled from
numerous conversations, and though respondents were invited to
add additional reasons which were not on the list, no one did, so
we believe the list to be quite comprehensive. Later, the twenty-
four items listed in Table 10-1 were selected as most representative and were included in the nonrespondent survey.

Table 10–1. Possible reasons for interest or involvement in multilateral marriage appearing in both nonrespondent survey questionnaire
and the Individual Summary for respondents.

> Sense of isolation in conventional relationship
> Variety of sexual partners
> Greater economic power of larger group
> More chance for vocational variety
> New aspects of personality emerge relating to more people
> Less individual responsibility
> Sense of belongingness
> Feeling loved, desired, or wanted more
> Greater intellectual variety
> Multiple adult models for children
> Protesting establishment
> Personal fulfillment
> Richer environment for children
> More stability than conventional family/marriage
> Satisfy missing elements in my present relationship
> Strengthen bond with my present spouse
> Sense of "community"
> Increased self-awareness
> Opportunity for personal growth

More personal freedom
Easier child-rearing
Eliminate boredom or staleness
Expression of existing love or friendship for certain people
Religious principles/beliefs

We were looking for indications of the extent to which respondents represented a subset of the larger group. We felt that reasons for involvement were more indicative of the basic type of people involved than other possible indices available for respondents. We did predict some differences, however. Specifically, we hypothesized that respondents, having a more established relationship with us, would be less likely to represent themselves in terms of the more socially acceptable reasons. Distortion in the direction of social desirability is common in surveys and tests. We were testing whether the relationship with respondents indeed reduced this tendency compared with others in multilateral marriages who were not respondents.

We agreed upon five reasons as being clearly more socially acceptable and four which were clearly less socially acceptable among the 24 reasons. The socially more acceptable reasons were:

Sense of isolation in conventional relationship
Greater economic power of larger group
More chance for vocational variety
Multiple adult models for children
Richer environment for children

The socially less acceptable reasons were:

Variety of sexual partners
Protesting establishment
More stability than conventional family/marriage
Satisfy missing elements in my present relationship

We expected the nonrespondent survey to include more returns checking socially acceptable reasons and fewer checking socially unacceptable ones. All the differences were in the expected directions, five of nine were *statistically significant** (isolation, eco-

* See Preface.

nomic power, multiple models, richer environment, and sexual variety), and one more approached statistical significance (vocational variety).

We must caution that other explanations for these differences are possible, although ours is an attractive hypothesis. The simplest alternative explanation is that nonrespondents simply had different reasons for getting involved. Additional credence is lent to our explanation by virtue of the fact that there were no other statistically significant differences in reasons given.

Despite these differences, the correlation, or extent of agreement, between respondents and nonrespondents was high and *statistically significant,* justifying our pooling the two sets of returns.

From a scale weighted by whether an item was checked as a strong reason or just a reason, a ranking was established. Sixty respondents and nonrespondents say they were motivated to try a multilateral marriage for the following reasons. The important reasons, in order of decreasing importance from the *most* important, *most* frequent response, are:

> Personal fulfillment
> Opportunity for personal growth
> New aspects of personality emerging in relating to more people
> Richer environment for children
> Sense of "community"
> Multiple adult models for children
> Variety of sexual partners
> Greater intellectual variety

Fifty out of sixty checked "personal fulfillment" as among reasons for trying multilateral marriage, and forty-five checked "variety of sexual partners." From the same data we can identify things which are *not* reasons why people are getting involved in multilateral marriages. The *least* important reasons in order of increasing importance from the least important, most infrequent response (only six said it was among reasons for interest), are:

> Protesting establishment
> More stability than conventional family/marriage

Less individual responsibility
Religious principles/beliefs
Strengthen bond with present spouse
Eliminate boredom or staleness
Satisfy missing elements in my present relationship
Easier child-rearing

Other reasons were obviously of intermediate importance.

As a group, participants are seeking growth, a better family for their children, a community, and sexual and intellectual variety; most of them are not rebelling, seeking escape, acting on religious principles, or improving what they consider to be unsatisfactory marriages.

We found the same content and emphasis in the taped individual interviews and in discussions with whole groups and individuals. We are confident that this fairly represents, collectively, the private motivations for most participants in multilateral marriage.

We anticipated there would be differences between the reasons given by men and those given by women. Conventional marriage is more restricting and confining to women than to men. Since conventional marriage represents the point of reference, we would predict more expression of deficit motivation from women than from men, as well as more responses from women to reasons regarding freedom. In the same vein, we hypothesized a greater association between the respondent's sex and choice of easier child-rearing as a reason than between sex and the desire for a richer environment or multiple adult models for children. There were four items representing deficit motivation:

Satisfy missing elements in present relationship
Strengthen bond with my present spouse
Eliminate boredom or staleness
Sense of isolation in conventional relationship

Male-female differences were in the expected direction and were *statistically significant* for the first two reasons above. Male-female differences were in the expected direction for "more chance for vocational variety" and "more personal freedom" but were *not statistically significant*, though the latter approached significance. More women than men said "easier child-rearing" was a reason, though *not significantly* more. As expected, the association with sex of the respondent was stronger for that item than for either "richer environment" or "multiple adult models."

All in all, male-female differences were few and slight. Among respondents, *significantly* more men than women said sexual variety was a strong reason, but the number for whom this was a reason was about the same for both sexes. Our hypothesis that the greater restrictiveness of conventional marriage for females is responsible for sex differences is further supported by the fact that no other significant sex differences were found in the combined sample.

Respondents alone were given a longer (fifty-six-item) list from which to select their reasons for participating in multilateral marriage; consequently the results are somewhat different. On a weighted score, the most important reason was "companionship," cited by more than four in every five respondents and as a *strong* reason by 42 percent. Nearly 90 percent included "variety of sexual partners" among reasons, but fewer than one in five reported it to be a strong reason. Of the next five reasons, all closely ranked, four were aspects or paraphrases of personal growth. Intellectual variety followed close behind.

Sixty-four percent listed among their reasons that they loved the particular people involved and 30 percent, second only to "companionship," indicated that love was a *strong* reason for their involvement. As many considered their children to be strong reasons for involvement as considered personal growth to be. At the very bottom of the list (only 9 percent) were "bisexual opportunities," "retreat from outside," and "religious principles/beliefs." Details will be found in Appendix IV.

The reasons given by respondents were analyzed to see if there were *significant* associations with the type of group formed, the duration of previous marriage, the ages of respondents, the number of children they had, and the duration of the multilateral marriage. The number of such associations discovered was so small compared to the several hundred relationships tested as to be attributable to mere chance. Table 11 in Appendix IV lists the associations found.

PROBLEMS AS REASONS. A few of the multilateral marriage participants (respondents and others) were motivated by or seeking solutions to personal or marital difficulties. While they are the exception, we have seen enough cases to discern some fragments of patterns. Because so few instances are involved, our understanding here is skeletal and tentative. The two foci common to more than one problem-motivated group have been security-insecurity issues and sexual inadequacy. More often than not, a wife has appeared to be the prime motivator for the group formation and for use of the group as a means to an improved situation. In most cases it seems that difficulties were felt more acutely by the wives.[2] Participants were not always aware of their problem-oriented motivations at the time the group formed.

Because there are more partners, a multilateral marriage may be seen as offering greater security than a conventional marriage. A spouse who considers his or her position in a dyadic marriage to be insecure may opt for a multilateral relationship as a means of achieving security. On the other hand, the potential participant may see the jealousy potential of multilateral marriage as adding to insecurity and choose it as a means to force encounter with his own or his spouse's insecurity. The multilateral marriage may be undertaken for its presumed effect on the spouse in giving an expanded, more intense base of love experience from which to grow or because of its "hothouse effect" in forcing growth.

One case is illustrative of the typical outcome. Among the many reasons that the four members of this group could give for wanting a multilateral marriage, one is that one of the women, Eleanor, did not feel her marriage to Malcolm gave her the security she desired. It is as if she thought that two partially committed husbands were better than one and maybe as good as one completely committed husband. It is not important whether her perception of her husband's commitment was correct; this is how she saw it. The rub in this case was that the group heightened her sense of insecurity. Malcolm's deep involvement with the other woman contrasted with her own lack of involvement with either the other man or the other woman. With a group of more equally, mutually committed people, the stratagem might have been functional, but for Eleanor the result was painful. Her jealous behavior resulting from heightened insecurity also added to the friction and tensions of the group.

Occasionally, sexual dysfunction figures among motivations for entering multilateral marriage. The sexual experience in the multilateral situation is sought because of its potential effects on whatever problem is presenting itself. In this respect, what is usually important to the instigator is the combination of the sexual experience with committed, supportive intimacy, hence other simpler and more purely sexual group experiences are viewed as unacceptable approaches to the presenting problem. We believe the experience of one young couple is fairly representative.

Winn and Lenore hoped to resolve their sexual difficulties through intimate involvement with the J———s. To Winn and Lenore, Nat and Eva J——— appeared to be much more sexually sophisticated. The problem from Lenore's standpoint was that Winn ejaculated prematurely; to Winn, the problem was that Lenore was slow to climax. Each thought that the other would learn from being sexually involved with a more sophisticated person. Indeed, Winn found that Eva J———'s faster responses enabled him to bring her to climax. Lenore learned that with Nat's slower responses, she could climax. This experience of success did build self-confidence, but each became more convinced that the problem must therefore lie with the other. When the group relationship dissolved, Lenore and Winn found that the problems in their marriage were worse. They sought counseling briefly and changed living situations in an effort to improve their relationship. Eventually they decided to separate, at first as an experiment, but later, on Winn's request, permanently.

Interestingly, we have found a common and somewhat unexpected outcome in most problem-motivated multilateral relationships, including the one just given. The wives, who often initiated the multilateral involvement and seemed more aware of dyadic problems, emerged having consolidated major personality gains, growing significantly in their sense of autonomy and self-worth. In several instances, the multilateral marriage, however unsatisfactory, led to a period of separation and independence which was very formative. Sometimes the women carried young children and major responsibilities with them to live completely on their own for the first time, and in the process discovered major strengths in themselves.[8]

MOTIVATION AND PERSONALITY. There is another way of looking at why people might actually enter an unusual form of marriage. What is in their personalities that could account for their choosing multilateral marriage? Do they share to some degree common personality characteristics which might represent basic, internal reasons for their participation?

For seeking answers to these questions, we felt that standard testing techniques based on accepted theories of personality would be superior to our observations and interviews. Undoubtedly, clinically trained personnel could elicit useful data on personality from clinical interviews, but even then there would remain questions of objectivity, distortions induced by the interviewer, and lack of strictly comparable results. Pencil-and-paper tests can be remarkably efficient in gathering personality data, and well-designed ones are resistant to bias and even to faking.

The *Edwards Personal Preference Schedule* (EPPS)[4] is among the most widely used personality instruments. It is based on a theory of personality which, in part, sees people in terms of the basic needs in their lives.[5] For instance, every person seems to manifest some need for order, some need to have order or pattern in life, though the amount of order a person seeks varies from person to person. Some people are satisfied to live in relative disarray, while others seem to need precise and detailed arrangement in every aspect of their lives. Most of us fall at various points in between. Each of us is prone to judge the behavior of others by our own needs. One with a very low need for order may see a neat and punctual person as compulsive, while the latter might call one who lived a relatively unordered life "slovenly" or "chaotic." Yet no point on the scale is more healthy than another.

The scales derived from the EPPS are more or less free of value judgments; it is an unthreatening inventory to take. The test consists of a large number of pairs of statements from which the taker must choose the one that better applies as an expression of his own preferences. From these a profile is derived of that person's level on each of fifteen normal personality needs. What the EPPS really does is feed back the person's own choices in a slightly different way, bringing together a large number of seemingly unrelated preferences (such as all those expressive of a need for order) into a single scale. Seeing oneself in this unusual mirror can be a valuable eye-opener. Consequently, the EPPS is extensively used in guidance and counseling.[6] The manifest needs reported in the EPPS are described in Table 10-2.

The pattern of needs exhibited by any one participant may say nothing about his reasons for becoming involved in a multilateral marriage. Similar patterns found among *many* participants could indicate common motivations at the level we have called "personal." It is at least plausible that participants were attracted to multilateral marriage because of its potential for fulfilling certain normal personality needs which for them were relatively strong. The relative absence of other needs may have facilitated involvement.

We hypothesized that we would see such relationships when scores were aggregated. We felt that the exceptional nature of multilateral marriage compared with prevailing social patterns would require, on the average, fairly high motivation in terms of basic personality. In individual cases, many other variables—such as the spouse's interest, opportunity, and the like—would have to be taken into account, but collectively, these would tend to diminish in importance.

The importance of sexual reasons revealed at the private level should show up at the personal level as well. The EPPS does not measure any "need for a variety of sexual partners," but it does include two scales which are relevant. The *het* (for heterosexuality) scale is essentially an assessment of sexual need. We hypothesized that respondents would have above-average sexual drive. The *chg* scale measures need for change. Significantly high scores on both scales could be given the interpretation of reflecting or including the need for sexual variety. We also saw multilateral marriage as a means of satisfying affiliative needs for people and so predicted high scores on the need for affiliation (*aff*).

To be in a multilateral marriage is to buck society. We predicted that participants would be low in the need to conform, which is included in the *def* (need for deference) scale of the

Table 10-2. Normal personality needs measured by the Edwards Personal Preference Schedule

Scale	Need for-	Description
ach	achievement	ambition, to succeed, to do one's best, to accomplish something of great significance.
def	deference	dependence, to follow orders (and others), to conform, to be dependable.
ord	order	neatness, to have organization, be systematic and plan in advance; orderly schedule.
exh	exhibition	attention, to be the center of things, to be noticed, to talk about oneself.
aut	autonomy	independence, to be free in decisions and actions; to be non-conforming, without obligations.
aff	affiliation	need for people, friends, groups; to form strong attachments.
int	intraception	need to know, to understand—what and why; to analyze others' motives and empathize.
suc	succorance	to *receive* help, encouragement, sympathy, kindness from others.
dom	dominance	to be a leader, to lead, direct and supervise; to persuade and influence others.
aba	abasement	conscience, to feel guilty and accept blame; to confess wrongs, admit inferiority.
nur	nurturance	to *give* help, sympathy, kindness to others, to be generous.
chg	change	variety, novelty; to experiment, try new things, experience change in routines.
end	endurance	perseverance, tenacity; to finish what is started, to stick with something even if unsuccessful.
het	sexuality	need for opposite sex, for sexual activities; to do things involving sex.
agg	aggression	to attack contrary views, to criticize, to tell what one thinks of others.

EPPS. They should tend to be independent, which would show up as a high need for autonomy (*aut*). Finally, inasmuch as multilateral marriage runs counter to the precepts of morality in which all of us are immersed, we anticipated that respondents would show low need for abasement (*aba*), that is, little *need* to feel guilty or to lay blame on themselves.

In some respects the need for change and the need for order are complementary. Having seen multilateral marriage as a departure from order and a distinctly less-ordered lifestyle than conventional marriage, we also hypothesized low need for order (*ord*).

One last hypothesis had to do with personal growth as a motivation. The need for intraception (*int*), that is, the need to know and understand, seems to be pertinent. Intraception includes the desire to know others and understand their motivations and as such can be related to the desire of participants to form authentic intimate relationships. For both reasons we felt that scores on *int* would be above average.

The profiles in Figs. 10-1 and 10-2 are composites of the nineteen males and twenty-three females for whom EPPS results were available. The profiles compare respondents to the nearly ten thousand adults on whom the EPPS was standardized. From the profiles it is evident that almost all the differences are as predicted. Only the need for affiliation was not as predicted. Apparently the need for people is not an important motivational factor in multilateral marriage. All the other differences were *statistically significant*.

Some *statistically significant* differences were found which had not been hypothesized. Both men and women showed very little need for endurance, that is, little need to persevere simply for the sake of persevering. They are unlikely to stick with something (even marriage) out of a need to see it through to its bloody conclusion. This in itself might be sufficient to account for the high rate of dissolution of multilateral marriages.

As compared with other women, women in multilateral marriages were found to be somewhat above average in the need to be succored and below in the need to give nurturance. Male participants were found to be significantly low in the need for aggressive behavior compared with most men. Their low *need* to be aggres-

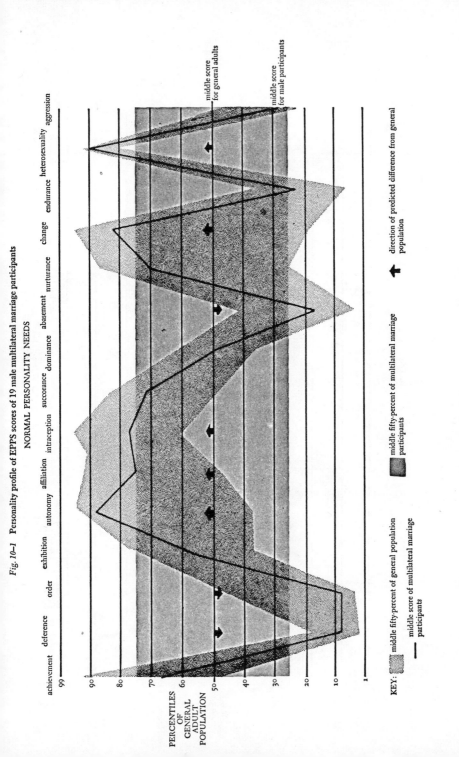

Fig. 10-1 Personality profile of EPPS scores of 19 male multilateral marriage participants

NORMAL PERSONALITY NEEDS

achievement   deference   order   exhibition   autonomy   affiliation   intraception   succorance   dominance   abasement   nurturance   change   endurance   heterosexuality   aggression

PERCENTILES
OF
GENERAL
ADULT
POPULATION

99
90
80
70
60
50
40
30
20
10
1

middle score
for general adults

middle score
for male participants

KEY: ▨ middle fifty-percent of general population
       participants

       ▦ middle fifty-percent of multilateral marriage
       participants

       —— middle score of multilateral marriage
       participants

       ← direction of predicted difference from general
       population

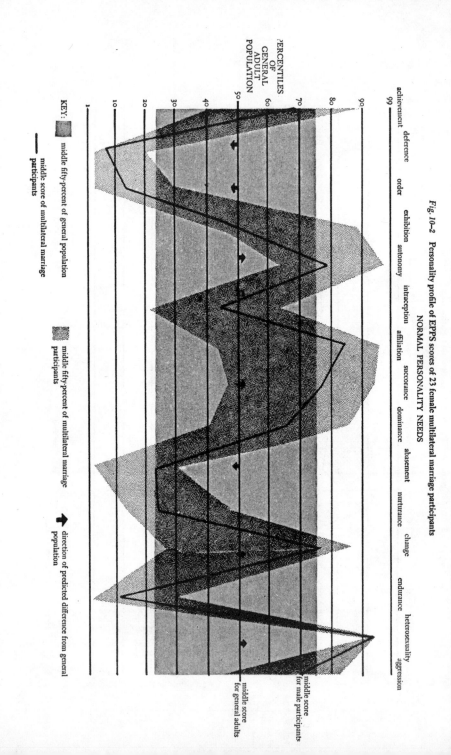

Fig. 10-2 Personality profile of EPPS scores of 23 female multilateral marriage participants

NORMAL PERSONALITY NEEDS

PERCENTILES OF GENERAL ADULT POPULATION

achievement   deference   order   exhibition   autonomy   intraception   affiliation   succorance   dominance   abasement   nurturance   change   endurance   heterosexuality   aggression

99
90
80
70
60
50
40
30
20
10
1

KEY:

middle fifty-percent of general population participants

middle fifty-percent of multilateral marriage participants

middle score of multilateral marriage participants

direction of predicted difference from general population

middle score for male participants

middle score for general adults

sive forms an interesting contrast with their normal *acceptance* of aggression as indicated by the POI results reported in the preceding chapter. Similarly, the normal needs for affiliation of both men and women can be compared with their exceptional capacity for intimacy revealed by the POI. Women in multilateral marriages, it should be noted, were, compared to other women, higher in sexual drive than were the men in comparison with other men. Thus women and men in multilateral marriages were more nearly sexually equal.

Once more we have a finely etched portrait of the personalities of many of the participants in multilateral marriages. The typical participant has a need to be free and independent, little need for dependence or conformity. He or she tends to seek change and variety without much need for an orderly life. Such a person is strongly sexual with a will to know and understand things, including the people with whom he or she is involved. A need to feel guilty or accept blame is not an important motivator.*

REPRISE AND CODA. The reasons some people try multilateral marriage form a consistent but convoluted pattern. It is very difficult to summarize the information from so many different channels. Considered in total, we would have to say that the reasons are as diverse as the people, and as varied as the reasons why other people choose conventional marriage. Love, sex, children, money, companionship, novelty, rebellion, and escape have all been important reasons for some people to enter into multilateral marriage. Some

* It is instructive to do as we suggested in the preceding chapter and reverse the comparison, asking what makes other people enter into monogamous marriages instead of marrying multilaterally. Compared to participants in multilateral marriage, most people would be described as having low needs for independence or freedom of decisions and actions and very high needs to conform, be dependent, follow, and to live neat and orderly lives. Compared to the multilaterally married, monogamously married persons don't need much in the way of variety or novelty and have a low sex drive. They do not seek really to know things or people. They have a genuine need to feel guilty. But they *are* likely to be persistent.

We feel that this somewhat tongue-in-cheek analysis is illustrative of intrinsic biases in making comparisons with norms. It is unusual but perfectly fair to define the norm with reference to exceptions.

few have had unsatisfying marriages which they sought to improve or to which they wished better alternatives. Some were motivated by abundance, some by deficits; some looked for extensions to good relationships, while others tried to fill holes. They were also attracted by the sexual advantages of multilateral marriage. There is little doubt, however, that the potential of the marriage to facilitate personal growth is a major reason for a majority to participate in multilateral marriage.

We would add another reason. Perhaps this new element is consequence rather than cause, or it may be the compound of other concepts. It comes up too frequently to be ignored, though. We see in most participants something which approaches being a genuine drive for intimacy, an active seeking for intimate contact and involvement with other human beings.* We wonder whether that isn't what marriage is about or is supposed to be about.

Intimacy.

We got married to be intimate.

REFERENCES

1. Reporter Ruthie Stein made similar observations in "Not Just an Ordinary Family," *San Francisco Chronicle* (August 28, 1970), p. 19.
2. Our paper, "Dissolution of Marriage in a Non-conventional Context," *The Family Coordinator* 21, 4 (October 1972).
3. For example, the case of the Allens and the Barnetts in "Dissolution of Marriage in a Non-conventional Context," *op. cit.*
4. Allen L. Edwards, *Manual for the Edwards Personal Preference Schedule* (New York: The Psychological Corporation, 1954).
5. The theory is Henry A. Murray's "personology." See Calvin S. Hall and Gardner Lindsey, *Theories of Personality* (New York: Wiley, 1970; 2nd edn.).
6. Kilgo's use ("The Use of the EPPS in Premarital and Marriage Counseling," presented at the 1969 meeting of the National Council on Family Relations, Washington, D.C., October 1969) was the immediate antecedent of our own use. See also Edwards, *op. cit.*
7. James Ramey, "Communes, Group Marriage, and the Upper-Middle Class," *Journal of Marriage and the Family* 34, 4 (November 1972).

* See Ramey's[7] observations on the desire for intimacy of people interested in expanded families and group marriage.

11

Growing

I remember my first marathon experience.* I was really surprised at how quickly I could really get to know people. We really got to caring about each other in those two days. At first we mostly sat around and talked about trivial things, played little verbal games with each other. But gradually, just being together, *having* to be together, all the time—I mean the tensions got pretty high—we began to break down some of the barriers and people started risking themselves, you know, really letting you in, inside. But it was so intense. Like everything was magnified. Angry feelings, love, everything. I think everyone felt drained, emotionally exhausted after only two days of that intensity of interaction. But there was something exhilarating about it, like one woman said at the end, a sense of having done a lot too, like we came a long way, sometimes a little painfully.

My group marriage is a lot like that. There's the same intensity, and we often get that good feeling that we are growing, becoming more "person," less "role." We know ourselves that much better and can be that much more.

Only the encounter doesn't end. I don't go back home Sunday at three. Peg and Hank are still there in the morning.

* A marathon encounter group, a group which meets around the clock, or nearly so, for one or two days, to foster growth and interpersonal risk-taking. The section on Skills in the Bibliography at the back of the book contains references on encounter groups.

Most of the respondents and survey informants sought out multilateral marriage for its potential for facilitating personal growth. One of the things they expect to get from the relationship is greater self-awareness through intimate interaction with other people. Through the process of the group they hope to further develop their fullest potential as human beings. Nearly four out of five had had previous experience in encounter groups.*

Neither encounter groups nor group marriages are forms of therapy. They are not at all for people with real emotional problems. Growth experiences can be profoundly therapeutic in helping just ordinary people enhance their strengths and overcome the blocks that keep them from realizing all their potential. Encounter groups serve other related purposes which are less important to participants in multilateral marriages. An encounter experience can reveal to people how much of themselves remains hidden and unknown to other people; it can show how the risks of openness and intimacy, though real, are greatly exaggerated and oftentimes more than compensated for by the rewards. These things must already have been learned before one can really consider a multilateral marriage. Valuing intimacy is among reasons why people have entered multilateral relations.

There are many varieties of planned and unplanned growth experiences. One thing which makes the multilateral marriage somewhat special is that "the encounter doesn't end." Actually, this can be both advantage and disadvantage. The intensity of involvement has become so great for many groups that they have had to take positive steps to keep it from getting out of hand, to limit the marathon to part, rather than all, of the time.

THE PROCESS. As we and most of our respondents use the term, "to encounter" means to meet person to person, disarmed and open, in an effort to communicate directly, honestly, and authentically; to be aware and spontaneously expressive of real feelings, and to understand and be understood at a deeply emotional level. Encounter is not confrontation, not a face-off or a simple venting of hostility. Anger is but one of the human emotions. The purpose of encounter is not to "break down" defenses as in oversimplified

---

* See Skills section in Bibliography for references on encounter groups.

popularized accounts of encounter groups. In the present sense, encounter is not possible unless people can be relatively defenseless with each other when the need for defenselessness arises. Neither is the encounter process very accurately described as "navel gazing" as some writers have suggested. It is a process of making genuine contact in order truly to know and be known beyond simply sharing activities and participating in common tasks, which may build a sense of cohesiveness and group identity, but not authentic intimacy.

THE INTERPERSONAL MIRROR. We believe that one of the most important ways in which multiple relationships, especially multilateral marriage, facilitates personality growth is through the process of mutual disclosure.* Real self-disclosure, exposure of what one really is, is in itself integrally related with emotional health and growth. Growth facilitates the ability to disclose, and self-disclosure facilitates growth.

Intimate interpersonal relationships play a special role in the process of the person's "becoming." As psychologist Sidney Jourard put it, "no man can come to know himself except as an outcome of disclosing himself to another person."[1] To disclose meaningful parts of oneself is a risk, and a growing intimacy leads to taking that risk. Disclosure by one person facilitates disclosure by the other and an accumulation of real knowledge of the other's personhood increases the sense of intimacy. In relationships in which people seek to be open and become intimate, a cumulative spiral is set up which builds self-knowledge and knowledge of the other person.

Each person is then a mirror in which one sees a part of oneself. What we see depends on what we can reveal, and we see it revealed in what the other can reflect to us. Whether we can see and make use of this reflection depends in large measure on our trust and regard for its source. It is sound folk wisdom that different people bring out different aspects of ourselves. We cannot be all of who we are with any one person, nor can any one person mirror except through what he is and what portion of that he can be with us.

* Our view of this process is a direct derivative of that of Sidney Jourard.[2]

It should be clear that multilateral relations are highly conducive to significant personal growth.

Kaye was married to a highly intelligent man. For whatever reasons, George tended to belittle Kaye's intellectual forays. In contrast to his quick theoretical mind, Kaye's could seem quite ordinary. She saw herself as somewhat slow. But Ned, who did not have a backlog of habituated exchanges with her, could see and appreciate the intellectual side of Kaye; in fact, her intellect was an aspect that most strongly attracted him. Ned himself was very intelligent and Kaye's relationship with him made her value what he said of himself and her. Through Ned, Kaye began to see, appreciate, and develop a neglected side of herself.

Once Kaye was talking with Mary, Ned's wife, with whom she had developed a strong friendship. She disclosed something about herself about which she seldom spoke. Her father had always pushed her to achieve. When she failed to live up to his expectations, he pushed her all the more and implied that had he had a son, he would not have been so disappointed. Kaye admitted to Mary that she had never felt very feminine. Mary could see how Kaye might get this feeling and she said so. Because Kaye regarded Mary as very feminine, Mary was able to help her to see the femininity in herself, in part by drawing attention to traits they shared.

WOMEN. All the evidence indicates that women are the major benefactors of the multilateral marriage experience, and they themselves generally evaluate their experience this way. Through the effects of interactions with intimates other than her husband, the woman begins to see more of who she is and more of her varied potential as a person. However liberated or not she may have been previously, she becomes more autonomous and defines her "self" less in terms of her husband and her role as wife, more in terms of her unique potential. Of course, growth of this nature could be facilitated by many experiences; we are not saying that multilateral marriage has a special claim on this. In fact, we would expect that almost any form of alternate intimate involvement would have some similar effect. But we would describe most of the women in our contacts with multilateral marriages as having consolidated major personality gains and become significantly more independent as the result of processes begun or taking place in the multilateral marriage.

Our analysis of reasons for participation suggests that women are often fully aware at the outset that they have the most to gain.

SLOWPOKES. The initial weeks and months of most multilateral marriages have been periods of tremendously rapid growth. More than one group has become so intensely involved in "process" that they neglected to have fun. The pace does slacken; at the same time it appears that problems seem to loom larger. At this point, groups have sometimes engaged in a form of scapegoating.

Almost every group has been able readily to identify some one person who was regarded by consensus as having made the least progress. Growing is good but often painful. Having barely consolidated their own gains, but seeing the group seemingly stuck in process, the faster-changing members turn to the identified straggler and exhort him to grow. After all, they have been through it, faced themselves, and changed for the better; now it is his turn.

At any time, the pressure can be very high for the person in the "hot seat" on whom process has focused. When the group zeroes in on one of its own as holding them up, the pressure can become unbearable. It is a mutually reinforcing, self-defeating process. The slowpoke is blocked from every direction. He cannot change, stay put, or go back. He cannot deny what others have accomplished nor shift the spotlight to them. He is caught. Some people respond positively to this dilemma, but not many. It is a common occurrence demanding sensitive anticipation and creative, consolidated efforts for the group to be able to deal with it productively. At the very time when they are most impatient, the group has to give their scapegoat room to maneuver and grow.

SEXUAL INTIMACY. We have come to believe that the sexual dimension of a multilateral marriage actually increases its worth as a growth-facilitating experience. When *The Radical Therapist* published Larry's paper on the subject of growth in multiperson marriages,[3] the editors bleeped the section on sex and growth. Later, when we were invited to respond, Larry wrote to the editor:

This is one way to state a part of how I view human sexuality. When people become authentically involved, they desire to communicate. And obviously, communication is a part of (all of?) the process of building authentic intimacy. Sex is one modality of communication. So are words, non-sexual touching, facial expressions, etc. In large part, how fully we experience ourselves is related to our freedom and ability in expressing ourselves and receiving feedback. A *priori* limitations on any modality may not only adversely affect relationships but the individual's experiencing of her/himself. Sex may be special in this regard; for most people sex is highly cathected and experienced as being close to their basic identity as a man or woman. Restricting one modality may temporarily enhance communication by forcing use of underused modalities (model: non-verbal sensitivity games). Sex may also be special in that sexual desire enters into even non-intimate relationships. What I am leading up to seems almost too obvious to state.

We find in our research on group marriages that sex does contribute to intimacy, though its exclusion is likely to have a more dramatic effect on relationships than its *inclusion*. Sex also may serve as a valuable trigger to force certain issues; the emergence of suppressed jealousy, for example.

The old model for male-female relations is: sex, especially sex that comes too early in a relationship, interferes with developing authentic intimacy. It is really based on: "If I play my cards right I can manipulate him (her) into bed on my own terms." On this premise, sex means that someone's maneuver has succeeded—manipulation not intimacy. But some people subscribe to a more viable model: "Only if I am myself and do *not* manipulate a particular end will the relationship mean anything." If real intimacy develops, sex is a very probable concomitant and sexual openness without manipulation can speed authentic intimacy.

In short, I do not believe that relationships which exclude sexual communication are more authentic than sexual relationships. Leaving all modalities as potential channels for communication is a better model for authentic intimacy. The very worst situation is where sex is excluded and there is also a taboo against even talking about the sexual attraction that will generally be there. Regrettably, this is the most common situation in social intercourse.

End of theory for now.

We are certainly not so naïve as to contend that sexual involvement *necessarily* enhances relationships, but in the right contexts with the right premises, the closeness and involvement that generally accompany sex can greatly facilitate intimacy. Multilateral marriage seems to be such a context.

Obviously, there can be direct growth in specifically sexual areas as the result of multilateral involvement. We have been told many times how the multilateral marriage was instrumental in freeing up participants sexually. Because of the close association between sex and jealousy for many people, growth from dysfunctional possessive jealousy has often been facilitated by sexual encounters which bring the issue to the fore or permit a person, through his own multiple involvement, to identify with the joy his spouse must get from the same experience.

COUPLES. Multilateral marriage has dramatic effects on the existing dyadic marriages. Every established couple has patterns of repetitious behavior that persist irrespective of their efforts. Some wonder why they keep fighting about the same things, never getting anywhere, why it is always "Here we go again!" Some couples may not be at all aware of the games they play, the intricate ways they act out their parts in a marital script which has its own special if hidden rewards. Eric Berne and his successors have contributed a great deal to our understanding of the games people play and their relationship to how we grew up and the kind of marriages we make.[4]

The multilateral marriage has advantages in that multiperson "games" are less easily established and played than "two-handed games."[5] And four-person games are less likely than three-person ones. We found support for this in our data; members of triads were substantially more likely than tetrads to indicate "dysfunctional 'cycles' of behavior" as one problem in the multilateral marriage.

It is hard for some couples to realize that the sorts of patterns we are writing about or which they read about in *Games People Play* apply to them as well, not just to sick people or troubled marriages. Besides the official marriage and its openly recognized basis, the couple also have a kind of unwritten marriage "contract" that was "signed" in secret and in which they agree to supply each other with certain satisfactions, playing specific roles that really suit the childlike parts of both husband and wife.[6] It is as if the final clause on the contract read: "Furthermore, the undersigned hereby agree never to discuss the terms of this contract nor to acknowledge its existence." Thus it is difficult for couples to be aware of this basis for their marriage. To make matters worse, outsiders can seldom get close enough to more than glimpse it. It takes the right balance between closeness and distance to be able to understand a couple's scripted behavior without becoming a part of it.

Repeatedly we found that the intense, intimate, open environment of the multilateral marriage exposed the scripts and the terms of the contract to the couples involved. The new context made old behaviors stand out in sharper contrast; habituated responses are difficult to see while situations remain unchanged. Most importantly, the other people in the multilateral marriage could come to know the couple well enough and see them enough in everyday circumstances to get some insight into the real nature of their relationship. The trust and intimacy within the group made it especially easy for couples to hear the feedback they received about what their marriage was really like.

Here is a common example. In many ostensibly equalitarian marriages, the hidden marital contract calls for the wife to defer to the husband in many instances and for the husband to be dominating and directive. This provides rewards to both by reinforcing basic feelings they have built up about themselves from childhood. Their behavior on the surface may appear to be fair and equal. In the spotlight of multilateral relationships, the hidden meaning of many exchanges becomes clear. The other couple notice that, when the chips are down, the marriage falls back on a pattern of dominance and deference. As the other couple give more, and more consistent feedback, husband and wife begin to see this aspect of their marriage.

But renegotiating contracts and changing old interactive habits can be most difficult. The other couple, eager to see problems in dyads solved so that the group can function better, are more likely to pressure than to be supportive or facilitative.

For many couples, including most survey informants, their marriage relationships changed for the better as the result of this process of exposure. The effects of such a confrontation have often been disruptive and, should the group dissolve, may take a long time to be resolved. In some cases, the result of this new awareness was for partners to conclude that their futures lay in different directions, so they separated. But both their reports and our observations lead us to believe that most of the dyads are eventually significantly improved as the result of the multilateral marriage experience.

Often a short-lived multilateral marriage has been the trigger for long-term growth efforts. Nearly two years after she and her husband left a foursome, one woman wrote us of her own growth in relationship to the multilateral marriage and her experience with transactional analysis:

I've been working in groups a lot the last nine months or more. . . . Group situations reminded me more or less of many childhood settings. I wasn't in touch with the here-and-now enough. I felt a lot of anger and pain that wasn't related to the present. [In the multilateral marriage] I was in touch with a lot of feelings that I was frightened of. I didn't know how to tell anyone how I was feeling until I felt like exploding.

As we all know the big explosion puts people up-tight. Many times after I got through my anger, though, I could really express how I was feeling. Most of my frustration was because I wouldn't let myself say what I was really feeling. . . . I'm learning . . . that it's OK to feel angry, turned on sexually and all feelings. There are my blocks of course, and I'll drift around awhile before I know what to do when something is bothering me.

I feel that people do need to get to know themselves well when they're in any kind of relationship. Openness is really important in all situations if closeness is the goal. I've found that it isn't easy for people to be open. I used to feel upset with those I lived with if I felt they weren't opening up, and of course my being upset (I know now) didn't help matters any. I learned just recently that the harder I push to open someone else up the worse feelings get, and I'm not really opening up myself. I just thought I was being open. The reality is I'm not saying what I'm feeling by pushing someone else. I really had to turn my head around to see this. I now respect other peoples' barriers because I know I have some, too.

Now, I'm working on my own barriers and learning to open up. My energy sure gets low sometimes. It isn't easy breaking down my barriers. When one finally goes away I sure feel good, though. I want to understand so much, but now I'm learning to be more patient. . . .

REFERENCES

1. Sidney Jourard, *The Transparent Self* (New York: Van Nostrand, 1969).
2. *Ibid.*
3. Larry Constantine, "Personal Growth in Multiperson Marriages," *op. cit.*
4. See Eric Berne, *Games People Play* (New York: Dell, 1967) and Thomas Harris, *I'm OK—You're OK: A Practical Guide to Transactional Analysis* (New York: Harper & Row, 1969).
5. See Eric Berne, *Transactional Analysis in Psychotherapy* (New York: Grove Press, 1961).
6. Discussed in Berne (*ibid.*) and in Harris (*ibid.*); in Robert Goulding, "New Directions in Transactional Analysis: Creating an Environment for Redecision and Change"; and in Sager, *et al.*, "The Marriage Contract," the latter two in Clifford J. Sager and Helen Singer Kaplan (eds.), *Progress in Group and Family Therapy* (New York: Brummer/Mazel, 1972).

12
Money Matters—Or Does It?

Walking through our own neighborhood of young, nuclear families, we notice that in nearly every back yard is a swing set. They are all much the same—a couple of swings, a slide, and some kind of glide ride. Sometimes they are only feet apart, the D———s yellow one on their side of the lot line, the K———s red one on the other side. Even during the heaviest play periods not one in six is in use; most of the time they sit idly guarding the empty yards.

The economic ramifications of expanded families could be profound and far-reaching. The nuclear family is a capital-intensive and inefficient enterprise with enormous excess capacity in almost all its facilities. A sizable shift toward cooperative and expanded family arrangements could markedly increase the efficiency of resource utilization. Such a shift would also require radical economic reorientation, and it would not be at all surprising to find the producers of consumer goods, especially appliances, aligned on the side of the traditional family against social change.

MONEY MANAGEMENT. Americans tend to value their private economic freedom no matter how constrained by budgets nor how much it may be invaded by taxation and government policy. In view of the fact that many marital battles are fought in the economic arena, there would seem to be a great potential for conflict over money management in multilateral marriages.

The M——s and the H——s had disparate economic habits before they got together. The M——s filled their living room with *objets d'art* and ran up substantial debts to maintain the standard of living they desired. The H——s were much more frugal. Pulling together, with the help of the H——s' savings, the group reduced the debts. But conflicting spending styles continued to be an area of tension, and Linda H—— often expressed resentment over their sacrifices for the M——s. This group had sizable interpersonal problems within the established dyads and between couples; these far outweighed the economic issues. As is often the case with conventional couples, money was more a battleground than the war itself.

Even this group was an exception. Most groups would go through an initial phase during which financial issues were important and occupied considerable attention. Then they would find a particular structure or scheme which accommodated most of the differences, and money would almost cease to be an issue.

The B——s and the G——s spent about the same portion of their earnings, but in different patterns. Whereas the B——s tended to make a continuous stream of small purchases, the G——s would more often save up for awhile, then make one big purchase. They reflected their different spending patterns in the economic arrangements for their multilateral marriage. They pooled less income than most groups and purchased such assets as high-fidelity equipment out of personal money, whereas most respondents would have used pooled funds for this purpose.

IDEOLOGY. Multilateral marriage, unlike the communal movement, lacks an economic ideology. The ideology of communes favors total economic sharing, and if the writers on the communal scene are taken at their word, most communes operate on this principle, or are feeling somewhat guilty and apologetic. The economic patterns of multilateral marriages are much more varied.

The reported economic structure among respondents is consistent with what we know of other groups from other sources. In one group of respondents, no individual income is pooled; in another, everything is pooled; but most said that one-half to two-thirds of individual income became part of the family-income pool. For most groups, pooled income was used to meet all or almost all household expenses. More than half purchased all their small and major assets from pooled income. Despite the absence of an economic ideology, the degree of economic integration for most multilateral families has been substantial. Most groups found they could decide on household budget issues and small-asset purchases informally or by whatever *ad hoc* approach seemed suitable. In most cases, consensual decisions were required for major assets.

ECONOMIES OF SCALE. For Mary and Arch K——, economic considerations played a significant role in starting their multilateral marriage. The K——s and the W——s were all interested in expanded families and had attended several meetings about group marriage. The K——s had already committed themselves to a lease on a large house in town, and they began to experience difficulty meeting the $380 monthly rent. In large part Meg and Saul moved in when they did to carry some of the financial load.

For most respondents and survey informants, though, economic arguments did *not* figure very high on the list of motivations. This is markedly different from Ramey's report on people interested in expanded families.[1] Basing his impressions on informal sources, Ramey described the two major concerns of husbands interested in expanded families as financial security and standard of living. A family with multiple breadwinners should be more secure financially and should be able to afford more collective luxuries, such as boats, summer homes, and swimming pools. Class differences (Ramey's informants were nearly all upper-middle class) and public-level versus private-level disclosures may account for the difference from our informants.

Respondents did report total collective incomes by group which were about the national median for income by families. The median total group income was $14,000 per year and it ranged from a low of $9,300, counting scholarships, for four adults without children, to a high of $190,000 for another tetrad without children. The median per-capita incomes were below average. In a couple of cases, we are aware that groups have more or less deliberately used their collective economic advantage to permit individuals to engage in less lucrative endeavors than they might if they were not in an expanded family situation. We noted instances of downward job mobility in Chapter 6.

We suspect that in the long run, most expanded families of whatever nature would strike a balance between higher family income and greater occupational freedom. Given the job situation as it exists today, the lower remuneration accorded to women may be justification within the nuclear family for the husband to work while the wife takes charge of the house and children. But the combined income of two women in a tetrad may be enough to nullify that argument. To date, no multilateral marriage known to us has reversed these male-female roles completely, though in many they are nearly equalized.

For two of the intact respondent groups, the economic situation has always been what we might call "tight," with some difficulty making ends meet for only a modest standard of living. Another group weathered a difficult period when they were all students with hardly pocket change to spare. Some couples and individuals from dissolved groups have also had to operate on very limited budgets. On the other hand, for several groups, money has never been a real problem.

For whatever reasons, our respondents have comparatively few of those extras the expanded family might be able to afford where the nuclear one could not. Collectively they own one swimming pool, two recreational vehicles, and a dirt-track racer.

HOUSE AND HOME. Builders do not construct houses or apartments for expanded families, or communes, or even "intentional neighborhoods." Most development responds to perceived averages and "trends" which substantially lag behind changing family needs even for nuclear families. But at least one highly successful and innovative developer has attended conferences on communal lifestyles, testing the direction of the wind, ascertaining the needs that might have to be anticipated by those in the forefront of his industry.

Of all the groups which have come to our attention, only one has ever been able to design and build a house for multilateral family living.* They had to sell it when they split up after a year and a half. Those with adequate wherewithal usually looked for mansionlike houses to be adapted to their large, multiadult families. Most made do with the larger or smaller conventional homes that they already had or could afford. Several groups arrived at the same remodeling solution and sacrificed attached garage space for the car to make room for an extra bedroom, an office, or a playroom, leaving the expansions neatly disguised behind permanently closed garage doors.

Very few groups, none among respondents, have legally shared homeownership among all partners. Most homes were mortgaged jointly by one legally married couple, though the group often regarded *de facto* ownership as extending to all partners. Leases have been handled similarly. Generally, groups have told us that the additional difficulty in obtaining four-way leases or mortgages and the risk of exposure were not justified by whatever marginal gain there might be in *de jure* joint ownership.

PECUNIARY PROBLEMS. Only one in sixteen respondents regarded money as a major problem within the group; one in eleven thought budgeting was. We asked each group to report on the economic problems the group had experienced. Most said too little money was a problem. Two each said they had trouble with budgeting or agreeing on specific expenditures. The other problems were all unique to a single group. One family, for example, had difficulty borrowing money because a character report cited their living arrangements.

In the fictional formula for multilateral marriage, money matters have been solved permanently by some sort of financial *deus ex machina*. For the real-life participants in multilateral marriage,

* Floor plans and house designs seem to be a major pastime for people who are thinking about multilateral marriage. See the plans in Rimmer's *Proposition 31* and *You and I . . . Searching for Tomorrow*.

no foundations, financiers, or fairy godmothers have appeared to foot the bill.

But, like the rest of us, they manage.

REFERENCES

1. James Ramey, "Communes, Group Marriage, and the Upper-Middle Class," *op. cit.*

13

Control, Conflict, and Consensus

The cover page was headed: "Basic Ground Rules for Residents." "Basically," it began, "the main point would probably be to clean up after yourself." It continued with a series of sections:

KITCHEN. If you dirty dishes . . . clean them up right away. We leave the dishes that we use daily in the strainer to drip dry. Do not leave dishes to drip dry that are not in constant use. . . . [F]ood in the refrigerator is available for munching. However, be careful about eating the family's next meal because you indulge in a hearty snack. If something looks special you might inquire before eating. . . . If you use ice cubes . . . refill the trays for the next guy. It may be you.

DINING. Meals are sometimes the only time that the family is all together. Try to stay free of other chores while you eat, especially reading, so as to devote attention to other members of the family. Some of us feel very strongly about this. . . . We don't throw away our napkins just because the meal is finished. If it is in good shape, neatly fold it and save it for the next meal. Good quality paper napkins can be used numerous times before they are in bad enough condition to throw away. We each have a glass of our specified color for use during each meal and between. Jocelyn's

color is blue. In fact, all of the blue glasses are Jocelyn's to do with
as she chooses. Andrew uses a red glass, Tina uses the pink glass.
. . Andrew always sits in the blue chair. . . . [T]hat is his chair
because it fits his back better. . . . Tina traditionally sits at the
grey chair. . . . Jocelyn sits on the bench across from Andrew. It
has been observed that reversal or change in this seating arrangement is apt to come about in different situations and that changes
in seating have an effect on the roles of the persons concerned.

And so it went, for four single-spaced pages. There were sections
for the bedroom ("There is a space left for the cat, . . . try to
leave it clear. Any clothes left lying around are available for the
cat to sleep on."), the bathroom, the garage, the trailer, and the
front and back yards. Each section presented the relevant rules
and regulations in minute detail. Had we not visited this family,
we would surely have believed theirs was a house full of cranky
anal-compulsives.

In truth, every family operates in part on rules and rituals,
habitualized behavior enacted daily with little if any variation. We
suspect it would be a surprising confrontation for most families
were they to see their own implicit, unspoken "ground rules"
neatly typed up as a set of regulations. Few of us are really conscious of the pervasiveness of routine in our lives.

What prompted this family to recast its routine as rules? For
one thing, the fine hand of a good social observer and interpreter
is evident throughout the document, and we suspect the availability of talent in itself was a factor. (A further example: "Although
she puts on an act of being gracious and hospitable about [her]
room, she is really quite possessive. She offers her bed, typewriter,
library, etc. for others to use, but she probably offers because it is
the 'right and proper' thing to do.") But this triad was also antici-
pating imminent expansion of their household to include new
members and felt the need for more obvious structure in order to
maintain personal integrity and smooth household functioning. The
author of these "ground rules" explained another reason for their
existence. The written rules, she felt, freed time for just "being"
with people they really liked.

STRUCTURE. Structure is a basic element of lifestyle, as well as a
human need. Some people, some families, seem to need a great

deal of structure, while others do better with very little. For some, structure must be visible and explicit for comfort, others prefer structure to be subdued and left implicit. Structure shows up in families in many ways—a corner of the counter which is always used for a random pile of junk mail to be sorted; a standard seating arrangement at the dinner table; labeled boxes for each child's school work; a special time for Dad to be with the children; a weekly night out for the parents. Structure does not always look orderly; some very messy families lead highly structured lives.

We learned that, other things being equal, the transition from a nuclear to a multilateral family carried the requirement of more structure and more explicit structure. Schedules for cleaning and cooking, sign-up sheets for repair jobs, rotation systems for baby-sitting were all common. Doors sometimes carried signs: "Go away, whoever you are! I'm trying to work." Or, "Enter, but take off your shoes first." One family had a weekly series of meetings. One night was for open encounter, to share feelings and get things off their chests. Another night was for budgetary and other practical matters. Still another was "kids' night," wherein the six children took the rostrum and aired their beefs or proposed new systems. Most groups found that frequent, if not regularly scheduled, group meetings were essential.

Though it became clear that the expanded family necessitated expanded structure, we also learned that there was some relationship between the need for a group to codify structure and its level of functioning. How much the members felt it necessary to have written rules spelling out minute details of proper behavior was often a rough index of how poorly they were functioning as a family. This was especially true of rules that dealt more with interpersonal behavior than with work and resource allocation. Generally the difficult formative period generated many rules and regulations which gradually fell into disuse as the people became more adept at dealing flexibly and sensitively with each other and more cognizant of each other's idiosyncrasies. Less than 6 percent of respondents felt that rules and rule-making were a serious or recurring problem.

The best strategy may be to implement the formal structure to aid in weathering stress until underlying issues can be resolved and the temporary rules abandoned. Unfortunately, rigidly formulated relationships do not facilitate creative growth or innovative solutions to problems. (We shall see this applied in the sexual area in Chapter 15.)

CONTROL AND COMPETITION. Patterns of leadership and control are a dimension of the structure of families. Traditionally, families have had a clear and dominant leader, more often the husband than the wife. One wonders whether multilateral marriage has any effect on the actual patterns of control, dominance, and leadership behavior of members. In a group there is potential competition for leadership. Research on *communes* has repeatedly stressed the importance of the single charismatic leader to circumvent competition. We base *our* conclusions regarding control, competition, and leadership patterns in multilateral marriages on prolonged direct observations.

On our first visit with one group, we are greeted by Rena. She had taken the initiative of writing to us and inviting us here, and now she takes the lead in introductions, directs (even dominates) the conversation, and answers when we put questions to the group as a whole. The group defers to Rena and clearly she is the leader. We shift the topic to participating in the research with us and suddenly Jack comes alive.

"Look," he says, leaning forward in his chair, a serious expression on his face, "I think we ought to have a meeting about this." With hand gestures he directs rearrangement of the seating. When everyone is assembled he appears to ponder for a moment and then tells us we probably should sit in on this. "Well, let's start." Evidently Jack is the real leader.

Arch, who had come in from the porch, turns to Darrell and asks, "What's up?" Darrell answers, stating the problem and issues involved in being part of our research. Jack continues to guide the flow of the discussion, but as the group closes in on consensus, Darrell is increasingly in the fore, analyzing the consequences of proposals and offering counter-proposals. At an impasse, Jack, Rena, and the others turn to Darrell, who relights his pipe, chews on it for half a minute, then spells out just what he wants from the decision. Everyone nods; Jack says, "Okay, so be it!" and people begin to disperse.

Those who stay begin to question us and it is a lively conversation which overlaps the supper hour. Karen stalks in and says, "Okay, people, let's get organized!" She starts handing out task assignments which go undisputed except that Arch and Rena trade. Later, when most of the family members are working on refinishing a table, Karen again seems to be in charge.

The majority of multilateral families had unselfconsciously evolved a pattern of control which Lou Mobley christened teleocratic[1] and futurist Alvin Toffler refers to as "adhocracy."[2] When we first observed it, we called it "pie-slicing." We thought of leadership in the groups we were observing in terms of a leadership pie, from which various individuals had carved out their own slices. In a teleocratic system, leadership depends on the task at hand; teleocratic means "purpose-centered." The leader is whoever has the talent or inclination relevent to what the group must do. Organization is *ad hoc* (hence Toffler's neologism) and there is not one but many leaders, though (usually) only one at a given moment. In the example above, Jack, Rena, Darrell, and Karen were all leaders, but in different functional areas. The roles observed on that one occasion would be repeated on many others. Jack was chairman, Rena represented the group to the rest of the world, Darrell was the guru whose wisdom in decision-making was seldom challenged, and Karen ran the task-oriented enterprise. Each one so disposed had a slice of the leadership pie. As talents and predilections became more clearly identified, the demarcation of the different functional areas of the leadership pie settled down. Leadership without competition and without fixed lines of dominance—it works, and we wish we had thought of it.

There is some variation in the way the pie is sliced. Sometimes people will trade slices or the boundaries will change with time. As a rule, however, we found certain functional leadership clusters to be common to many families. These are:

Chairman/parliamentarian/moderator: he or she calls and adjourns meetings, tries to keep things to the point, comments on "points of order," recognizes people wishing to speak, etc.

Spokesman/liaison/representative: he or she carries on correspondence on behalf of the group, initiates and mediates outside contacts, acts as gatekeeper, handles "public relations," represents group opinion, etc.

Foreman/manager/organizer: he or she usually takes charge when work is to be done, sets up and maintains schedules, gets after laggards, "gets the show on the road," etc.

Treasurer/financial manager: he or she monitors finances, keeps the budget, usually makes minor financial decisions alone and sometimes major ones, pays bills, etc.

Intellectual/theoretician/philosopher: intellectual leader, often formulates policy, source of ideology for family, frequently turned to for aid in decision-making, etc.

Guru/sagamore: frequently but not always same person as intellectual leader, he or she is source of "wisdom," last resort in disputes, etc.

An index of their success in slicing the pie is the low frequency with which respondents cited "competitiveness" and "dominance or leadership" as problems; less than 10 percent considered either to be serious.

Teleocratic leadership is not universal among respondents and other multilateral marriages. Some families have a single, more or less unchallenged, leader, but these are in the minority. We have not found any association between leadership/dominance patterns and either the size of the multilateral marriage or the ratio of women to men. For example, one triad manifested a clearly patriarchal pattern even though one woman was confident and highly independent. A marital *quid pro quo* had been established, but with more accommodations to the man than to either woman. It was *his* house, *his* chair "as traditional male head of the household." In another such triad, the man said he was in control and acknowledged sultanic fantasies of being master of a veritable harem, but inter-reactions in the family disconfirmed that. In reality, the women ruled by a coalition which excluded him from most real decision making, while at the same time they actively supported his fantasies of being in control. In still a third such triad, the pattern was teleocratic.

DECISIONS. One of the persistent arguments for the necessity of having a head of household or a charismatic leader in a community is that *somebody* has to make the decisions. More than half of reporting respondents indicated decision-making as a problem, but it was almost never thought to be a serious one. In multilateral families, minor decisions tend to be made teleocratically, that is, by the person whose piece of the pie is involved or who happens to be in charge at the moment. Major and family-oriented decisions are more often made by consensus.

A consensual decision is not a majority choice, everybody must agree. The trick is to find some option which is acceptable to everyone. We could construct an ideal composite of consensual decision-making in multilateral families, but based on our observations, only one or two families would come close to that ideal. We have identified two contributing factors to more effective consensual decision-making in our responding groups and elsewhere. We shall give only the barest outline of the first and go into detail on the second.

Informally we have used the phrase "creative problem solving" to refer to a specific set of approaches in interpersonal conflict resolution. A better term might be "no-lose problem solving."[3] In the no-lose approach, all parties (1) are responsible for identifying their own needs and interests and for seeing that the group decision meets these; (2) are committed to continuing, indefinitely if needed, until an adequate solution is reached; (3) disavow the use of power, influence, control, or the threat of power of any kind; (4) are prepared to use every creative resource in seeking a solution; and (5) agree never to compromise, never to be satisfied with anything less than winning, that is, achieving a solution that is completely satisfactory to themselves. Along with the last point goes the understanding that no one enters the process set on "getting his way" with respect to some specific outcome. Compromise is not permitted because compromise undermines relationships and group cohesiveness, leaves important needs unmet, leads to resentment, and, most importantly, is unnecessary. Most human conflicts of interest either yield to power, compromise, or remain unresolved for two reasons. The contest is over specific outcomes rather than needs, as it should be; and the contestants do not mobilize their creative abilities to generate new, previously unrecognized solutions which can meet everyone's needs. In the traditional way most couples resolve decisions, somebody always loses and fails to get what they want. What the traditional way misses is that besides choices A, B, and half-A half-B, there are C, D, E, F, and an infinitude of other possible outcomes, some of which will give them both what they want in terms of meeting their needs, though the outcome is not likely to be what either set out to get.

This is the essence of the no-lose approach to consensual decision-making. It has worked for some of our respondents and we shall say no more.

PROCESSED AND UNPROCESSED DATA. An effective and efficient decision process requires adequate, valid data as input. A number of the respondent groups discovered the importance of this and went on to evolve means of getting the needed data. When the issue to be decided is sensitive or emotionally charged, this can be most difficult.

Ed and Sandy have just brought coffee and cups to the table. They sit down with Trish. Amy seems to be flitting around like a moth looking for a place to light until Sandy extends a chair to her and scowls, suggesting that the time has come. All four pass time in silence through the ritual of pouring coffee, adding cream and sugar, stirring, sipping, and nodding approval. The silence continues. Trish is trying to appear involved without catching anybody's eyes.

"Um, well, we oughta," Ed begins, but suddenly the others are facing him expectantly and he trails off.

"What do we want to do tonight?" Sandy tries next. "What would you like to do Trish? I mean, anything's fine with me." Trish looks disapprovingly. "Well, I don't mean I don't *care*, I just mean I don't have strong feelings one way or another."

"What *do* you want, even if it isn't a strong preference?" asks Amy. Sandy bites his lip, shrugs, but says nothing.

"Well somebody has to start," Ed begins. "I get the impression from all the lovey-dovey stuff that Sandy and Trish want to be together tonight so my choice is Amy." Sandy and Trish look at each other; Amy's face is unreadable.

Sandy nods, then pauses, waiting for some response from Trish or Amy. He gets none. "Trish *has* been pretty romantic with me today. Yeah, I think I'd like that. That what you want, Trish?" he asks.

"Sure, sure, whatever you guys like is okay by me. But Amy hasn't said anything. Amy you hardly ever express a preference, why don't you say what *you* would really like?"

"What would you like me to say?"

This conversation from a beginning group resulted in a seemingly unimportant, not-too-difficult decision that Sandy and Trish would spend the night in one room and Ed and Amy in the other. Each in fact believed that he or she had sacrificed to the majority and was the only one not satisfied by the outcome. This came out in a big fight the next night. The sleeping arrangements on a single night should hardly be crucial, but it certainly is regrettable that all four of them ended up unhappy when they could have all had what they preferred. What happened?

Ed, who began and who gave his choice first, was really the most indifferent. He had a lower stake in the outcome and could honestly reverse his choice later if necessary. His risk was lowest. Even so, he did not really express *his* feelings but what he interpreted to be the desires of Sandy and Trish. He was wrong, of course. Sandy was somewhat turned off to Trish at that moment because, to him, she had been a bit too clinging. He preferred to sleep with Amy that night. When she didn't speak up, Sandy concluded the odds were against him and, not wanting to hurt Trish's feelings, really answered for her rather than for himself. Trish, it turns out, had been paying a lot of attention to Sandy because she thought she sensed that he was feeling rejected by her. She was even a little resentful of having to meet these needs when she would rather have been outside with Ed. By the time the ball reached her, Ed and Sandy had stated the same preference and Amy had assented through silence, so Trish merely echoed what she heard to be the group sentiment. As for Amy, she had been trying to get her feelings across to Sandy but couldn't get past Trish who was always around him. She, more than any of them, did not express herself. In fact, she usually asked what the other person wanted her to say.

Quite ordinary couples can go for years not knowing that they have never heard a spouse's real wishes. For someone who has not been in similar group situations it could be difficult to appreciate the agonizing delicacy with which such mazes must be negotiated or the ease with which one can fall into not speaking for oneself.

People in general don't express their real, personal, unmodified feelings much of the time because to do so involves risk. Whoever goes first is vulnerable. Others may be critical or reject one's preferences too readily. People fear that they may hurt other people's feelings if they are candid about their own. So groups of all kinds dance around issues, make tentative and highly processed approaches. Each member attempts to ascertain the group's feeling before expressing his own. No one can do that, however, since no one else is really expressing their own feelings. What is needed, and what several responding groups invented on their own, is a set of formalisms or mechanisms which facilitate the expression of unprocessed data.

Unprocessed data are a person's own, unmodified, private feelings, wishes, or desires about some subject. As one group put it, "What would you want to do if there were no one else's feelings to take into account, if you were totally free and could have anything you wanted? What do *you* want, totally disregarding what you *think* that others may want?"

Here are some rules we have collected that reduce the risk of expressing unprocessed data:

1. Rotate or select by lot who goes first in expressing his or her unprocessed data.

2. Prohibit comment on expressed proposals or preferences until all unprocessed data are in.

3. Feelings do not have to be justified, explained, or rationalized. Whatever they are, they are legitimate. Criticism of feelings is not legitimate.

4. Everyone should clearly understand the difference between unprocessed and processed statements and the group should monitor itself, encouraging anyone offering a processed statement to substitute an unprocessed one.

5. It may help if it is known that unprocessed statements will not be held against anyone. Having stated his or her unprocessed data as input to the decision process, each person can be allowed later to choose a position which is really processed without the group referring back to the original statement.

A group is not guaranteed smooth sailing even if everyone can and does give unprocessed statements as input to the decision process. Unprocessed preferences can conflict just as much as processed ones, and reaching consensus can be just as difficult. At least the group will be basing its decisions on what members really want and will not be wasting time just trying to uncover this information.

People familiar with group dynamics, family theory, or encounter groups will recognize related concepts under different names—congruent communication, straight-talk, "I-statements," being responsible for oneself—to mention a few. We are reporting the approach as our own respondents have found it to be relevant to the decision processes in multilateral marriages.

CONFLICT RESOLUTION. Not all conflicts of interest in multilateral marriages could legitimately be discussed under the rational-sounding heading of "decision-making." Conflicts in expanded families are rife and the intimacy of multilateral marriage adds intensity. We have seen no real patterns in style of conflict resolution. From a functional standpoint, the group interested in staying together faces no more important task than to develop an effective style of conflict resolution. Such a style is certain to be unique to its participants, but we suspect that those marriages which are happiest and most functional will adopt some form of strategy that neither avoids nor seeks fights and sees in conflicts an opportunity for learning.[4]

REFERENCES

1. Lou Mobley, in reporting to the October 1970 Kirkridge Symposium, "Responsible Communal Life Styles," on his year of visiting communes.
2. Alvin Toffler, *Future Shock* (New York: Random House, 1970).
3. Thomas Gordon, *Parent Effectiveness Training* (New York: Peter H. Wyden, 1970).
4. George Bach and Peter Wyden, *The Intimate Enemy; How to Fight Fair in Love and Marriage* (New York: Avon, 1970).

14

Children in the Group

I<small>MAGES—YOUNG CHILDREN, THEIR</small> tanned bodies stippled by salt spray, running from the surf, laughing at the roiling cold and their own awkward high-stepped gait as they lose the race. A proud-shy ten-year-old face, round, smiling, crowned by close-cropped hair, a rough-tumble, fishing boy and the rhythm and eloquence of his poem "Butterfly." Eighty seconds like three hours of gazing into her six-year-old eyes, four inches away, gazing back through rivulets of long blonde hair and pool-water. A swinging stick that glances off the *piñata*, though blue eyes peek out between the slipping blindfold and his hair of dry fieldgrass. Three once-eager seekers of shock, asking to be allowed to stay in the refreshment stand while the long awaited climax of *Willard* plays to a lot full of cars and one camper, empty save for a sleeping six-year-old and their once-reluctant but now-hooked chaperone. Solemn voices, holding back anger, choking back tears, a dead kitten and a small boy, straight-standing, with serious, clever eyes.

Images—of some of the children we know, all of them children of our respondents.

From the perspective of the typical adult's psychological difficulties, the nuclear family is easily indicted as a poor way to raise children, yet from the perspective of almost everyone—raised and still in nuclear-family situations—multilateral marriage could appear to be an even greater threat to children.

From the beginning, we were interested in how children really fared when their parents were married to more than one person. Early observations led us to believe that children were major benefactors in the multilateral family.[1] Yet we knew that the observational and interview skills we had developed were aimed at adults, and we doubted our ability to make meaningful evaluations from the children's perspective.

The Merrill-Palmer Institute in Detroit runs a remarkable program permitting students in family-related areas to spend a year of intensive study combined with change-oriented work in the community. For a few days we stayed in one of the student houses while attending the annual conference on the family. Amid bread-baking, speech-giving, discussion-leading, and music-sharing we met Angela Hunt. Her background in child development (Iowa State University) fitted our needs, but most importantly somehow all three of us thought we could get along. So Angela joined the project for the summer to undertake an intensive study of the children in multilateral families. She joined us as colleague and became a real part of our family, building a special bond with Heather, who was only two weeks old when Angie moved in. Most of what we know about the children in groups comes from the study which she designed and executed with a modest amount of aid and interference from us.

We found her viewpoint to be very compatible with our methodology. She defined her primary goal to be understanding how multilateral marriage looked to children in such families. How, if at all, did the parents' multilateral marriage influence each child's concept of himself, his family, and his peers? As with the rest of the study, a variety of objective and subjective techniques were used, including standardized tests, interviews, and very careful observations. In our opinion, Angela's work may well be the most important outcome of the entire Study Project.*

---

* What we present in this chapter is a distillation of major elements and findings from the substudy. The full report runs to over eighty pages.[2] Full details are expected to be prepared for professional publication.

THE KIDS. Forty children in twelve multilateral families, half of which were intact, were involved in the substudy. Nine of these families were respondents in the base study. All but one of the children had been born into nuclear families before their parents formed a multilateral marriage. They ranged in age from nineteen months up to twenty years. Nine preschoolers and twenty-one of elementary-school age were included; there was one high school graduate, the rest being in secondary school. Twenty-five were still living in the multilateral situation at the time of the substudy. In the absence of significant differences we have aggregated children from intact and dissolved groups in reporting results. Like any bunch of kids of this size and diverse ages, they would be difficult to characterize.

CARE. Certainly parents care for their children. But parents frequently hide fears and insecurities under the guise of concern for children, using them as excuses for actions and attitudes. Parents may continue emotionally dead marriages "for the sake of the children." They retain prejudices, revealing latent fears when they append, "but I wouldn't want my daughter to. . . ." Relationships with children are as highly cathected as sex but more socially acceptable as motivation for action. It is no wonder then that concern for the long-term effects on children is the single most frequently professed objection to multilateral marriages and other family variants. Many people have assumed *a priori* that anyone participating in an altered marital pattern, but especially one which includes multiple sexual relationships, must not care much for their children. All respondents have been open with their children about the deep and intimate nature of their multilateral marriage commitment. Openness about sexual involvement goes especially counter to prevailing parental practice.

We found that participants in multilateral marriages were very concerned for their children. Most considered potential benefits to children as among the most important reasons for becoming involved in a multilateral family. Angela's structured observations corroborated this. She observed that child-rearing was given high priority, that much concern was expressed by parents for the needs and well-being of their children. Of families returning questionnaires in the base study, half reported that they hoped for children by cross-marital pairs as a part of their multilateral marriage, and two more (of nine families) considered this a remote possibility.

RATINGS. What is child-rearing like in a multilateral family? Five of six base-study groups reported that child care and relating with children were easier as the result of their multilateral marriage; the other thought things had remained the same. But, child-rearing is a complex, multidimensional aspect of family life. To sharpen our observations and be able to quantify aspects of child-rearing, ratings were devised on the four dimensions shown in Fig. 14-1 using the respected Fels Parent Behavior Rating Scales[3] as a guide. All three of us learned to observe and make independent ratings which were in *significantly** close agreement on the four scales.

The first scale covers the restrictive-permissive dimension òf child-rearing style. At one end is completely restrictive/authoritarian child-rearing, at the other, permissive/laissez-faire. In the exact middle is a style of child-rearing called "free." A free approach designates practices which allow for each child's uniqueness and support the child's efforts to reach his own expectations, yet which openly express limitations necessary for the maintenance of adult individuality and comfort. "Free" practices are essentially what A. S. Neill termed "freedom without license"[4] and behaviorally are as much in contrast with permissive practices as with restrictive ones.

Families were also evaluated on a scale of consistency or inconsistency in child-rearing, on the extent to which they exhibited a high or low degree of child orientation, and on the children's role in the family—whether children were treated more as accepted partners in the family or as rejected burdens. We were least consistent in rating consistency (the correlation or extent of agreement among us did not quite reach the level of statistical significance we sought) and most consistent in rating child orientation and children's role. The relationships between scales was such as

* See Preface.

Fig. 14–1. Means of ratings by three judges of child-rearing structure of thirteen multilateral families and fragments of dissolved families.

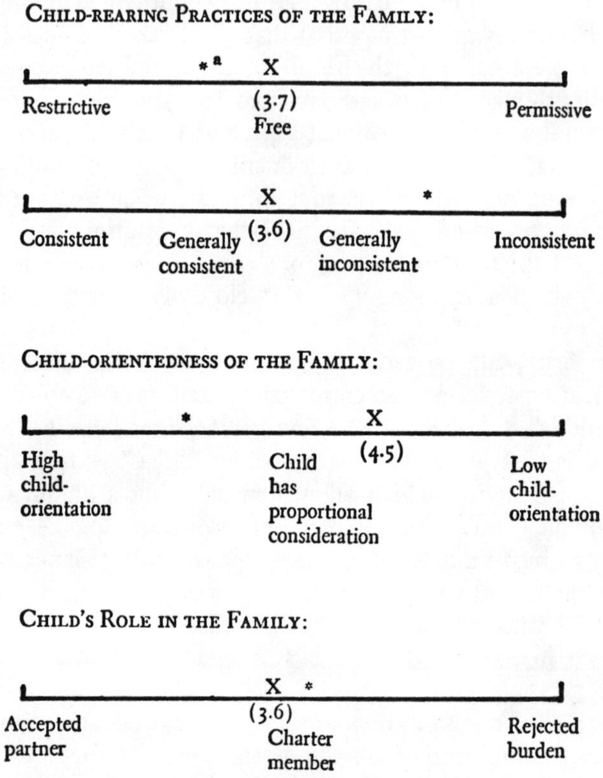

CHILD-REARING PRACTICES OF THE FAMILY:

```
|_____*_ᵃ___X_____|
Restrictive        (3.7)                      Permissive
                   Free
```

```
|_____X_____*_____|
Consistent   Generally (3.6)  Generally        Inconsistent
             consistent       inconsistent
```

CHILD-ORIENTEDNESS OF THE FAMILY:

```
|_____*_____X_____|
High                    Child   (4.5)         Low
child-                  has                    child-
orientation             proportional          orientation
                        consideration
```

CHILD'S ROLE IN THE FAMILY:

```
|_____X__*_____|
Accepted          (3.6)                  Rejected
partner           Charter                burden
                  member
```

ᵃ Hunt's ratings of "typical" nuclear families included here solely as a subjective point of reference.

to justify treating them as independent factors, except in the case of high child orientation/low child orientation compared with acceptance/rejection. These were *significantly* interrelated. (See Appendix IX.)

Before seeing any of the multilateral families, Angela made some highly subjective estimates of where she thought "typical" nuclear families would fall on these scales. We are making no special claims about the estimates, which were never intended as more than a subjective point of reference. Her estimates seem plausible, but a comparison sample is really needed.

The results in Fig. 14-1 show that children in multilateral families get proportional consideration, but the families are slightly less child-centered than we would guess most nuclear families are. On the other hand, children are "charter members" of the family and are perhaps more accepted than their counterparts in nuclear families. Whatever the real comparison might be, children in multilateral families, with rare exceptions, are at least not being ignored or rejected.

On the average, we rated parents who were in or had been in multilateral marriages as having "free" child-rearing practices, leaning ever so slightly to the restrictive side. Almost certainly they are less authoritarian than most parents, but taken as a group they are not permissive parents. It came as a big surprise that they were also fairly consistent, much more so than we would guess the average family to be. Consistency with only two parents is hard enough, but merging two or more families with well-established independent styles would seem to make consistency less likely.

In an earlier substudy, we had asked respondents to check off terms they thought descriptive of their group's child-rearing. In still another, we supplied the same list but asked them to check those applying to their own upbringing. These data are not strictly comparable to the direct observational ratings from the child substudy, but do help to round out the picture.

From their adult perspective, the families in which participants grew up were more strict and authoritarian than permissive, lax, or free, and more inconsistent than consistent. This may reflect simply the consensus of a whole generation or it may be a tendency special to this group of people. It hints at a remarkable feat in their moving more toward essentially free child-rearing that is also more consistent. The six base-study families which rated themselves did tend to see their child-rearing as consistent, though flexible. The infrequency with which "free" was chosen is probably due at least in part to our failure to define or clarify the term on the original questionnaire.

SEEING IS BELIEVING. Before beginning the extended field trip with us in which she visited the families for periods varying from two-and-a-half days to a week, Angela worked out careful objective definitions in seven areas of observation. From her copious notes taken during the field trip, some patterns became apparent in these areas.

Children from multilateral families tended toward a high degree of independence, needing minimal guidance. Of those who didn't fit this pattern, half showed an even more mature pattern of interdependent behavior (free to take independent action or be reciprocally reliant on others as appropriate to the given situation). In the same line, the children's work and play habits tended somewhat toward the self-motivated end of the scale, rather than toward requiring supervision; and they accepted responsibility more than they avoided it.

Their aggressive behavior was middle-of-the-road, rather than extreme and their interactions with peers revealed a complete range of behavior from leadership to withdrawal, although the latter was found to be characteristic of only two children.*

In a child's development, two vital issues are with whom the child identifies and how he feels about himself. A child's feeling about himself—does he see himself as a worthwhile person, has he confidence—is an important index of his emotional well-being. In some sense, a good self-concept *is* emotional well-being. A positive self-image is a prime ingredient of continued growth. Seven of the thirty-eight children for whom sufficient observations were

---

* In fact, both these young teenagers were being ignored and had become so withdrawn as to lead us to suggest the need for clinical help. However, neither of them was in an actual multilateral family. Their family situations had much in common. Each father had brought home a woman with whom he had become involved and neither mother was a completely willing participant. This is in sharp contrast to the situation in true multilateral families.

available would not be described as having good self-images. About half of the remainder had middle-ground, average senses of their own worth.

The bulk of the children were described by Angela as being very much "in contact with themselves" with a highly positive image of themselves as valuable persons combined with a realistic perception of their own abilities. They accepted and valued differences in other people. In short, most of them are confident, healthy, in-touch kids.

MEASUREMENT. We are inclined now to agree with Angela and a mentor of hers at Merrill-Palmer. They both felt that her professional observations and personal interactions with children would yield the most meaningful data. But we were not always so inclined and even so, we would probably still desire some hard numbers to augment Angela's skill at wresting insight from a child's everyday behavior. After reviewing many standard methods of measuring adjustment and development in children, we settled on two that dovetailed with our methodology in the larger study and with the purposes of the child substudy.

Preschool children present special challenges (and no doubt special rewards) to the developmentalist. Gaining access to the preschooler's concept of himself can be a most arduous task. Fortunately, for the young child much more so than as he matures, sense of self is closely linked to his mastery of himself and his environment. Being able to do something gives him the sense of confidence which usually in turn leads him to attempt and master new things. The young child with internal difficulties, who has a very negative image of himself, is generally one who falls behind in development. Naturally, there is great variation within what is both "normal" and devoid of cause for alarm. Only consistent patterns of ability or inability for very carefully chosen tasks can be given a reliable interpretation. Even then, only skilled professionals are likely to be able to interpret variance in development.

Angela brought with her from Detroit a green zipper bag filled with such temptations to our two kids as a rubber ball, pieces of colored yarn, a toy telephone, and a box of raisins. These were some of the props used in administering the Denver Development Screening Test (DDST), a composite of more than a hundred carefully chosen, graduated, standardized tasks for assessing the development of children from birth to six years.[5]

Eight of the nine preschool children performed beyond their age level in all four areas of the DDST: personal-social skills, fine motor skills (like manipulating small objects), language skills, and gross motor skills (like standing on one foot). The other preschooler, nineteen months old, was ahead in two areas, behind in two. This aggregate degree of advancement is *statistically significant.**

For older children it becomes possible to ask questions which explore more or less directly their concept of themselves. Carl Rogers, well known for his identification with basic encounter groups, devised a test called the Personal Adjustment Inventory (PAI)[6] the original intent of which was to put onto paper much of the process that a skilled clinical psychologist would use in interviewing a child to assess his degree of maladjustment. The PAI is a conservative instrument with some hoary assumptions about the well-adjusted child. It is difficult to score and the norms for comparison are inadequate, but it was the least among many evils for us. It did have one special attraction; it assessed the three areas Personal Inferiority, Social Maladjustment, and Family Maladjustment, the self-peer-family variables of our interest.

The assessment of self-concept derived from observation and interview was reinforced by the PAI: the seventeen school-age children from multilateral marriages averaged very low (i.e., better) Personal Inferiority.

Both Social Maladjustment and Family Maladjustment were marginally above what is considered by Rogers to be normal. A detailed analysis of individual responses revealed that the difference was accounted for by certain questions consistently answered in a particular way. On one scale children were asked whom they would like to live with on a desert isle, and on the other, whom they would most like to go with to a circus. Most of the children in this study named one or more members of their family for companions. Naming family members rather than age-mates is taken as a sign of maladjustment and adds up to four points to the scores.

---

* If the assumption is that children in multilateral families are as likely to be ahead as behind the expected levels, the probability of this many being ahead is .0195.

We question whether this is a truly valid assumption, though it is undoubtedly common for children to name peers. Angela also drew attention to the fact that this test was developed in the school environment while we administered it in the summer when children spend more time with their families and might be less likely than at other times to name peers. Another question of interest was "Do you like having someone else tell you how to do things?" We wonder whether liking it or not caring are truly signs of adjustment, but at any rate, our families' independent kids answered predictably (and "wrongly") and said they would rather do things their own way.

Well, we had been warned about such tests.

PICTURES. One goal of this substudy was to find out what multilateral families looked like to the children. In her interviews, Angela asked each child to draw a picture of his family and explain it. From what they told her as well as such detailed observations as the order in which family members were drawn, their positions and size, Angela was able to piece together a remarkably clear child's-eye view of multilateral marriage. There is probably no better way to convey this than through a drawing of our own.

The drawing in Fig. 14-2 was not done by one of the children, though perhaps it could have been. It does represent what they

Fig. 14-2 Conceptualization of multilateral family by child, showing "inner" and "outer" family.

told us of their families. Typically, children from multilateral families thought of themselves as having a family within a family. The clearest division between "my family" and "the rest of the world" included their parents, coparents, siblings, and cosiblings. They would persist in seeing these people in family roles even after their biological parents separated from the other adults of the multilateral marriage. They would form child-parent or sister-brother type relationships even in cases where the group did not all share the same household.

Yet there was a distinction, something like this:

INTERVIEWER: Who's that you're drawing?
CHILD: That's Dad.
I: And who's this over here?
C: Umm, Jim.
I: Who is Jim?
C: He's Jim, you know.
I: Yeah, I know but I mean this man here you said is a daddy to you, but who is Jim to you?
C: Well, he's kinda like a daddy. Well he *is* a daddy, but sorta.

While children generally clearly identified other adults in parental roles with respect to them, and other children in sibling roles (and, in fact, related to them in expected patterns of behavior), they almost always qualified these roles to show their similarity with roles of members of their inner (nuclear) family but at the same time distinguishing them as somehow different. In our drawing, this is represented by the less-sharp boundary around the child's inner family.

Typically, children in these families identified closely with a biological parent, usually their mother. We do not see in this proof of the centrality of the nuclear family. Too many variables are uncontrolled, not the least of which is duration. Only one of the children in the substudy had lived for a substantial portion of his life in a multilateral family household. Fifteen of them had returned to living in conventional households as the result of dissolution of the multilateral marriage. We have nothing which would allow us to determine the persistency of the inner-family/

outer-family distinction. If anything, it is rather striking how read-ily children seem to accept expanded-family members and how their perception of the expanded family survives separation.

WHAT WILL THE NEIGHBORS THINK? Even when people are not overly concerned about the effects of multilateral marriage on children, they anticipate problems children may face in relating with other children. Will they be ostracized? Will their unusual home-life become a source of shame and the object of resentment because of the reactions of other children? Will they ever be able to bring their friends home? And (horrors) what if a teacher should find out?

Virtually every child was found to have ample peer interaction, and they brought friends home to their house as often as they went to friends' houses. Most or all of their friends live in conventional families, since multilateral marriage is so rare. Five of the kids said that friends had commented on their family as weird or strange, but then the same number mentioned that their friends had really *liked* the family setup. The rest said their friends either simply accepted or didn't comment on the family situation. For the kids, social pressure was not a major concern, though it appeared to be an area of sensitive awareness.

Neither was it a major concern for the parents in the multi-lateral families, though they had talked about it and discussed it with their children. In our opinion, their parents' openness about the multilateral relationships and candid discussions about rela-tions with the outside world were essential to the absence of prob-lems from the kids' points of view. We also found that even the young children, like their parents, were able to use good judgment in disclosing or not disclosing details of family life, being open with friends they could trust and circumspect with ones they could not. One of six families indicated on questionnaires that children had had problems in school or neighborhood; three of six indi-cated that children related well in school and neighborhood. Prob-lems with peers were not totally absent, but they were compara-tively uncommon and undramatic.

GROWING UP. To most of the kids, having multiple parents has been a mixed bag. While they dig the abundance of adult resources and recognize that strain is lowered by distributing parental responsibility, they have sometimes become lost in the blaze of new relationships and frequently have been the target of multiple, perhaps even conflicting demands. We cannot say that multilateral marriage presents clear advantages for children, though the latent potential may yet be there.

Without repeated, long-term udies which include elaborate controls, nothing can be said with confidence about what effect multilateral marriage has on children. These limited data are suggestive of some relationships into which continued inquiry is justified. A child's experience in a multilateral family does not appear to be significantly related to patterns of aggression, work and play habits, or the assumption of responsibility, but it does appear that this environment might foster independence and a strongly positive self-concept. Ironically, it may also be associated with close identification by the child with biological parents.

On most issues, the structure of the family has little bearing on the children's development. What does affect them is the nature and the quality of their parents' interactions with them and with each other. As in nuclear families, good marriages are good for children, bad marriages are not.

It is safe to say, however, what multilateral marriage is *not* doing to kids. There appears to be absolutely no justification for fears that this "deviant" form of marriage is screwing up kids. And the healthy self-concept of children in these families leads us to believe that fears for the long term are also unfounded. We would be hesitant to claim many beneficial effects, but we do feel that any significant pattern of trauma or disturbance would have been revealed by our probings.

TO THE PARENTS. Children are much more resilient than most parents think. Marriages can have destructive effects, but when certain essentials are met—such as clear, open, direct communication between parents, and affectionate validation of children—many other conditions are of little importance for the healthy development of children.

Multilateral marriage can be very attractive for parents. Our study reveals that among adults who share similar child-rearing values sharing responsibility for child care is a real benefit. Shared among more cooperating adults, children become much less a responsibility, much more an opportunity. Problems related to children and child-rearing were among the very least frequently checked problems on questionnaires. Of specific child-oriented problems from the Family Summary questionnaire, jealousy was cited most often.

We might say that parenthood is much too much for only two people. When there are alternate sources, children are less likely to want for attention and adults are less resentful of inopportune demands. Many times we would have personally valued some independent inputs from other intimately involved adults in resolving child-related issues within our own family.

We would caution the would-be multilaterally-married to give thought to the negative potentials. These are not, in our opinion, the destructive influence of parental sexual involvement or the thwarting of single-father-mother identification. But there is the potential for the emotional intensity and benefits for adults to lead to short-changing the children.

In the end, there is one very telling question. Would those in multilateral marriages want their children to follow suit? In our survey of attitudes, collectively the men said Yes and the women said Yes, perhaps; but 61 percent of both sexes were in the middle and added very similar qualifications. They said that really, it would have to be their children's decision. This sounds to us like a pretty good qualification to add.

REFERENCES

1. First reported in Larry and Joan Constantine, "Where Is Marriage Going?" *op. cit.*
2. What we report here are only some of the findings from her eighty-page report, "Multilateral Marriage from the Child's Perspective: Lotsa Good —Lotsa Bad." Detailed excerpts are expected to be published in the future.
3. Chapney, "The Measurement of Parental Behavior," *Child Development* 12 (1941).

4. A. S. Neill, *Summerhill: A Radical Approach to Child Rearing* (New York: Hart, 1960).
5. William K. Frankenburg and Josiah B. Dodd, "Denver Developmental Screening Test" (Boulder, Colorado: University of Colorado Medical Center, 1969).
6. Carl Rogers, *P. A. Inventory* (New York: Association Press, 1961).

15

Sex in the Group

To TAKE THE DIRECT route to the heart of the matter, the answer is Yes. They do. That is, in every responding group, there has been cross-marital sexual involvement and partners have engaged in sexual intercourse with people other than their legal spouse. This is a *finding* in that the operational definition we use for multilateral marriage does not require that partners be sexually involved with anyone. A committed multilateral relationship without sex is possible; we just have never found one.

The equalitarian ethic of participants carries over into the sexual area as well. Both sexes agreed strongly that women should be free to initiate sex and disagreed that women enjoy sex less than men. On both items they were more equalitarian than Athanasiou's informants[1] but only *significantly** so on the second.

In fact, as many women as men considered that a variety of sexual partners was among their reasons for getting into multilateral marriage, although among respondents, *significantly* more men indicated that this was one of their strong reasons. The high EPPS *heterosexuality* scores of women in the groups, when compared with other women, further suggests that sex is as much

---

* See Preface.

motivation for the women as for the men. There were no significant male-female differences in sexual experience; both men and women were quite experienced sexually. (See Appendix IV, Table 10.) More than half of respondents reported previous extramarital sex. Just under half of survey informants reported previous sexually intimate friendships, about the same proportion as reported in Ramey's study of people interested in expanded families.

CHANGE PARTNERS. Sex in the group is an essential element of multilateral marriage. How do they handle it? How is it decided who sleeps with whom? Half the groups reported using some form of fixed rotation with provisions for exceptions. Typically this meant that the same pair would sleep together for three or four nights in succession, then switch partners. Among all tetrads on which we have information, a three days-four days, four days-three days schedule has been reported most often where a fixed rotation scheme was in use. For groups not using a fixed rotation scheme, the decision-making process was either left unstructured or was undertaken by the group as a whole.

Most groups have been well aware of trade-offs between less-structured and more-structured means of determining sleeping arrangements. Fixed rotation is an equalizer and leaves no one out, minimizing the potential for jealousy, or so its proponents argue. Some form of free choice gives more freedom and permits spontaneity, its advocates argue. Our observations partially confirm either position. That two people are sleeping in the same bed does not guarantee they will have sexual relations. The rotation schedule can be completely balanced while disguising great disparities in sexual preferences and actual sexual involvement. Fixed rotation of partners does permit members to avoid or postpone dealing with inequalities, feelings of rejection, or insecurity. A formal rotation scheme also conserves energy. The seemingly free choice of an unstructured approach may commit the group to a heavy investment in resolving the daily issue of who's in which bed. On occasion we have observed tentative probes concerning preferences and multiple maneuvering and negotiating beginning quite early in the day, though by bedtime everybody seemed to have a pretty clear implicit understanding of where he was to move his pillow. We have also seen arduous attempts by some groups as groups to negotiate the nightly process with maximal satisfaction and minimal hurt feelings. In either case, the actual amount of spontaneity and gain in freedom are moot.

This is an especially clear example of the trade-offs in complexity and structure articulated in Chapter 13. Keenly aware of the inefficiency of their informal methods or stinging from repeated flare-ups of rejected feelings, groups turn to structure. Groups with good communication, whose members can confront each other and deal with their feelings of insecurity and rejection, have little need of fixed rotation. Participants in groups that stuck with an unstructured or group-decision process tended to become more effective as they acquired appropriate skills. But the rule has vivid exceptions. There are groups for whom rotation is merely a comfortable choice, not a postponement of problems. More nights may depart from the schedule than conform to it. And some groups have stubbornly stuck with a strained free-form approach.

Some creative compromises are possible. In one group, first women then men were responsible for the decision on alternate months. We have suggested an "exception management" procedure in which arrangements are assumed to remain the same until someone calls for a change, at which time the group decides a new arrangement by consensus. This would preserve flexibility and conserve energy. Frankly, we found most groups did not take full advantages of their flexible resources in permitting everyone the sexual interactions they desired. Because Ashley and Senta, for instance, are not paired for the night need not prevent them from disappearing for an hour when they come home from work. Where highly structured systems are really serving to cover up symptoms, we would not expect threatening departures like this.

Groups reported that partners paired according to their primary relationship about as often as otherwise, independent of the scheme for rotating. Some of those with fixed rotational schemes gave primary-bond partners some preference. Every group provided for heterosexual pairs sleeping together, none for same-sex pairs. Most had provision for people to sleep alone if they wished.

GROUP SEX. It is an easy cognitive step from group *marriage* to group *sex*. Half of our responding groups provided for group sleeping in their sleeping arrangements, but this need not imply group sexual activities. Most respondents have tried group sexual activity, and collectively they agreed that within a group marriage it is desirable. Nevertheless, in most groups, group sex occurred only rarely or occasionally, if at all.

We can best illuminate this paradoxical area by attempting to convey something of group sex as experienced by respondents.

Many respondents have reported to us group sexual encounters which were profoundly beautiful. Their descriptions and the effects that these encounters have had on their lives, qualify many instances as what Abraham Maslow called "peak experiences"— the highest and most significant experiences in life. Not all the group sexual encounters would qualify. Some were merely exciting or enjoyable; some were complicated by problems of competition, sexual hangups, or simple anxiety. But we believe that the peak experience in group sexual encounter is characteristic, even if not typical, of this group of people. In this respect, they are sharply differentiated from swingers, among whom group sexual encounters are widely preferred but seem to be more mundane.

We find it difficult to convey the sense that we have got of this experience. Joy, in her mid-twenties, does it better:

I shall never forget that first time. It just happened. The three of us were lying around in the living room, feeling very close and kinda groovy. From time to time Adam kissed each of us. Then Adam lifted my blouse and started kissing my breast, and he was touching me while Karina kissed my other breast. I was floating, lost in waves of feelings without even a thought about what we were really doing. We went into the bedroom and all made love. It didn't seem like Adam made love to me and Adam made love to Karina; we *all* made love, all three of us. None of us had ever done anything like this and wouldn't have had the faintest idea of what to do or how to handle things if we had thought about it. But it just happened. It was the most natural thing in the world. Afterward we all sat around on the bed just looking at each other saying, "Wow! Wow!" All through it we had this sense of oneness. At times I couldn't really tell where I left off and somebody else began. It was an overwhelming experience and we felt changed by it, somehow set apart from the rest of the world. We were literally high for days afterward, walking around with grins on our faces, feeling totally satisfied by what had happened and the most alive we had ever been. I could feel the love they both felt for me and I loved them both so much. I still do.

Where group sex is either such an intense experience or a significant problem, groups have not opted for it as a steady diet. A few have maintained that group sex is "just not where we're at," though in private it has come out that some members would like to try it while others are fearful. Sex in separate bedrooms, behind closed doors, may avoid confrontation with latent or suppressed feelings of insecurity.

Some peculiar dynamics pertain to the number of people involved in a group sexual encounter. Threesomes are the most common experience among respondents. They report that a subjective experience of unity is more common with three people than with four. Two men and two women all making love together seem to have a decided tendency to become two couples who just happened to be side by side. Without any intention, some sense of competition and comparison often arises from this configuration.

However uncommon group sex may be in the population as a whole (and we suspect it is far more common than society would like to admit), it is definitely not unnatural. The content of sexual fantasies suggests that most men and women have some interest in simultaneous love-making with two or more partners at once. If the sexual expression of affection is a "natural" concomitant of marriage, then group sexual expressions are thoroughly to be expected in group marriage.

SAME AND DIFFERENT. The importance of the same-sex relationships to the healthy functioning of a multilateral marriage has already been discussed. Where deep bonds of affection develop between two women or between two men, or where group sexual encounters bring about close physical proximity, sexual contact between members of the same sex in a multilateral marriage would be an unsurprising outcome. At the very least, we would expect that nonsexual physical expressions of affection would be exchanged between members of the same sex who have a close relationship.

Both male and female respondents felt very strongly that people should be able to express affection physically to individuals of both sexes. Both sexes also agreed that the ability to relate sexually to individuals of both sexes is healthy and desirable, though they were *significantly* more certain about physical affection than sex. So, as a group, they believe that ambisexuality—the capacity to relate sexually to either sex as appropriate to the circumstances—is a healthy attribute. What about their actual behavior?

Only rarely have there been direct sexual encounters between just two people of the same sex within a multilateral marriage. Just one-third of the men and the same fraction of women reported having once had some homosexual encounter (which is about normal), but these were not within the multilateral marriage. The same-sex interaction which does occur, almost always takes place in a group sexual setting. Reports of the subjective experience of these encounters are almost perfectly consistent. Nearly everyone who has been involved experienced the sexual interaction *among* several partners (hence in part between members of the same sex) as different from sex *between* just two members of the same sex. The one is "ambisexual," the other is "homosexual."

Joy's account of her experience with Karina and Adam given above contains an element of this distinction. That respondents organize these experiences differently does not seem to us to represent an aversion to, or hangup over, homosexuality (neither their attitudes nor their behavior support that), but rather, a real phenomenological difference between multilateral, ambisexual encounters and bilateral, homosexual ones.

Three-person sex more frequently has involved two women and a man than two men and a woman. Women in this society resolve their feelings about their ambisexual potential much more easily than do men. The studies of swinging have concluded similarly.[2]

MULTILATERAL AND OPEN. In contrast to fictional multilateral marriages, many of the multilateral marriages with which we have had contact have also been open-ended, that is, members were open to intimate friendships and sexual involvement outside the multilateral marriage. At the time they completed questionnaires, only about a third of reporting respondents said they maintained intimate friendships outside the group, but we know that this proportion grew with time. Collectively, they felt strongly that outside involvement was *not* a sign that something was wrong with the group marriage, but they were uncertain as to whether this might threaten the stability of the group. Comparing still intact groups to those which eventually dissolved, the former were *significantly* less likely to report outside intimate involvement.

Our knowledge of the details of the majority of these outside relationships does not reveal a cause-and-effect relationship in either direction between open-endedness and instability. We suspect that the majority of multilateral marriages which survive will eventually become open-ended. Whatever led or permitted participants to enter multiple intimate relationships is not likely to cease with the establishment of a multilateral marriage. In fact, most members of those groups which did not have an open-ended ethic thought that alternate intimate relationships were at least conceivable in the future.

SEX AS A PROBLEM. Just over half of reporting respondents indicated that there had been problems with sleeping arrangements. Though only a couple thought this was a major problem. A similar fraction said that choice of sexual partners was a problem. Only about a third reported that sex per se was a problem in the group. Only a few thought sexual problems were major or recurring. There have been isolated instances of various sexual difficulties with expected frequency.[3] In most such instances the sexual difficulty has been found, through counseling or spontaneous changes in relationships, to be largely symptomatic of interpersonal problems. Combining all the available data from different sources on these groups, we are forced to conclude that sex is rarely a real problem. Even Kilgo in her pessimistic prognosis for group marriages was led to this same conclusion.[4]

Indeed, respondents reported that their satisfaction with their sex life increased somewhat to greatly as the result of the multilateral marriage. They were not just enjoying it more but also reported engaging in it more. (See Appendix VII, Table 2.)

It is as if people who are closely involved interpersonally might as well be sexually involved, too, for in the long run sex is seldom a detriment to relationships; sometimes it facilitates growthful involvement, and at the very least it feels good.

REFERENCES

1. Robert Athanasiou *et al.*, "Sex," *op. cit.*
2. See, among others, Gilbert Bartell, *Group Sex* (New York: Peter H. Wyden, 1971).
3. Larry L. and Joan M. Constantine, "Sexual Aspects of Multilateral Relations," *Journal of Sex Research* 7, 3 (August 1971).
4. Reese Danley Kilgo "Can Group Marriage Work?" *Sexual Behavior* 2, 3 (March 1972).

16
Seeing Green

JEALOUSY IS A PART of normal human experience. Almost everyone in our culture has experienced that sudden sense of insecurity when someone with whom they had a personally important relationship, turned, however briefly, to another. Though the propensity for jealous behavior is probably not innate and certainly not cross-culturally universal, it is common. In multilateral marriage simultaneous, multiple intimate relationships provide an abundance of settings for the emergence of jealousy and a continued arena for focus on jealous behavior. Four out of five participants reported problems with jealousy, ranking it third among all problems of multilateral marriages; only one in five, however, specifically listed it as a major problem. Respondents were significantly more likely to report it as a major problem earlier in their groups' histories than later. Jealousy as a problem was also significantly associated with age; older respondents reported it as a problem less often than younger ones.[1] Our observations and interviews revealed that most jealous responses were outgrown and groups developed increasingly effective means of dealing with jealousy as the group continued and members matured. Recurrent or major problems with jealousy were almost never an important factor in the demise of a group.

Both sociological and psychological data on jealousy are lacking. Attitudes on jealousy are often ambivalent or mercurial. In this culture, jealousy is alternately praised and pronounced pathological. Premaritally, jealous behavior may be regarded as an index of commitment or its provocation an instrument for inducing commitment. After marriage, it may be a source of marital stress.

While there is no single model of jealousy which can be legitimately called the accepted theory, most traditional conceptualizations in the literature have certain common features.[2] (1) Jealousy is an emotion, like anger or joy. (2) Property, possession, ownership, and rights are regarded as underlying bases. (3) Sexual relationships are the context in which jealousy is localized or, in some formulations, legitimized. (4) Whether innate or conditioned, adult jealousy is considered to be so deeply ingrained as to be all but inevitable.

OBSERVATION. The nature of jealousy, its origins, its effect on the jealous party and the objects of jealousy, and the degree to which it is an inseparable part of one's nature could be determining factors in the long-term viability of multilateral marriage and other patterns of open multiple involvement. Consequently, we made extensive systematic observations and inquiries on the experience of jealousy within multilateral marriages but also in other relationships, which ultimately resulted in a new formulation of the concept of jealousy.

In our observations we were struck by the frequency with which the "emotion" was first labeled by a person other than the ostensibly jealous one. Usually, when jealousy was not involved, people we were observing labeled their own feelings in an interaction. They did so whether these were hedonic ("positive") feelings like joy or affection, or anhedonic ("negative") feelings such as anger or fear. In our personal experience, too, we could recall many instances of statements like "You sure are acting jealous!" or "I think you're jealous!" or "He must be jealous!" but few instances of the jealous person labeling his own feelings.

The frequency of external labeling could stem from social habit, deficient awareness associated with "being jealous," denial by the jealous person of feelings which he may regard as illegitimate, or even the absence of such feelings in the person who has been labeled jealous. To us, recognition of the labeling process was a call for deeper probing into what the labeled person was indeed experiencing.

Another key insight is best expressed as a metaphor.[3] Let us say that you are eating dinner when you look up to see through the window that someone is quietly rolling your car down the driveway and into the street. You leap from the table and run out the door, screaming, "Hey you! What do you think you're doing!" To other family members who were not facing the window, your behavior may seem rather bizarre, creating as it did an unpleasant disruption in the dinner routine. Nevertheless, the odds are that your behavior would be effective in inducing the would-be thief to abandon his attempt and flee. On the other hand, you may have been thinking about how some character could sneak up behind the azaleas, release the parking brake, and push your car away without your knowing. You keep looking anxiously out the window, becoming increasingly convinced that the car is moving almost imperceptibly. Unable to bear the tension any longer, you race out the door, screaming, "Help! Police! Stop thief!" To other family members, the two situations would appear to be very similar if not identical, yet in one case your behavior was functional—serving you—and in the other it was not. Both performances, however, were in response to threats which you perceived as real.

Gradually, from these insights and the additional material we unearthed as a result, we have evolved a rather comprehensive model of jealousy which accounts not only for the data better than earlier theories but has already been useful in a clinical sense in providing means for people to deal more effectively and growthfully with jealousy. At present it is a tentative working model which draws upon previous models in some areas and departs radically in others. We have made no explicit provision for the inclusion of so-called pathological jealousy, either in itself or as part of a pattern of other psychological difficulty. Without attempting to define "normal," we will simply characterize this as a theory or model of normal human jealousy.

JEALOUSY—A MODEL

Jealousy is a label applied to one of several clusters of context-dependent behavior patterns usually exhibited by one person in response to a situation involving loss or potential loss of something valued in some relationship with another person. The elements of this *jealousy situation* always involve an Actor, the person who is "acting jealous"; the Object, the person in the relationship with Actor; and the Agent, the person, persons, or thing which is identified as the cause or source of the threat or loss. Although the Agent is usually a person, behavior in response to loss as the result of other things, such as a job, a pet, or a hobby might also be labeled as jealousy. It is convenient simply to call whatever Actor values and has lost, is losing, or may lose, the *loss element.*

This identifies the essential elements. Most importantly, jealousy is *not* an emotion, something that is felt, but rather, it is behavior, a way of acting. What is actually felt or experienced by Actor when he is behaving jealously is one of a number of emotions or moods which are in part dependent on the nature of the loss or impending loss, or at least on his perception of it. Sometimes there may be no underlying emotional basis. The emotional response to the situation has both primary and secondary components. The behavior and the emotion involved are highly sensitive to situational context, individual predisposition, and external expectations.

JEALOUS BEHAVIOR. The behavioral patterns that are labeled as jealousy are varied. There are two primary clusters which we will identify later in different contexts. One cluster consists of behavior associated with anger, rage, and similar feelings. The other is related to depression, despair, and grief. The behavior may appear to be primarily communicated toward either Object or Agent. The "jealous" wife may take her anger out at the husband who has "betrayed" her or attempt revenge on the mistress.

Jealous behavior is always highly context-dependent, that is, whether or not an individual behaves jealously in a given situation depends on the specifics of the situation, not just on whether or not it is a situation usually associated with jealousy for the individual involved or for most individuals. Jealous behavior may be divided into two major kinds, depending on whether the behavior does or does not have an emotional basis in strong feelings which Actor experiences. Much jealous behavior does not come from strong feelings but is the habituated or expected response in that situation. "People . . . feel jealous because the norms of our monogamic society teach them to, expect them to, *force* them to."[4] Often we have heard individuals say, "I suppose I should be jealous," or, after behaving jealously, "I really didn't *feel* jealous, but I felt I *should* feel jealous. After all, I wouldn't want it to seem like I don't care."

The social context, cultural conditioning, and expectations of Actor as well as others who are present play significant roles in determining jealous behavior. The traditional view of this is summed up thusly:

> Jealousy does not occur in "natural situations" . . . those defined [by] established institutions. Our malignant emotions . . . greet any illicit attempt. . . . They do not manifest themselves when a licit attempt is made, partly because we do not have the subjective feeling of "being wronged," and partly because their expression would receive the disapprobation of the community.[5]

Another example of this effect is the woman who maintains the pretext of not knowing of her husband's infidelity because she does not want to have to behave jealously as her society demands. Jealous behavior which is less "programmed" and more a genuinely felt response to the immediate situation may be called *situation responsive*.

LOSSES. The loss element associated with jealousy may be anything Actor values in the relationship with Object or as the result of the relationship. A man might lose status either because his partner was a source of status or because losing a woman in itself diminishes status in his community. One person may lose control over another. If the relationship includes the perception of possession or ownership of one by the other, this too may be lost. The loss of need satisfaction may be the loss element in a jealousy situation. A person may identify his/her *self* with another person and could experience the loss of that person as a loss of self. A traditionally married woman's sense of identity may be almost totally defined by her husband and children. Sometimes exclusivity, exclusive use of or access to, may be valued in itself, and to this extent a loss of exclusivity could be the loss element.

The value of the loss element is defined by Actor and its actual or pending loss is always real to him. On the other hand, there may be no actual danger of his ever losing what he values with respect to Object. In the case of potential loss, jealous behavior in the face of a real threat is probably functional, while jealous behavior in response to an unreal threat is probably dysfunctional. It is quite obvious that in a multilateral marriage it is always to the group's best interest to identify the extent of reality or unreality of any jealousy-provoking loss. When the loss potential is real, it is of further interest whether the loss has been actualized or not, and if so whether that loss is recoverable or not, as these determine what subsequent actions are most functional to the group and to the individuals, especially to Actor.

THE EXPERIENCE OF JEALOUSY. In our study, we began to gather material on the feelings associated with jealousy as the result of observing the modes of coping which some of the more functional groups had developed. When one member of such a group was seen to behave in a way which could be labeled jealous, other members would respond with neither approval nor disapproval, but would begin helping the person to probe and identify his own feelings. At first, we confused the actual experience of jealousy with possible loss elements—status, control, possession, ownership, need-satisfaction, self-identity, and exclusivity—until we noted that these were merely subjectively valuable things which one might feel one has lost or is losing. The primary feeling-basis of jealousy reduced to a few common things, namely, anxiety, hurt, and loss.

Anxiety is an emotional state associated with anhedonic sensations of anticipation. We have all experienced anxiety and can give detailed accounts of its tension, the more rapid pulse and breathing, the knot-in-the-stomach, lump-in-the-throat feelings.

We learned that anxiety over perceptions of potential or impending loss was the most common "feeling" experienced when someone "felt" jealous, that is, when his behavior was so labeled. (It is conceivable for someone to experience anxiety over an uncertain future as the result of an actualized rather than a potential loss, but we have not observed this.) When the loss is already actualized, the most common experience was usually described as a sense of emptiness, aloneness, or incompleteness, which we have chosen simply to call a sense of loss. Less common than either anxiety or loss was for the "jealous" person to feel hurt or "betrayed" (sometimes described as "in pain") over a loss.

Secondary feelings are feelings that people have about their primary feelings or into which they transform or displace their primary feelings. Secondary feelings may arise so readily that primary feelings are barely experienced or translated into behavior. Secondary feelings in response to the jealousy situation are more varied than primary ones and include anger, rage, sadness, despair, depression, and grief. The jealously behaving person may even have feelings about these feelings, such as guilt or shame if "feeling jealous" is perceived as illegitimate.

The diversity suggested by this catalogue of primary and secondary feelings associated with jealousy belies the fact that *the majority of situation-responsive jealousy was found to consist of anxiety accompanying the perception of imminent loss.*

Anxiety is quite well understood and is known to be associated with certain physiological indicators. It is interesting that Davis described symptoms of jealousy (adrenalin production, tachycardia, increased blood sugar, striated muscle tonus) and associates them with physical mobilization but not with anxiety, perhaps because anxiety is usually considered to be less specific.[6]

For the potential for jealousy to emerge into actual behavior, there must be a stimulus of sufficient clarity and intensity. It is as if each of us has a threshold or barrier beyond which any involvement or accumulation of involvement is considered a violation. Sexual interraction frequently serves as the immediate trigger for jealous behavior. Equally often, sex is the arena in which other modes of jealousy may be expressed.

Alternate sexual involvement in our society is considered to be a clear and unambiguous justification for jealousy. Indeed, the absence of a jealous response to recognized sexual relations outside a marriage is greeted with disbelief or disapprobation. The clarity of the sexual context may lead to jealous behavior when little, if any, anxiety is experienced. Augmenting this programmed response is the fact that for most of us, sex is an especially highly cathected area of experience. That is, we are heavily emotionally invested in sex, identifying it as somehow unique, more important, and closer to our sense of personhood than other modes of human encounter.

For both of the foregoing reasons, jealousy over sexual matters often turns out to have its basis in other areas, such as maintenance of control.

coping. Ultimately Actor takes some action in an attempt to cope with and modify the intense feelings experienced in jealousy or the situation evoking them. The range of real-life behaviors is enormous, but generally fall into one of several categories: antagonistic behavior, isolational behavior, redefinitional behavior, and problem-solving. If we assume there to be ongoing relationship between Actor and Object (not excluding the possibilities of one between Actor and Agent and/or Object and Agent as well), then we are interested in the effects of the actions upon the relationship. In particular, for a continued viable, contactful relationship, Actor and Object must remain in contact throughout the period of jealous behavior or reintegrate again later.

Antagonistic behavior includes fighting and quarreling, shouting, and other expressions of anger or rage, violence,[7] attempts to take revenge, etc. These may be directed toward Agent, the "other party," but as often as not they are directed toward Object. Isolational behavior includes separation from Object and withdrawal. Withdrawal may be complete, or Actor may simply withdraw from the relationship things which Object values. In a conventional marriage, a wife may respond to her husband's indiscretion by withdrawing affection or refusing sexual favors. From this it should be clear that isolational behavior, especially in that it may become habituated, hinders reintegration.[8] Even strongly antagonistic behavior, unless extreme and prolonged, keeps the parties in contact.

Fighting is a special case because, though it is partially antagonistic, it may also be a means of problem-solving. Except in the most extreme and ritualized examples, fights between intimates involve some communication, that is, some exchange of information, and this can be enhanced by specific fighting skills such as those espoused by George Bach.[9] In any event, fights are often followed by moves toward reintegration.

As sociologist Robert Whitehurst has noted, some people, in response to a jealousy situation, direct their feelings and behavior toward neither Object nor Agent. They externalize the cause of the situation, identifying extramarital sex as the common enemy, for example.[10] We have also observed jealously labeled individuals intellectualizing or rationalizing away their jealousy. Both displacement onto outside causes and intellectualization represent attempts to redefine the problem. Redefinition does not in itself hamper reintegration, but neither is it likely to be highly functional.

Creative problem-solving to cope with jealousy is, of course, uncommon on the greater American scene. It is obviously both integrative and highly functional for a couple to respond to jealousy by sitting down and beginning to talk rationally about the meaning and possible resolution of the situation. Our study has led to the refinement of an especially effective problem-solving response to jealousy which involves clarification of the experience of jealousy for the person whose behavior has been labeled.

In the process of clarification, it is the responsibility of other parties to assist Actor in identifying his real feelings in the situation. They can simply respond to the early signs of jealousy by asking him how he feels or they may encourage him to "get into" and express his feelings. The aim is to get not only a clarification of feelings but the identity of the loss element. Further exploration with Object and Agent can clarify the reality or unreality of any loss of this element, and all parties can then work on a resolution of the situation.

INTERVENING VARIABLES. The occurrence of jealousy in otherwise equivalent circumstances will be mediated by whether or not Actor perceives a loss potential. This in turn will be a function of the way he construes reality and how secure he is in the relationship with Object. If Actor does not consider exclusive sexual access to be of value in itself or if he is very secure in his belief that he will not totally lose Object, he will be less likely to behave jealously when Object has intercourse with Agent.

A number of factors have been found to enhance security, hence reduce the likelihood of jealousy.

A strong commitment or covenant between individuals can increase the sense of security. The more intense the commitment, the more it is expressed in terms of permanence, the lower will be the threat of loss. Commitment has several forms, and the form of commitment can also be a factor. If Actor perceives Object to be committed on the basis of an emotional investment in him, this is likely to be more cogent than if the commitment is on the basis of "As long as things are groovy." Commitment based on ideology ("Marriages are essential to happiness and ought to last a lifetime") is probably intermediate in effect.[11]

The longer a relationship lasts, the more secure its participants are likely to be. We believe this to be the explanation for the decrease in reports of jealousy from longer-lasting groups in our study and for similar results in the Kinsey surveys and in clinical studies.[12]

A person may be secure in his relationship with someone if he considers each person to be unique, hence irreplaceable. Since Agent is not the same as Actor, Agent cannot replace Actor in the relationship with Object, hence there is no threat to Actor. This way of looking at people and relationships has been called individuation and is effective in reducing jealousy if really believed.[13]

In a complementary vein, if Agent has alternate sources of whatever he values in the relationship with Object, there is no threat of loss. This is especially relevant to multilateral marriages, as it can be assumed that the multilateral involvement provides alternate sources. This view is compatible with individuation; each individual may be unique in total, yet be the source of many things, each of which might also be obtained from another person.

Finally, we observe, as have others, that jealousy declines with maturity. Age often brings security in many respects. Developmentally, jealous behavior has its origins in sibling rivalry. In the jealousy of an older sibling for the new baby we can see the same elements as in normal adult jealousy: loss of attention, feared additional loss, the desire for exclusivity. The healthy child outgrows this as he sees that parents can love and provide for more than one child. While some time may be lost, there are gains which are more than compensatory. Unfortunately, this experience is not usually generalized to other adult relationships.

IMPLICATIONS OF A NEW MODEL OF JEALOUSY

We could summarize our model of jealousy as follows: Jealousy is learned behavior exhibited in response to certain types of situations involving three "parties," one of whom perceives the loss or potential loss of something valued in the relationship with a second person through the action of the third party. Jealous behavior in response to real, actualized losses which are perceived as completed and irreversible usually has its origins in a sense of loss, perhaps transformed into grief. Most jealous behavior has its origins in anxiety, in unpleasant anticipation due to insecurity. The potential for loss need not be real. Because it is learned behavior, jealousy may occur in response merely to the nature of the situation without any strong basis in feelings. Anything valued may be the trigger for jealousy; what is valued in the relationship need not make sense, need not even be real. Individuals may exhibit jealousy over a loss of status, diminished control over the other person, loss of actual possession or the quasi-legal sense of ownership, loss of sources of need gratification (or loss of need gratification), or even the loss of time spent with the person. The experience of jealousy leads to a variety of secondary feelings and coping behavior, some of which are markedly more productive than others.

APPLICATION. The value of this model is apparent when it is applied to real situations, especially those derived from multilateral relations.

Eva and Jack C—— owned a roomy townhouse. When Carl W——, a close friend of Jack's, could find no work in the city, he and Helen were offered the use of an extra room at the

C———s until their finances improved. Propinquity rapidly generated strong attractions among all of them, and one night, after another long evening of excitedly exploring their feelings for each other, the four of them decided to try having Eva and Carl spend the night together in the spare room while Helen went with Jack to the C———s' bedroom. Over the next week, the cross-marital relationships became increasingly intense and sexual. For Eva, especially, the experience with Carl was in sharp contrast to what she regarded as difficulties, sexual and otherwise, in her marriage. Carl began pushing for a group marriage, an all-out commitment. His relationship with Eva appeared to become almost an obsession to him.

One night, as the evening drifted into the earliest morning hours, Carl and Eva lay talking in her bed, continuing their almost nonstop exploration of the limits of their forming relationship. Once, they both shifted position at the same time and the bed creaked noisily, bringing on laughter from both of them.

Suddenly the dark exploded in a nova of electrical sparks announced by the cymbal-crash of a shattering light bulb. When the other light was turned on, Jack, who had been in the other room with Helen, was standing over the bed, and a table lamp lay where he had thrown it across the startled pair.

On the surface, this appears to be a simple case of a violently jealous husband reacting (many would say justifiably) to his wife's intimacy with another man. His jealous behavior seems to have been triggered by the sound of the bed and accompanying laughter, which suggested sexual intimacy. It is equally superficial to note that Jack responded to an imaginary threat in that Carl and Eva were not then engaged in intercourse.

At the time, neither Jack, nor Eva, nor Helen, nor Carl were in a position to confront and analyze their situation. They had neither experience with the model nor the presence of mind to engage in problem-solving. Eva, knowing Jack best, responded by immediately discontinuing her intimacy with Carl almost *in toto*, though the W———s continued to live with the C———s for a few months more.

What we can piece together from various sources is a more complex picture. The audible hint of sexual intimacy was, of course, merely the trigger for Jack's behavior, and sexual intimacy itself was only the arena in which feelings were identified and permitted to emerge in behavior. Jack was as aware as Eva of problems in their marriage. The group process springing from their involvement with Carl and Helen had brought them all face to face with their scripted behavior and ways in which they maintained an image of marriage which disguised reality. Of immediate importance was Jack's emerging feeling that his marriage with Eva was not based on love and that both of them in the past had used sex in a manipulative manner or to express hostility or control. It appears that to Eva, sex with Carl seemed like a new, more total experience, less adulterated by disaffection than sex with Jack had been. To *all* concerned, sex was a defining element of their relationships.

What Jack feared was losing Eva, an especially unpleasant prospect at a time when new material was surfacing which held the promise of an improved marriage with her. Losing Eva would mean the loss of satisfaction of many needs. To him, and perhaps even to Eva, her defection to Carl was a real potential. Eva's dramatic response, curtailing an intense, accelerating intimacy with Carl, presents a seemingly paradoxical contrast with her involvement with him. Yet it makes sense if she sensed what Jack feared and recognized—that she could conceivably choose Carl over him; only complete abrogation would be convincing.

These four people did not explore Jack's feeling or deal with whatever threat he was responding to, so our analysis can remain only one of the more plausible among several explanations. The unpleasant final dissolution of their foursome might have been somewhat modified had they been better able to deal with jealousy and the relationship between exclusivity and nonexclusivity as well as their insecurities.

The next situation is a composite, representative of more functional dealing with jealousy.

Geraldine was an anxious wife who coped with uncertainty by taking control. She would talk incessantly and attempt to maneuver situations into predictable outcomes, whether pleasant or not, rather than face uncertainty. Soon after she became involved with Donald, Donald's wife, Suzanne, began to get involved with

Geraldine's husband, Pete. Though Donald and Geraldine had started the cross-marital relationships and were the early enthusiasts of a group marriage, their relationship was soon eclipsed by the one between Pete and Suzanne. The four of them and their three children had moved in together in an old farmhouse, but more and more, Suzanne would persuade Pete to go with her alone on various junkets. She had never before had any deep sexual relationship except with Donald, and after eleven years of marriage was totally absorbed by the novelty of her relationship with Pete.

When Pete and Suzanne walked in after spending a weekend camping together, they found their spouses waiting. Donald seemed on the verge of exploding as he paced in tight ovals in front of the fireplace; Geraldine sat on the arm of an overstuffed chair, smoking nervously. Let us follow this situation to see what it would be like if the four of them developed an effective style of coping with jealousy.

"You look like a caged tiger," Pete said, addressing Donald. "What's up?"

"Nothing's up, that's just it. You guys were supposed to be back from your cavort with Mother Nature an hour and a half ago so we could all take the kids into town," Don answered angrily, but he was interrupted by Geraldine.

"Listen, what about me? Nobody seems to be interested in what *I* feel, you just walk past me and start up with Don. Look, I think we all ought to sit down and have a big talk. There are a lot of things that people aren't talking about." ("Like what?" Suzanne asked as Geraldine went on obliviously.) "Suzanne, why don't you put on some coffee while the boys move the chairs out to the porch. I want you all to start facing the issue. I think ——"

"Wait!" Don interrupted, "just what *is* the issue? No, wait, don't answer. Something strikes me funny, Suzie. What are you doing?"

"Putting out my cigarette."

"No, before that, I mean. Weren't you doing just what you did when the neighbors dropped in last Thursday, talking like an express train and choreographing everyone and everything?" Don paused and glanced at Pete. "She does that when she's nervous, doesn't she?"

"Look, ask her. She's right here."

Suzanne intervened and addressed Geraldine. "You look pretty nervous and up-tight, Gerrie."

"Yeh, well I guess I am. Wouldn't you be? I mean, after all, I tell Pete to get home by six and I depend on him to do things and he doesn't seem to care about what *I* want and . . ."

"You're acting pretty jealous if you ask me," Pete put in as he lit his pipe.

"Cool and collected as usual, ready with the labels," Geraldine sneered.

Suzanne raised both hands above her head in a gesture of attention. "Hey, you guys!" she exclaimed. "Look, Geraldine, both you and Donald are acting pretty jealous. That ought to be a clue for us. Something *is* going on. What is it? What are you feeling? Like Don said, you're behaving the same way you did with the snoopy neighbors. What do you feel?"

Gerrie smiled. "Give me a chance and maybe I can tell you." She paused and put a hand on Suzanne's arm, making it clear she was not mad. "I feel—well, I feel like nothing's happening the way I plan it. Everything is getting away from me. I'm angry at Pete. And I'm angry at you because Pete wasn't supposed to respond to you this way. You two are running amuck and I don't know where it's going to lead."

"Maybe you're afraid you might lose Pete," Don put in.

Pete walked over to Geraldine. "Is that it? Do you think I'll leave you for Suzanne?" She didn't answer but frowned slightly. He went on, "You keep talking about not being able to depend on me, about me not doing what you want, stuff like that. What's that sound like to you?"

"Control stuff. Sounds like I'm losing control over you. Or afraid I will. But," the calm certainty in her voice changed again to nervous tension, "what about Don? He's not losing control over Suzanne. What's his issue?"

Don snorted. "Never had control." He sat down, looked puzzled for half a minute and then began hesitantly, "I can't quite put my finger on it. I get this uncomfortable, angry knot in my stomach at some times but not others."

"Do you remember other times when you felt jealous about someone Suzanne was into?" Geraldine prompted.

"Well, not some*one*, some*thing*. Remember," he asked Suzanne, "when you first got into yoga? It was yoga this, yoga that. Exercises for an hour and a half before bed, yoga classes three times a week, all day Saturday reading a book on yoga. I hardly even saw you. It's the same now."

"You mean, honey, you're not seeing enough of me?"

"Right, I just don't have any time with you. It was okay as long as the four of us would spend time together and I would at least sleep with you every few nights, but now you two are always off by yourselves. I don't care so much what you and Pete do together, but I want some of you, too. Funny, that goes for you, too, Pete. We haven't talked or worked on the boat in two weeks."

This group is well on its way to improving their situation for all concerned. They will be working on the control issue for a long time and they will again find themselves with problems in distributing time, but they are well past the level of labeling behavior and the alienation which that brings about.

Though what we have presented is somewhat compressed, the interaction among Pete, Suzanne, Geraldine, and Donald is representative of what we have seen emerging from the more highly functional multilateral marriages. We see no reason why this technique cannot be applied in conventional dyadic relationships. The object is to remove the pejorative connotation from jealousy and view it as a behavioral cue signaling an opportunity for exploration into the nature of a relationship. Undertaken repetitively, the effect is not only to illuminate the fears and insecurity over immediate threats, whether objectively real or merely perceived, but to build security and confidence in the ability of the relationship to cope with threat.

In the long run, we find that people in multiple relationships who develop effective exploratory styles of dealing with jealousy outgrow certain forms of jealousy. In this sense we would regard jealousy based on status, control, possession, ownership, and exclusivity as less mature. Jealous behavior in response to real losses in need satisfaction and time jealousy appear to be an intrinsic functional residue. Time jealousy occurs when Actor experiences a real reduction below some critical threshold in the amount of time spent with Object because of Object's involvement with Agent *and* without any other relationship to involve Actor's time.

People do not seem to outgrow these latter forms of jealousy, nor does it seem to us that it would be in their best interests to do so.

GROWTH. Probably the most important constituent in growth from jealousy is security. Regrettably, insecure people in insecure relationships continue to have unproductive encounters with jealousy. The question then becomes one of how to become secure when one's experience is that of continuing threat.

Attitude and mental set can assist in the growth process and we find certain of these to be common in the early experience of people who have emerged from possessive jealousy. Sometimes very early in their dyadic marriages they came to view the attention of others directed toward their spouses as enhancing themselves. That others would find a spouse attractive was taken as ego-enhancing, status-elevating, or as validation of mate choice. While these may not in themselves be highly mature forms of gratification, such things seem to have played a role in forming early positive associations with multiple involvement, albeit very mild involvement.

Some people also genuinely take pleasure in the pleasure of someone they love, thus responding positively to a relationship which the spouse finds to be rewarding, joyful, or growthful. One may also focus on the secondary, more personal, gains which can accrue from having a happier spouse. Finally, sometimes we find a form of ego extension in which one person regards the experiences of an intimate as being in some sense his own.

To grow beyond possessive, controlling jealousy is a worthy goal for anyone.

REFERENCES

1. Larry L. and Joan M. Constantine, "Sexual Aspects of Multilateral Relations," *op. cit.*, pp. 204–225.
2. For a carefully reasoned traditional model of jealousy, see the paper by Kingsley Davis, "Jealousy and Sexual Property," *Social Forces* 14 (1936), pp. 395–405. See also Jessie Bernard, "Jealousy in Marriage," *Medical Aspects of Human Sexuality* (April 1971).
3. Psychologist Victor Garlock first drew our attention to the functional/

dysfunctional aspects of jealousy as related to the reality/unreality of the provoking threat.

4. Bernard, *op. cit.*

5. Davis, *op. cit.*

6. *Ibid.*

7. See Robert Whitehurst, "Violently Jealous Husbands," *Sexual Behavior* (July 1971).

8. Two analyses of coping behavior and its effects on relationships are found in Robert Whitehurst, "Violence Potential in Extramarital Sexual Responses," *Journal of Marriage and the Family* 33, 4 (November 1971), and "Jealous Wives and Extramarital Sex," *Medical Aspects of Human Sexuality* (accepted for publication).

9. Bach, *The Intimate Enemy, op. cit.*

10. Whitehurst, "Violence Potential in Extramarital Sexual Responses."

11. Rosabeth Kanter applies the concept of differing commitment mechanisms to an analysis of communes in "Commitment and Social Organization: A Study of Commitment Mechanisms in Utopian Communities," *American Sociological Review* 33, 4 (August 1968).

12. Bernard (above, n. 2) cites A. C. Kinsey, *et al.*, *Sexual Behavior in the Human Female* (Philadelphia: Saunders, 1953) and M. R. Sapirstein, *Emotional Security* (New York: Crown, 1948).

13. Charles and Rebecca Palson, "Swinging in Wedlock," *Society* 9, 4 (February 1972).

17

The Group Marriage in Society

Whether they live in an anonymous brick-front town-house in a major city or on an isolated farm on the outskirts of a village, the multilateral family will have to interface with the larger community and must be viable in a real, not altogether friendly, society.

Our personal encounters with the public have taught us the intricacy of the interface with society. We recall a church-related picnic to which we had been invited by friends. The young suburbanite seated next to us continued to probe into just what we did professionally until we told him we were researching multilateral marriage. He seemed fascinated by the idea and began asking questions about how men fared with other men and with multiple wives. It was clear to us that he was "trying on" the idea for himself. But very rapidly, others at the long redwood table picked up words here and there and started listening in. His wife leaned forward to speak around him. "Isn't that *bigamy*?" she asked, giving a peculiar emphasis to the last word. "I mean two wives, I mean, it just isn't right!"

"Well, they aren't bigamists because bigamy is a legal concept," we answered. "None of those in group marriages has actually tried to take out multiple licenses and such."

"Well then, they're not really married are they? I mean to be really married means having a wedding and being able to prove it. Really they're just sleeping around." She turned her face expectantly to her husband.

"That's just what I was thinking," he announced. "What could anyone possibly see in it?" Thereafter he was alternately the most derogative and the most fascinated of the conversants, depending on whether his wife had joined in or had returned to talking about schools with the woman next to her. When she was in the conversation, she kept returning to the distinction between legal "real" marriage (her relationship with her husband) and "lesser" relationships. The objections were voiced more often on legal or social principles than on moral grounds.

THE LAW OF THE LAND. In most states, members of multilateral marriages will indeed be in violation of the law on multiple counts. The exceptions are those states which have removed from the law restrictions on sexual relations between consenting adults. No state directly prohibits group or multilateral marriage, though many have bigamy statutes; and a rejected constitutional reform in New Mexico would have explicitly banned multiple marriages. In most states, partners in a multilateral marriage could be charged with adultery, fornication, or cohabitation. In many places vague catch-all statutes remain on the books and might potentially apply to multilateral marriages. Keeping a disorderly house, lewd cohabitation, open and gross lewdness are among the titles of these provisions. In addition, most localities have health and zoning ordinances which have sometimes been used to limit the number of "unrelated" adults in a single dwelling.

True, most of these laws are little used, many may in fact be unconstitutional either because they are vague or because they invade the privacy of marriage. To be guilty of bigamy, one must "legally" marry two different people, not merely declare one's commitment. While such laws remain, the threat of direct legal reprisals or extralegal pressure exists. Zoning and health restrictions have been used against communes in many places.

The long-term trend appears to be toward "consenting adults" laws. This type of legal reform has been slow and inconsistent. Ironically, in California, single adults engaged in casual, secretive swinging would not be in violation of the law, while two legally married couples in a committed multilateral marriage would be guilty of at least adultery and open and lewd cohabitation in the eyes of the law.[1] On the other hand, a bill to legalize group marriage has been introduced perennially in the California legislature. In Wisconsin, Assembly Bills 1396 and 1398 would have explicitly legalized polygamous and probably multilateral marriages.[2]

All but one respondent completing the Attitude Survey agreed very strongly that the law has no business regulating private sexual behavior between consenting adults. All felt very strongly that religious groups should not impose their standards on others, and on this issue respondents were significantly more liberal than informants in Athanasiou's survey, which is to be expected in view of respondents' relatively nonreligious orientations. They felt strongly that group marriage should be legalized but felt *significantly* more strongly that *any* form of marriage should be legal, reflecting their liberalism and concern for the broader issues. Public nudity was acceptable and should be legal, they felt, but they balked slightly at public sex. They agreed, but *significantly* less, that public as well as private sexual behavior between consenting adults should be legal.

To date, the law has left multilateral marriages alone. No respondent has had legal difficulties associated with their multilateral marriage. Two couples formerly in multilateral marriages encountered some difficulty in trying to adopt or obtain guardianship over children. Their difficulties seemed to be related to aspects of their marital lifestyle but probably not to their multilateral marriage experience.

Cambridge, Massachusetts, was the setting for prosecution of members of a small commune, on charges of open and gross lewdness and lascivious behavior, stemming from reaction to their entire lifestyle but especially their predilection for nude sunbathing on the porch of their urban home. A judge found them guilty, but in the retrial, the jury acquitted them despite their open admission to having been nude but not lewd.* It is this sort of

* Their trial is of broad social significance. The transcript has been published in paperback (*Lewd: The Inquisition of Seth and Carolyn*, [Boston: Beacon Press, 1972])

harassment which poses the biggest legal threat for multilateral marriages.

NEIGHBORS. The law represents only the official interface with society. Most contacts take place at the neighborhood level. What *will* the neighbors think?

In many cases, the neighbors may not have anything to think *about*. Five of nine groups reporting said that the neighbors probably knew nothing. Our other sources suggest that many groups survive in part through invisibility. Yet, when groups have been open in the selective pattern of disclosure we have most often seen, neighbors and neighborhoods have been quite accepting. On one particular block that we know, chances are you will find any missing youngster if you go to the big colonial in the middle of the block. It houses one-half a multilateral marriage (the other half is two blocks away) and is the favorite rendezvous of neighborhood kids, most of whom know of the unconventional family situation. Their parents do, too, but do not see reason to isolate their children. This neighborhood is in a notoriously conservative section of urban sprawl. Whether the neighbors know or not, most multilateral families get along well in their communities. Seventy-eight percent characterize relations as good to excellent, for both adults and children.

FAMILY, FRIENDS, AND FRIENDS OF THE FAMILY. People in multilateral marriages are hardly social isolates. Almost every reporting respondent maintains close contacts outside the group. More than 60 percent said that all their friends knew of their multilateral marriage and an additional 15 percent reported that most of their friends knew. Fewer than one in ten had no friends who knew. All but one group had friends with whom the group interfaced as a group, and the number of such friends reported ranged from six to twenty-five.

Nor does their multilateral marriage isolate them from their relatives. Nearly two-thirds said their parents knew, or knew something, of their relationship; almost a quarter said their parents knew completely. The replies were virtually the same when we asked about other family members. When we talked with them, all but a very few hoped they could share with their parents what they were or had been into. Some parents were very openly accepting of their sons' and daughters' "deviant" marital choices; others had great difficulty; a few asked not even to be told. But all in all, things are pretty good with their families: 69 percent said they were on good to excellent terms with their parents and families; another 34 percent said things were satisfactory or as good as could be expected.

Generally, where parents have first met their offsprings' multilateral partners in a more or less normal social context, without knowing the extent of involvement (or before it comes about), they tend to react favorably. We also find that many people of the last generation, when first encountering the idea of multilateral relations, try to make some association with an experience in their own lives. Surprisingly (or perhaps not surprisingly) most people find some related situation in their lives. One set of parents recalled a very close friendship with another couple which they acknowledged might have developed into some kind of intimate involvement had they all been brought up differently. One man remembered a boyhood friendship shared with another boy and girl. These experiences were remembered warmly and, we feel, aided in developing a positive association with the idea of multilateral marriage, if not for themselves, at least for others. But one woman associated multilateral relations with a difficult period in her life when she was trying to break an engagement with one man while she was dating another who was pressuring her into a new engagement. One father could only associate multiple relations with the agonizing sense of betrayal he felt when he accidentally walked in on his wife and her lover. We found that such negative first associations were sufficient in themselves to account for most of the parents who had difficulty accepting the idea of multilateral marriage.

BUSINESS AS USUAL. Business and job contacts represent another sector of the interface with society. Economic risk and the American tradition of separating job and family would lead us to predict that comparatively few people in unconventional family styles would be open about them with business contacts, yet most employed respondents said some business contacts knew of their multilateral marriage. Three said all their business contacts knew and two more said that most knew. Respondents in still-intact groups have been *significantly* more circumspect with business associates than those whose groups dissolved. We do not believe this association holds generally; we know of other intact groups of comparable duration which have been much less reticent. One professional has had the head of the department in which he is employed over for dinner to meet both his wives. And in one instance, supervisor and subordinate are both involved in the same group!

Families must successfully negotiate many transactions with other social systems. Schools and financial institutions are ones which are likely to be particularly sticky.

The A———s and the S———s, a newly formed group, decided that their houses were too small and set about finding one with enough room for four adults and five kids. They specifically sought out a sympathetic real estate agent who helped them find just such a house. Then they had to secure a mortgage. They wanted to own the house jointly. The first bank turned them down flat. Previously, the bank explained, it had taken a chance with a similar joint mortgage arrangement. When the couples broke up, the bank was left holding the bag. By applying to eleven banks at once, the A———s-S———s were able to get their mortgage.

Once everyone was moved in, the group decided to be selectively open about their lifestyle. They felt it was important that the childrens' teachers know about their expanded family, especially so that the teachers would understand any references to two mommies and two daddies. So the parents approached each of the teachers. One reacted by saying she appreciated knowing of the situation and offered to set up parent-teacher conferences for all four parents to be present. She said that the school would need the names of the additional parents for emergency notification. She asked other pertinent questions as though their family situation was the most natural thing in the world.

Their minister, too, was very accepting when they told him of their unconventional lifestyle. In fact, in addition to being a friend, at various times he became their counselor.

This group was not only sensitive about to whom they disclosed, but also how and what they disclosed. For example, they referred to their group as an expanded family ("who would be against family-ness?"), since the term "group marriage" is all too easily equated with group sex and adults only. At worst, reactions have appeared to be neutral. So for this group, being open but selective has been acceptable and at times helpful.

One Mother's Day the children of one group were making cards in elementary school. All the children insisted to their teachers that they wanted to make three cards, one for each mother. The teachers developed personal interpretations which they found acceptable—they were children with divorced and remarried parents, the family treated favorite aunts as substitute mothers, the children didn't differentiate between mother and *grand*mothers. People believe only so much as they are capable of believing. This tendency in others functions as protective camouflage.

Confrontations with financial institutions have not been devoid of extra red tape, but have usually finally worked out satisfactorily. It surprised us to learn how many multilateral marriages had three- or four-way joint bank accounts and printed checks listing all the names. Bank tellers sometimes had to call over their supervisor to okay the account and explain how to set it up, but to our knowledge, no bank has turned down such an account.

THE CAUSE AND CONFLICT. As a rule, respondents and most others we have met from multilateral marriages have deliberately avoided what they see to be unnecessary conflicts with the community and society. They have not sought legal recognition of their relationships nor drawn attention to themselves through four-way joint-income-tax returns. Printed checks would seem to be an exception, since they are certain to raise eyebrows in normal transactions. It appears that transactions proceed more smoothly when the name of every signer is printed on the check.

With few exceptions, respondents have not been very active politically, almost never in terms of political and social change directly related to their multilateral marriage. Most have placed the priority on their own family. As one man expressed it, "I don't think any of us want to wage legal battles against the rest of the world unless we have to. We are neither the crusade type nor the martyr type; we just want to lead the style of life that we have found, without interference. Any teaching we are likely to do is by example."

And yet they are concerned about the larger causes. They felt that legalization of all marital alternatives was *significantly* more important than legalization of their own choice, multilateral marriage. Some are actively involved in the peace movement, population control, and minority liberation. We polled respondents in connection with the rising flood of requests we get from media people wanting help on programs or stories pertaining to multilateral marriage. The reaction was without dissent; the time is ripe, they told us; popularization is needed now as a step toward acceptance.

Multilateral families can fade into the community background only so long as there are too few to notice. The real confrontations with banks, Birchers, and bureaucracies are yet to come for multilateral marriage and other emerging family forms.

REFERENCES

1. Gary Solis, "Group Marriage and California Law," *Harrad*, 1, 1 (January 1970).
2. Pat LaFollette, *Family Synergy Newsletter* 1, 12 (May, 1972), p. 6.

18
Mixing and Matching

Not too many weeks after the honeymoon comes the "toothpaste-tube trauma." For the sixth or seventh time, the young husband tells his wife not to squeeze the tube in the middle. Only he insists that it is the hundredth time and launches into a demonstration of the proper technique for rolling the tube from the end, punctuating the lecture with inquiries into the sanity or intelligence of anyone who would squeeze a toothpaste tube in the middle. She calls him an anal-compulsive. He calls her a slob.

After years of marriage, conflict over such trifles may appear as silly, precisely because of years of building a joint lifestyle in which most such trivia have been merged into a mutual style or each partner has become resigned to living with a conflicting style. By "marrying age," most adults carry an enormous accretion of behavior and expectations about style of life including detailed specification of such trivia as the proper way to get the toothpaste from the tube. An important task for the young couple is to fashion a comfortable joint lifestyle from habits and hopes that are certain to conflict in many areas.

It should not be hard to imagine the greater complications in resolving conflicts in lifestyle among, say, four adults. Two married couples getting together could conceivably have an advantage in having already been through the process once with their dyadic marriage. Instead, having been through it once, couples proved to be even more reluctant to make significant accommodations in order to establish still another compromise style. Two people together could cling twice as closely to their established lifestyle. "Lifestyles" was among the five most frequently cited problem areas in multilateral marriages.

SOLITUDE AND PRIVACY. Most of the lifestyle issues we observed were really mismatches between partners; the propensities of one conflicting with those of another. Sometimes, the conflict was really between the individual and the group. This was most especially apparent in the conflict between an individual's desire to be alone at times and his or the group's desire for togetherness.

Larger families usually have a shortage of space and time for family members to have privacy; multilateral marriage families are no exception. Generally, it took a group until the tension in the one with the highest need for time alone or privacy built up to an explosion level to become fully aware of this problem. Most participants found they had to be very sensitive to their own and each other's needs in these areas, taking definite steps to provide the time and the facilities. All but a few of the groups felt that their homes were really inadequate in provisions for private space. Remodeled garages and trailers in the back yard expanded the facilities for some, but most houses are just not designed for multiple-adult families.

LIFESTYLE TRAITS. The nature of multilateral marriage and the ability of some members to tolerate long periods with little privacy helped to lose the privacy issue in other areas of conflict. Observing numbers of groups over extended periods, we began to see that many individual, idiosyncratic behaviors and isolated conflicts fit into clusters that appeared to have common, underlying bases.

Ted and Ernie, for example, just did not seem to get along. They argued over the use of the desk in the den; they couldn't agree on whether necessary repairs should be done by one or both together; Ted got upset when Ernie barged in on him reading in the bathroom; Ernie objected to Ted "pestering" him while he was working on his car. Their whole relationship seemed to deteriorate until the den was turned over to Ted as a private office and a portion of the basement was walled off as Ernie's shop. Suddenly dozens of separate areas ceased to be areas of conflict as Ted and Ernie's underlying needs for private space were satisfied.

The common elements for clusters of individual lifestyle conflicts have many of the characteristics of basic personality needs like those discussed in Chapter 10. We have identified and developed tentative definitions for eight of these "needs" which are strongly manifest in people's lifestyles and which underlie many of the lifestyle conflicts experienced by respondents. We found that what appeared to be matches and mismatches in these areas accounted for much of the friction or ease in establishing a joint lifestyle. We identified what might be called a need for *play* and a complementary *task* need which varied considerably from person to person and seemed to be a factor in conflicts over how groups spent time. ("Get serious Frank!" "All you seem to care about is getting the job done.") Differing needs for *structure* were noted in previous chapters as being important. In the interpersonal dimension, we identified two subcomponents: a need for simple *companionship* and for deep *relationships* which seemed to vary independently. And we noted three separate aspects of privacy which we labeled *ownership, territory,* and *solitude.*

We regard the eight lifestyle needs in Table 18-1 as personality traits which shape a person's choice of lifestyle. Some of these are more "surface" than "deep" characteristics. Although these needs were developed to explain patterns observed in multilateral marriages, we suspect that such lifestyle needs have quite a bit to do with almost any group-living situation. We would not regard even substantial differences in these needs as necessarily determining incompatibility, but any close group would eventually have to find ways of dealing with disparities and would certainly be helped by an awareness of how important each area was to each member.*

* We have begun work on a short inventory measuring such needs for unsupervised use by people trying to get to know each other, especially in anticipation of living together.

Table 18-1.   Some areas of personality which have apparently strong
influences on lifestyle.

The Need For:

PLAY	—the need for nonpurposive activity, to do things for fun; to laugh, make jokes, and relax from stress
TASK	—the need for purposive activity, to do things with an end goal; to work and be busy (probably related to needs for achievement and order)
STRUCTURE	—the need for rules and order; to have things orderly, planned, and organized in time and space (essentially the need for order)
COMPANIONSHIP	—the need to have other people around; for groups and belonging
RELATIONSHIP	—the need for deep, committed attachments; for close relationships with others, for intimacy (with Companionship related to the need for affiliation)
OWNERSHIP	—the need to own or possess things; to have exclusive use of or control over things
TERRITORY	—the need for a private, personal place or area; to exclude or partially exclude others
SOLITUDE	—the need for alone time; to be by oneself, to withdraw, even with others present (possibly related to the need for autonomy)

THE "NEED" TO BE PRIMARY. In triads we have observed some special problems which have not occurred in larger groups. All but one of the triads on which we have any information have been formed of an established couple and a single person rather than of three single people. Whatever the efforts of the participants to compensate, there is an intrinsic asymmetry in such a situation. The legal status of the couple's relationship is an element of the asymmetry, as is their longer experience with each other. Respondents in triads were much more likely to consider "existing marriages" a problem. At the heart, though, the experience of an imbalance is often expressed by the single partner as having to do with a "need to be primary."

Many people have told us that they felt a need to be first in somebody's heart, to be in one relationship in which they are the most important person to the other. Every triad we have encountered has been aware of this problem and most have dealt with it through a strong commitment to an equal-love ethic and/or through measures designed to minimize the practical and perceptual differences in the relationships. One triad has plans for taking some rather dramatic measures to this end. Carla and Patrick, legally married, are getting divorced. Patrick will remarry to Betty; then all three will have the same last name. Carla already has a child by Patrick; Betty plans to have one after the divorce and remarriage. Their needs all mesh well, for Carla feels that the sense of freedom associated with not being legally married to Patrick but still being in a committed relationship with him is important to her in her growing autonomy. Patrick has wanted more children, but Carla hasn't wanted to get pregnant again, so Betty's desire for a child also fits.

COMMITMENT. A multilateral marriage, even without the elaborations envisioned by this last group, is a major undertaking requiring a high level of commitment by all participants. They must be thoroughly committed not only to the multilateral marriage but to each other personally. Frequently we found within a single group forms of commitment which did not match. "Commitment" was listed as a problem area even more often than "lifestyles."

The function of commitment in interpersonal relationships is to conserve energy and to carry the relationship through times of stress. When one is committed to something, one does not need to reevaluate the necessity or wisdom of sticking with it until or unless problems exceed the threshold represented by the degree of commitment. And more important, commitment keeps people working on their relationships even when they are having considerable difficulty, giving them an opportunity to learn how to cope with such difficulties. Were people always to continue relationships only so long as things are groovy, they would never learn how to deal with "ungroovy" things. Of course, people can be overcommitted, continuing a destructive relationship.

Probably the match in commitment is more important for group success than the type of commitment. We suspect, though, that commitment to the particular people involved is more functional in a multilateral marriage than is commitment to the *idea* of the multilateral marriage.

Commitment does not solve problems or resolve mismatches in lifestyles, but without it, a multilateral marriage is not likely to last very long.

19

Endings

Less than a year ago the M———s and the C———s were caught in a whirlwind of romantic involvement and a sense of pioneering a new form of family. They bought a house together, made love together, cared for their children together, encountered . . . and now the M———s are preparing to move out. The house will go up for sale.

In the long run, most multilateral marriages do break up; at least to date. It would be unfair to call all of them failures. Even supposed failures often teach the participants and the rest of us something important which may make future relationships more productive and longer lasting. For our part, to stay together for the longest possible time is a poor goal for marriage. Other ends— growth, fulfillment, happiness, among others—are more important and may demand shorter relationships if they are given priority. People change and the marriage that was valid at one time may lose its validity. Where growth is accelerated, as in multilateral marriages, relationships may lose validity even more rapidly.

In our survey of attitudes, most respondents felt that multilateral marriage need not necessarily be a lifetime commitment. They strongly disagreed that dissolution implied failure. In the final analysis, though, the dissolved group has at least failed to continue to live together, which is a kind of failure even if longevity is not a very important goal in itself. Why didn't or couldn't they continue? What happens next?

WHAT HAPPENED. We spent many hours talking with people from dissolved multilateral marriages, trying to understand with them what went wrong, why their multilateral marriage didn't last. They reported the same problems with the same frequency that lasting groups reported. Sometimes there were special circumstances, such as overly heavy work commitments, that contributed to breakups. But, in most cases, we found that dissolution could be traced to rather basic things about who the people were and what they were able to do. Interpersonal skills—consensual decision-making, giving unprocessed data, giving and receiving feedback, and the like—emerged as essential. Groups that didn't master these skills had much more difficulty, and our impression was that they didn't last as long. Some participants were the wrong people for group marriage, some were the wrong people for each other. A few felt they had learned by trying, that they were not cut out for multilateral marriage.

Personality theories of marital success, especially those based on complementarity of needs, have fallen into disfavor.[1] To understand multilateral-marriage dissolutions, we have had to resurrect and modify this viewpoint. Basically, we have concluded that most multilateral marriages that dissolve do so because the people simply couldn't live together. While interpersonal skills were a factor, most often they couldn't live together because of basic personality characteristics. In fact, "friction in personalities" ranked second among problems reported by respondents; 36 percent said it had been a serious or recurring problem.

We divide the relevant personality factors into surface, or life-style, traits and deeper personality characteristics, with the intended implication that surface traits are both less essential elements of compatibility and more easily modified than deeper ones. A person's lifestyle in part reflects relevant surface-personality needs of the sort outlined in Chapter 18. Dramatically different lifestyle needs require much greater energy and skill to reconcile into a common living situation. The match between people's propensities for play, for structure, for territory, ownership, and solitude appears to have a great deal to do with how successful a group will be in day-to-day living.

The personality needs purportedly measured by the Edwards Personal Preference Schedule (see Chapter 10) are examples of what we mean by deeper characteristics. In the final analysis, we are simply saying that, for the most part, groups broke up because the people in them were basically not compatible.

It should be clear that we part company from both behaviorists and romanticists, who for different reasons believe that any group of people can live together. To one, only interpersonal behavior is relevant, and this can be modified by changing the contingencies; to the other, all that is needed is sufficient love, desire, or commitment. We believe there are some people who cannot live together nondestructively, that there are many more who cannot live together comfortably, and that the number in both categories is much higher if the criterion is to live together *and* maintain authentically intimate relationships. Among our respondents are dissolved groups from both camps, who couldn't make it despite Skinnerian regimens or all-out love.

Of specific problem areas contributing to dissolution, sex was rarely a factor, jealousy somewhat more common. Many groups with children spoke of conflicts in child-rearing style. This, we believe, lends credence to our thesis about personality compatibility. Few things speak more fully and plainly about who a person really is than the way he or she relates with and raises children.

WHAT HAPPENS NEXT? For most couples, the end of the multilateral marriage has meant a return to their previous dyadic relationship. Out of twenty-four couples from fourteen dissolved groups, four couples divorced following the group breakup and in two additional couples the husband has asked for a divorce. Four other couples separated informally, one for only a short time. In four of these ten broken dyads the split came about primarily as the result of growth and growing awareness on the part of the wife. The same number, but not all the same couples, had acknowledged previous marital difficulties. The multilateral marriage may only have served to enable the partners to take action. In at least one multilateral marriage we have reason to believe that at some level the participants intended the group to serve as a transition from unsatisfactory dyadic relationships to other, better ones.

The C——s were married when Carol was in her midteens and they had two sons shortly afterward. Cal is comparatively nonverbal, a semiskilled technician of average intelligence, whose nonwork interest is virtually limited to hunting. Carol is verbal, intelligent, of varied interests, and has continued to educate herself. She expressed long-term realization of a total lack of communication and common interest in their marriage. It appears that she was considerably more dissatisfied than Cal, although much later it came out that Cal had been involved extramaritally.

Largely at Carol's initiative, they became involved first with Don, a single student with little previous sexual experience and no deep relationships, and Ellen, at that time married but separated. She had married a GI on the eve of his going overseas and there had never really been a marriage. The multilateral involvement provided the excuse, opportunity, and support for her to terminate an unsatisfactory and meaningless relationship.

Ellen never did relate well with Don and did not become sexually involved with him over the entire sixteen-month history of the group. Slowly, the group became more distinctly two dyads with Ellen and Cal siding against Carol and Don. Carol became pregnant under circumstances that left paternity in doubt. Suspicions were that it was Don's child rather than her legal husband's. It was Don who accompanied her during the delivery.

The group disintegrated shortly after the birth of the baby. Don stayed with Carol in the C——s' house; Cal and Ellen moved out. The C——s initiated divorce proceedings, and eventually Cal and Ellen were married.

Numerous clues suggest that this was the intended outcome. Assessing the "damage" we find Don having formed his first deep, stable relationship with a woman. Carol is now in a fulfilling relationship with her intellectual equal. They share philosophy, goals (both are pursuing further education), and seem to have good communication. A year after the group dissolution, their prognosis is good. Ellen ended a token marriage and wedded Cal. In every observable way, she and Cal have more in common and are better matched than Cal and Carol ever were.[2]

Almost all the couples reported that following the group dissolution they had some difficulties in their marriage, which they attributed in some way either to the multilateral-marriage experience or to the breakup. People have been changed by the multilateral-marriage experience and, as a result, are unable merely to return to the conventional marriage as it existed before. They must go through a period of readjustment and renegotiation of their roles in the marriage and their modes of relating. Frequently, what a couple have lost are some of their unproductive, scripted behaviors and rigid roles, but establishing new contracts can be a protracted process.

FRIENDLY RELATIONS. Almost two-thirds of the dissolved groups remain friends, some of them quite close. Only about a third of the individuals expressed strong resentment toward other partners following the breakup. Participants definitely rejected the notion that a multilateral marriage should be preserved for the sake of the children, but as a rule, children regretted the breakup of the group. Our observations do not show that dissolution of the multilateral marriage has seriously hurt children, but certainly divorce is no joy for kids even in conventional marriage. A group dissolution followed by divorce of the biological parents could be worse.

AND AGAIN. One way or another, multilaterally married people worked out the details of separation when that became necessary. They were as emotionally and financially entangled as any conventional couples, yet they were able to decide about all the messy issues of divorce without the aid or interference of divorce proceedings. Charged with full responsibility and freed of legal intervention, we suspect that many more divorcing couples would part amicably and remain friends.

Despite everything, only two of twenty-nine respondents reporting said they wouldn't do it again. More than half said the answer was "perhaps." All but one of those seventeen spontaneously added explanations echoing our theory of what was wrong the first time. Eight of them said it would depend upon the people, on the *right* people. Four wrote that they would need to have a close, deep relationship or be in love first. Many emphasized that they would be more cautious or selective next time.

REFERENCES

1. Carlfred B. Broderick, "Beyond the Five Conceptual Frameworks: A Decade of Development in Family Theory," *Journal of Marriage and the Family 33*, 1 (February 1971).
2. Larry L. and Joan M. Constantine, "Dissolution of Marriage in a Nonconventional Context," *The Family Coordinator 21*, 4 (October 1972).

PART IV
BEYOND

20

Excursus on Human Loving

Strong feelings and active loving have been an integral part of the multilateral-marriage experiences of almost all the participants with whom we have talked. Nearly two-thirds said they got into multilateral marriage in part because of love. We would be seriously remiss if we did not at least attempt to sort out something of the relationship of love to multiple intimacy.

THE GROWTH OF LOVE. The roots of love are in infancy. Our ability to love and be loving, as well as the ways we love and express love are substantially shaped by our experience of love during childhood. Love is also contingent on one's love of oneself. This ancient wisdom is repeatedly rediscovered in modern behavioral science. If you do not truly love yourself, you cannot truly love another.

Most people experience love with different people differently. Each human relationship is unique, and the content of relationships is influenced by societal norms for the roles of the people involved. Society expects fathers to love daughters differently from how they love their wives and may even incarcerate them if they fail to differentiate. Yet there is also an underlying common element in every truly loving relationship—in brotherly love, in conjugal love, in motherly love—which is what love is really about.

LOVE IS. Without *defining* love, we would characterize the common elements of love quite specifically.* Love involves an *active* caring for the life, growth, and happiness of another person; the essence of real love is *loving*, verb rather than noun, behavior more than feeling. Powerful feelings, intense longing for closeness and union, are love's concomitants, but in themselves these feelings are not what we have come to call love. Implicitly, loving includes acceptance of the other person in his unique personhood, to love him for himself. To love is also to be committed to another person in a significant way. Caring—committed, facilitative, active caring—is characteristic of *all* kinds of love.

LOVE AND HEALTH. To be able to love at all is at the very least a sign of some degree of emotional health; not to be able to love at all is at least a sign of some degree of nonhealth. An abundant ability to love must be correlated with greater health, and a meager capacity with less. However, there is healthy love and unhealthy love. We would identify healthy love with its effects on lover and loved. Healthy love is growthful and facilitative, enhancing the achievement of each person's fullest potential as a human being.

We see healthy love as characterized by an absence of extremes —productive, potent, motivated by abundance more than deficit. Healthy love is intense and impassioned but not all-consuming. One who loves productively wishes to be near but is not miserable without the beloved, thinks often but is not obsessively-compulsively preoccupied with thoughts of the lover, sees and forgives faults but is not blind to them, is attracted but not driven. The healthy love relationship is one of interdependence rather than either total dependence or independence.[4] In his studies of love in healthy people, Maslow found that self-actualizing individuals *sought* and *preferred* love and loving relationships, but they did not *need* or *demand* them.[5]

* Our views derive from an inextricable admixture of Fromm,[1] Ellis,[2] and Maslow.[3] The debt is obvious and continuous; we shall not repay it at each use.

ONE, TWO, . . . MANY. Can we really and truly love more than one person at once? The answer is "Of course!" Almost any normal, healthy adult loves many people: son, daughter, spouse, mother, father, brother, sister, friend. Fromm would even say that one must love a number of others besides oneself if one is to be considered truly healthy. Ellis maintains instead that "if one *only* obsessively-compulsively loves *one* other, the chances are that one really loves no one, including and especially oneself."[6]

The normal, healthy adult would insist that though she loved many people, she could not love more than one person in the same way. After all, conjugal love *is* different from parental love . . . isn't it? Yet this person loves both Joey and Tad, her sons, loving them as a parent loves a child; and she loves Maria and Tony as a sister loves siblings. Then one *can* love more than one person "in the same way" can one not?

There is, we confess, a certain amount of "sleight of hand" in the foregoing paragraphs, for we have been deliberately skirting the central issue, whether the kind of love between wife and husband can exist with more than one other person at a time.

In our society, marital—intimate adult sexual—love is accorded unique status. Allegedly, it cannot be felt with more than one person at a time. When Davis asked if "affection" is "divisible" he found that most sexologists answered affirmatively. He cited sources stating that cases of "simultaneous passion" are common.[7] Literature is filled with plots the essence of which is the "triangle." Literature has not denied that one can romantically, sexually love more than one person at a time, though the resolution which writers have thrust upon their protagonists have almost always been that they must choose. One to a customer.

The contemporary hangup is not over whether genuine multiple love is possible, it is over multiple sexual love, and it is not over whether such love can be experienced concurrently but whether it should be *allowed*. In the rational and religious arguments against the possibility of multiple intimate love relations, we also hear the suppressed plaint, "But I only got *one!*" The possibility that one might be able to love two adults in a similar, deep, involved, and sexual way is threatening. If *people* can do that, then one's spouse might, and one could lose the total, exclusive quality of that relationship. Worse, if one sees relationships in either/or terms—"You *must* choose! It's him or me!"—then the choice just might be "him"!

Do some people really love more than one other person in the committed, intimate manner usually reserved for spouses? We must answer an emphatic Yes! We could answer for ourselves personally or we could answer for our respondents. But how can you know whether Dean *really* loves both Anna and Jeanette? Neither you nor we can *be* Dean and feel what he feels, any more than we can experience his loving as Anna and Jeanette do. There are only three ways, all inadequate, we can "know." We can ask. We can observe to see if his behavior is congruent with what he says. We can study him closely, psychologically, seeking to understand the way he organizes reality and his meaning of love. There is no fourth way. So we have asked. People do tell us that they genuinely love each of several people. We watch and see them behaving lovingly, acting in ways that bespeak deep, committed caring. And we try to understand, through long talks, even through tests. Once more the answer is Yes.

It is now our considered opinion that people who do not grow intimately close to more than one person do so only by actively avoiding intimacy. One need merely be open to the potential for growing to love, and it will come all but inevitably. People avoid growing closer by using the rituals and rules which maintain social distance. They head off pending intimacy by playing interpersonal games. As Eric Berne put it, the absence of games is intimacy, which is both more rewarding and also riskier. In real loving is openness, exposure of what we really are, nakedness. And if we are committed to caring, we might find ourselves responsible, interdependent, rather than in illusory independence.

LIMITS. Where does it all end? How many can we love? In some ways we believe there *are* limits and these limits seem to follow certain relationships. The limit is greater than one. As one loves, one's capacity for loving increases. Almost universally, those who have loved more than one and more than once have said that love becomes easier. Every human activity follows some kind of learning curve. If we did not find loving easier, did not love better as we loved more, love would be the single exception to this rule of human behavior. Parents' relationships with their children are a legitimate model. Most parents experience their capacity for love as growing to accommodate their additional children. From this same model it is clear that there are some ultimate constraints. Time is finite; space is finite. When dividing one's time among several children, each gets less time than if there were only one. However, priorities can be shifted, freeing time, space, and energy. People learn.

Love is also knowing, it is knowledge of another person in an intimate way, knowing and accepting the core of his being. But our capacity to hold images, to deal with information simultaneously, to remember complex relationships are all known to have limits which are not as large as one might think. It is reasonable to expect that our ability to hold onto that complex construct that constitutes our knowledge of the self of another person would also involve these limits. Most of us have experienced situations in which we felt there were just too many people to deal with at once.

When all the separate factors are integrated, we suspect that the effect for most people is to limit to a few the number of ongoing intimate love relationships in which they can actively participate at one time without substantially diluting intensity and quality. It is doubtful whether most people could handle as many as six or seven adult relationships, though, if relationships can be intermittent and periodically renewed as circumstances permit, and need not be continuous, then the number must be greater.

YOU, ME, AND THE OTHER GUY. There are certain to be substantial individual differences in the ability to love and the capacity for multiple loving. Most of us have known people whom we would describe as very loving and others we would say were not very loving. Every known manifestation of human personality and ability spreads over a considerable range. It is possible, we suggest, that just as there are creative artistic geniuses, people gifted in logical thinking, and those with exceptional manual skills, there could be people who are "interpersonal geniuses" as it were, capable of more readily forming and maintaining committed loving relationships than most of us.

SYNERGY. For many people there is a lag between recognition of one's own capacity for multiple love and comfort with that capacity in the people one loves. A key is the concept of synergy. To see things synergically is to be able to transcend dichotomies, to see the integral interdependence of opposites, and to fuse falsely divided concepts. The transcendence of dichotomies is characteristic of self-actualizing people, the very healthiest of people.*

Synergic love transcends the dichotomy of self and other in the act of loving. This kind of synergic perception of loving is one way of enabling growth into multilateral relations. We do not think it coincidental that synergy is a sign of emotional maturity. Abe Maslow gave this example:

> If I get more pleasure out of feeding my strawberries into the mouth of my little beloved child, who loves strawberries, and who smacks her lips over them, and if I thereby have a wonderful time and enjoy myself watching her eat the strawberries, which would certainly give me pleasure if I myself ate them, then what shall I say about the selfishness or the unselfishness of this act? . . . Obviously, the best way to say this is that the words selfish and unselfish as opposites, as mutually exclusive, have become meaningless. The two words have fused together. My action is neither selfish exclusively, nor unselfish exclusively, or it can be said to be both selfish and unselfish simultaneously. Or, as I prefer the more sophisticated way of saying it, the action is synergic. That is, what is good for my child is good for me, what is good for me is good for the child, what gives the child pleasure gives me pleasure, what gives me pleasure gives the child pleasure, . . . shoes on the feet of one make the other's feet feel good. . . .[8]

This is what loving is really all about.

REFERENCES

1. Erich Fromm, *The Art of Loving* (New York: Bantam Books, 1963).
2. Albert Ellis, "Sick and Healthy Love," *The Independent* issue 132 and

---

* Abraham Maslow first used the term in this sense, borrowing it from anthropologist Ruth Benedict who characterized the healthy society as synergic. The synergic society is one whose social structures are such that when the individual acts out of self-interest he inevitably acts in the common interest as well. Ours is a very unsynergic society.

133 (April and May 1963); reprinted in Ellis, *If This Be Sexual Heresy* (New York: Lyle Stuart, 1963).

3. Abraham Maslow, *Toward a Psychology of Being* (New York: Van Nostrand, 1962).

4. Ellis, "Sick and Healthy Love," *op. cit.*

5. Maslow, *Motivation and Personality.*

6. Ellis, "Sick and Healthy Love," *op. cit.*

7. Kingsley Davis, "Jealousy and Sexual Property," *op. cit.*, pp. 395–405.

8. Abraham Maslow, *Eupsychian Management* (Homewood, Ill.: Irwin and Dorsey Press, 1965), pp. 88–89.

21

Footnote on the Nature
of Human Sexuality

OUR PURPOSE IN RETURNING once more to the subject of sex is to bring about a synthesis of what might be called an integral view of human sexuality. Though we believe that cohesive theory in human sexual nature is realizable, our present undertaking is considerably more modest. We merely want to pull together some ideas which form an intriguing pattern in juxtaposition.

ELSYNDIA. We shall bring about this juxtaposition in a fictional but not wholly fabricated social context. The tiny intentional community of Elsyndia was formed as an experiment in the exploration of new styles of human relating. Like many of the real communes of today, Elsyndia is imbedded within a larger society from which it is partially isolated. Its founders' aim was to form a "new society" which is more responsive, more human, more synergic. Its members have to greater or less degrees been liberated from parts of their earlier cultural conditioning, or at least they believe they have. Through creative innovation put to the actual test of social trial-and-error, they hope to evolve a better social order.

At Elsyndia, rules and social forms are developed only when the community sees the necessity in response to real felt needs within what is revealed of their own human nature. In every social arena, the initial state is unstructured, unprogrammed.

Sex is no exception. At the outset, Elsyndians elect to foster an openly sexual community without special restrictions on sexual behavior. Force or other infringement of the freedom of others is prohibited, but no differently from other areas of behavior. Sex is to be permitted to occur as it occurs, free, spontaneous, unfettered.

Elsyndia is a close, equalitarian community whose members value open, authentic encounter. There is much interpersonal intimacy. Sexual attraction becomes rife and soon almost every member is attracted to and sexually involved with many other members. The Elsyndians find that women no less than men have abundant capacity and appetite for sexual encounters, given opportunity in an accepting atmosphere. Nor are the children exempt; in the openly sexual environment they happily participate with their age-mates and others. The range of sexual behaviors exhibited by the unrestricted community members is substantial.

As provided for in their charter, the Elsyndians assemble at year's end to evaluate their experiences and decide future social policy. When the agenda turns to sex, discussion is long and loud. In their structureless twelve months Elsyndians have learned something of the social consequences of sex. There are complaints that planting fell behind because Joe frequently interrupted his plowing to dally. There are expressions of dismay that involvements have become so convoluted as to defy cognition. There were fights. Sexual preferences were not always reciprocal. Sometimes people were left out. Some Elsyndians had tried to restrict the sexual involvement of others. The contagion of anger, arguments, and depression had carried their effects beyond the immediate parties to problems.

The assembly concludes that sex is too much of a problem to be left unrestricted. It is complex; it consumes energy; it embodies potential conflict and competition. Through rules of sexual conduct, the Elsyndians hope to reduce the cost to the community. Norms are established restricting sex to encounters with outsiders except in the case of two people who agree permanently to limit their sexual relations to each other. All sexual encounters are to take place in private.

What Elsyndia has really done is attempt to remove sex from social space. They have tried to move it outside the community or isolate and contain it. The visible manifestations of sex in the social arena have been dramatically reduced. Confident that they have solved a major social problem, the Elsyndians adjourn to their new, more controlled lives. No one asks to what extent the community cost has actually been lowered, nor where the sexual problems, having been banished from the social arena, may have gone.

Years later someone may ask that question, perhaps a young doctor seeking insight into the poor functioning of some community members. Color him Freud.

Elsyndia is a parable of the existential conflict faced by countless human communities through the ages, from ancient nomadic tribes to contemporary communes, from tiny families to vast nations. The most realistic part of our parable is the outcome. Reviewing history, it is evident that most human communities, especially the family itself, have chosen to put sex as much as possible into personal and private space rather than in the social space of the community. Even the controls over sexual behavior are internalized norms which operate for the most part within individuals and require social intervention only as they break down.

The explanation for the preponderance of outcomes which tend to take sex out of social space is simple. The consequences of open, public, multiple sexual involvement are highly visible, the cost to the community readily observed. The community does not have to see or incur much of the cost of sex in private and personal space. There are consequences, nonetheless; the costs are accrued by each and every individual in the community. Sigmund Freud's contribution to understanding human sexuality was to expose some of these intrapsychic costs. We might say that sex cannot be made to go away, but disruptive effects can be made less visible.

IN THE FAMILY. The family is a kind of community, an especially small, close, and intimate community. As inevitably as in Elsyndia, manifold sexual attractions develop within families. Viewed in this way, the incest taboo is not a unique cultural phenomenon, but merely another example of group choice to limit the social contingencies of sex. The near universality of the incest taboo attests to the ubiquitous nature of intrafamilial sexual attraction. The forcefulness with which the taboo is ingrained and with which violations are met reveals the strength of the drives which it attempts to limit. Psychiatry has provided further evidence that almost all individuals are sexually attracted to members of their own family.

Analogs of the incest taboo are common in familylike groups. Modern communes which have experienced difficulty with intragroup sex—jealousy, competition, etc.—have often reverted to a form of exogamy, limiting sex to liaisons with outsiders.* Among *kibbutzniks* seldom does marriage or sex occur between members of the same age group, a group which has shared sleeping quarters and showers since infancy. Intimacy is almost always between members of different cohorts or different *kibbutzim*.

Few adults can discuss incest rationally or open-mindedly. That we should even raise the issue in this book is certain to lead to comment and adverse reaction. But we see the family as archetypical of human sexual relations. There is a subtle, converse connection between the premises of multilateral relations and the premises of the incest taboo which is best approached through a cohesive conceptualization of human sexual nature.

THESIS. At the risk of alienating many readers, we begin by succinctly stating what we feel to be well-supported though not necessarily universally accepted hypotheses about human sexual nature.

The normal human being is a pervasively sexual being throughout life, capable of sexual response to other human beings of

---

* We have a hypothesis about the response of intentional communities to intragroup sexual stress. To the extent that the community sees itself as a family, we expect it to favor exogamic solutions; to the extent that it sees itself as a community/society, we would expect it to favor monogamic variants of endogamy. The referent models are the family, which permits only exogamous relations except for the marital dyad, and the subculture, which traditionally favors "marrying their own kind." Clearly size is a factor, too.

either sex and any age. Sexual attraction is a complex aggregate of biologically, socially, and individually determined predispositions, but is primarily mediated and modified by two factors. First, sexual attraction and the desire for sexual expression of affection is the (all but) inevitable consequence of propinquity and intimacy. Second, within the field defined by either predisposition or propinquity and intimacy, novelty is the principal enhancer of attraction and desire for sexual encounter. All these factors favor a resultant intrinsic polysexual propensity, a human tendency in the absence of exogenous constraints for sexual involvement with more than one partner.

Even the infant is a sexual, erotic being, and sexual encounters by children are widespread and well-documented.[1] Where the culture is permissive and supportive, most children spontaneously engage in sexual activities even to intercourse among older children.[2] With counterevidence growing, the concept of a period of sexual latency prior to puberty is falling into disfavor.[3] The sexual needs and capacities of the elderly at last are being given recognition.[4]

Psychiatry since Freud has recognized the "polymorphous perverse" nature of children, their tendency and ability to derive sexual pleasure from almost any part of their sensual apparatus in encounters with a host of different sexual objects.[5] This sexual potential is not age specific, definitely not limited to attractions between peers. The commonness of May-September (or even April-September or March-September) attractions is evidence for variability with respect to age of the object of sexual attraction. Counseling and therapeutic practice shows that immediately prepubertal and postpubertal periods for children are very likely to bring into awareness sexual attractions across very great age differences.

The ambisexual potential of normal healthy human beings is, in some respects, the best kept secret of human sexuality. Ethological data from primate studies reveals that most individuals of most species will interact sexually with members of the same sex in appropriate circumstances and that even with available partners of the opposite sex, same-sex encounters are not wholly absent.[6] In human cultures and subcultures where ambisexuality is validated, almost all individuals engage in repeated same-sex encounters while showing marked heterosexual preferences.[7] In a society such as ours which dichotomizes sexuality along purely heterosexual and homosexual lines, denigrating the latter, acknowledgment of one's own ambisexual nature can be difficult.

The case for human polysexuality was presented in Chapter 2 and most primate data are supportive. Not only is there good reason to believe that men and women share equally high sexual drives and equal desire for partner variety, but at least one plausible theory argues for female sexuality and polysexuality being much the higher. The Sherfey Syndrome[8] is an assumed female response to unrestrained sexual opportunity in which females reveal almost boundless and insatiable sexual appetites. Dr. Mary Jane Sherfey argues that females have been more strongly repressed and constrained sexually in most cultures precisely because their drive is stronger. Experiences of swingers give some support to some aspects of the Sherfey Syndrome,[9] though the associated theory of the origins of the family is more questionable.

INCESTUOUS. The reasons generally given, even those by social scientists, for the incest taboo are more often results than reasons. Religions reflect, justify, and perpetuate the decisions of societies. Anthropologist Claude Levi-Strauss makes the consummate point that widespread incest would tend over the ages to breed out deleterious and fatal recessive traits, thus their presence today is a consequence of the incest taboo, not a reason for its instigation.[10]

At heart, the incest taboo is based on the assumption that the father and the son cannot both be sexually involved with the mother, or similarly for mother and daughter, consequently the so-called "Oedipal complex" must be resolved by the child and parent renouncing (repressing, suppressing) their sexual desire for each other. The assumption derives, in turn, from the obviousness of the social costs of various forms of conflict which can arise when multiple involvement is permitted. It is imperative to observe that the taboo is founded on two premises. The first is that only the visible (social) costs are real. Put in comparative terms, the cost in social space is assumed to be greater than the aggregate individual intrapsychic costs. On an absolute basis the first premise is clearly false, and psychiatric and psychological evidence gives serious cause to question even its relativistic form. The second premise is that the difficulties concomitant with multiple sexual relations are inevitable and insurmountable, or speaking relativistically, where multiple relations are permitted, the energy which would be consumed in resolving interpersonal issues exceeds the energy spent in suppression, avoidance, or diversion of the natural sexual desires. The existence of successful and fulfilling multilateral relations, some of which have reached a "maintenance level" of energy demands, calls this second premise into question in either form.

There is, then, a very essential connection between multilateral relationships and incest, not because they are both examples of "deviant" behavior or because acceptance of either is evidence of radical sexual attitudes, but because the taboo against incest is ultimately founded on assumptions that multiple sexual involvement is too costly, unworkable, or intrinsically conflict-ridden, and because the incest taboo is merely one example of social attempts to minimize the obvious effects in social space of multiple sexual attractions. The family is merely one group in which such attractions are probable.*

There is no shortage of theories of incest and the incest taboo.[11] We are not so naïve as to presume our analysis is complete—there are vast untouched regions in the area of parent-child sexuality, for example—but we do believe that it is novel and valuable. We are not arguing for incest, nor have we proven or disproven any central theses concerning human sexuality. We believe, however, that the very existence of some of the emergent marital/sexual patterns among healthy participants is sufficient to justify reopening and reexamining some long-closed questions.

It is at least possible that sexually open marriages with opportunity for ambisexual expression in group sexual encounter are fundamentally more congruent with human sexual nature than are conventional marriages, but at this point we are merely calling for a rapprochement with difficult issues.

---

* Our survey of respondents' attitudes revealed an awareness of this connection. They did not see intrafamilial sex as necessarily bad. See Appendix VI.

YOU AND THE NEIGHBORS. The essential points of our thesis are probably better appreciated through a less threatening example than incest. Our contention is that certain relationships are operable in every close group situation. Let us imagine that two neighboring families, the Castles and the Benedicts, have become close friends. The kids migrate between houses; the families eat dinner together several nights a week, exchange parental responsibilities, and spend weekends and summer vacation sharing the lake property they financed by pooling their resources. We assert that in virtually any such "intimate in-group" there will be multiple sexual attractions. The kids are probably not unaffected, but we shall leave them aside and focus in on the two couples.

The Castles and the Benedicts cannot choose whether or not they will become sexually desirous of each other; this will happen or not pretty much independent of their wishes. They *can* choose whether or not to acknowledge their desires to their spouses, or to the object of their attraction, or to the group. They can choose whether or not to actualize their sexual desires and whether to do so openly or clandestinely, but they cannot avoid impact on their relationships. We maintain that even to "do nothing" consumes energy and takes its toll on the group.

Suppose they choose not to permit their sexual attractions to be actualized.* There is now an important element of the group relationship which is not talked about. There will almost certainly be a considerable amount of kidding, semisexual play, and innuendo, all of which is designed to discharge the sexual energy in their cross-marital attractions. There will always remain a substantial residue of nonspecific sexual tension which will be demonstrated if the sexual kidding ever gets a little too real for comfort. One can recognize these points by the sudden silence, nervous coughs, and inept attempts to return the context to "just kidding." In electing not to actualize sexual attraction, the group gains only in that it avoids openly dealing in group space and within their marriages

---

* The chances are that this occurs without their ever being aware that they have made a choice, certainly without talking about it. In fact, we suspect that if they talk about it openly it may only be a matter of time before they do something about it.

with sexual and related issues, such as control needs and insecurity.

Should the Castles and the Benedicts decide that they will become actually physically and not just psychically sexually involved, they may be in for some stressful times and some difficult revelations about themselves and their marriages. On the other hand, they could learn and grow from these and from the greater openness and honesty in their group relationship. They may find that they can transcend these difficulties. They will have avoided a low-level but perpetual tension and displacement of energy. Quite likely, they will have had at least some pleasant, perhaps even some profound, sexual experiences.

We are not arguing for either resolution, but for a viewpoint that recognizes in such situations the manifestations of common if not inherent human sexual propensities and which is aware that neither option is a priori superior. The one option is simply much more probable because its disadvantages are less visible. What is best depends on all the complex individual and situational factors and the priorities or goals of the people involved. What is new, or at least important, is that a group *can* share sex and still be friends, still be happy and healthy.

REFERENCES

1. Floyd Martinson has compiled available data in his forthcoming book, *Sexual Encounters of Infants, Children, Preadolescents, and Adolescents* (in preparation).
2. Ford and Beach, *Patterns of Sexual Behavior*, pp. 195–199.
3. Carlfred Broderick, "Children's Romances," *Sexual Behavior* 2, 5 (May 1972).
4. Mary S. Calderone, "The Sexuality of Aging," *SIECUS Newsletter* 7, 1 (October 1971). See also Eric Pfeiffer, "Sex and Aging," *Sexual Behavior* 2, 10 (October 1972).
5. Sigmund Freud, "Three Essays on the Theory of Sexuality," Ch. 2 "Infantile Sexuality, in Strackey, ed., *Standard Edition of the Complete Psychological Works of Sigmund Freud*, vol. VII (London: Hogarth Press).
6. Ford and Beach, *op. cit.*, pp. 143–147.
7. The "X-group" in Melanesia is an example of a culture validating male ambisexuality. William Davenport, "Sexual Patterns in a Southwest Pacific Society," in Frank A. Beach, ed., *Sex and Behavior* (New York:

Wiley & Sons, 1965). The swinging subculture validates female but not male bisexuality. See Bartell, *Group Sex*.

8. Mary Jane Sherfey, "The Evolution and Nature of Female Sexuality in Relation to Psychoanalytic Theory," in *J. American Psychoanalytic Association 14*, pp. 28–128, 1966.

9. See Edward Brecher's report in *The Sex Researchers* (Boston: Little, Brown, 1966).

10. Lévi-Strauss in Skolnick and Skolnick, *Family in Transition*.

11. S. Kirson Weinberg, *Incest Behavior* (New York: Citadel Press, 1955), pp. 224–248.

22

Toward Tomorrow's Families

THE IMPACT THAT EMERGING marriage and family forms have on the great bulk of contemporary families is slight. But we believe that their impact on tomorrow's families will be enormous.

It would be an enjoyable exercise to catalogue our personal predictions in dozens of areas relating to marriage and family life, but we do not believe this would be especially valuable. Our guesses in many areas are not likely to be any better than anyone else's. On the other hand, our position at the edge of the family field, at the horizon of developing patterns, gives us a special perspective from which to see family structure.

Viewed from this perspective, patterns are evident from which we have been able to synthesize a unifying conceptualization of family change in certain dimensions. Inferences drawn from this model are, we believe, more than just guesses. The prognoses and the model are integral, and the former cannot be appreciated without the latter.*

* There are many views of the future of marriage and the family. Our purpose is not to compile and compare these, though that is certainly a task worth undertaking. We have chosen not to complicate our central purpose in presenting a new synthesis with citations to numerous alternative views, few of which deal with cohesive models of the type we are attempting

THE CHANGING FAMILY BOUNDARY

The family is a system and the marital dyad is a system within a system. Each of the parts—mother, father, son, however many there are—interacts with all the other parts, affecting behavior and being affected. The family together, as a system, is more than just the sum of the individuals within it. Collectively, through the interrelationships and interactional processes among its members, the family becomes an entity in itself, with unique functions and special capabilities.

One of the essential functions of the family is to be a family, to define itself. This function of establishing an identity apart from the rest of the universe must be fulfilled by every human system for it to be viable. A separate identity means that one can tell the insiders from the outsiders—or the insiders and outsiders can tell. This means that there is a boundary around a system such as the family, intangible but nevertheless real and observable. Boundaries of this sort may be delineated by many processes—by special requirements and procedures for gaining entrance, or for leaving; by behavior that is different within from without, or which is dependent on whether or not outsiders are present; by topics which are private to within the system, or taboo in it; by limitations on the kinds of exchanges which may take place between insiders and outsiders.

The boundary function is vital. Many communes seemed to have failed largely because they inadequately defined their boundaries, and many of the most successful communes in history concentrated on activities which may be viewed as boundary-maintaining processes.[1]

Families, expectably, vary considerably in how sharply they define their boundaries. There are families which readily accept new members or in which members may relate with many friends

---

here. The Bibliography contains references to much of the literature on the future of marriage and the family.

The family-systems concepts which we present are standard and widely used. Our theory of the changing boundary and analysis of the convergent nature of various emerging family forms is, to the best of our knowledge, original.

essentially no differently from the way they do with each other. Such families make one feel "like one of the family." Other families are very closed systems, with heavily defended borders permitting only certain predetermined kinds of interactions with outsiders. Boundaries which are more closed or more open are aspects of family style; whether one is better—more functional—than the other depends on numerous situational factors.

Rarely is a family truly socially isolated, however closed its boundaries might be. Family members hold jobs, attend school, conduct business in the community. The family boundary is selectively permeable, however, passing some transactions and blocking others, depending on the situational context, the message content, and the means of communication involved. Packages are unwelcome at 4:00 A.M.; a neighbor may be allowed to shout greetings but not obscenities; a friend may be blocked from expressing his affection for your wife by caressing her, though it may be okay for him to say, "You're quite a woman!" On the average, contemporary family boundaries are closed to most intimate transactions, though open to most instrumental or empty ones, thus they are closed in essential and highly meaningful areas.

There is one way in which the function of the family requires loose boundaries. A family has failed as a family if its boundaries do not permit the exchanges necessary for the young ultimately to leave.

Common social forces and environmental factors interact with the boundaries of families to influence the relative effectiveness of solid versus permeable, defined versus diffused boundaries in promoting vital family units. Large families, clans, generationally extended families can tolerate tighter boundaries than can small ones yet still meet the many needs of their members. When members share with their society a sense of alienation and isolation, solid, impermeable family boundaries are less tolerable than when the ambience is one of involvement and integration. Families, like living systems, must be capable of adaptation to changes in environmental requirements. To respond effectively in any way to rapid change, family systems must be highly interactive and permeable to inputs from the outside. Where the family unit is geographically mobile and can be frequently uprooted, its boundaries must be diffuse and permeable enough to enable it to establish new roots with comparative ease.

The conditions which demand more open family boundaries— alienation, isolation, small size, rapid change, and mobility—are precisely the conditions of the modern family. In a kind of stubborn irony these same conditions lead many families to react overtly by tightening their boundaries, closing in on themselves, and more sharply delineating the acceptable interfaces with society. Society and its representatives mirror the same tendencies. The threatened family institution is shored up by togetherness and calls for traditionalism. By vetoing comprehensive child care, the President acts to *close* the family boundary *against* changing situational requirements.

The solidifying family boundary *cannot* reach an equilibrium with the forces creating pressure upon it because some of those forces are acting from within and are strengthened by tighter boundaries. The family as currently modeled is unstable under these conditions.

EMERGENCE. Emerging marital and family patterns, such as group marriage, communal living, and swinging, are analogs on a social scale of the reactions taken by individuals in single-family systems. *The unifying feature of all these innovations is that they act on the family boundary, making it more diffuse and permeable. Rather than deviance, these forms represent family systems seeking to establish new, viable equilibria within radically altered (and still changing) environmental conditions.*

In the case of swinging, the family boundary for the marital dyad is rendered selectively more permeable, permitting virtually free sexual exchange across it while remaining essentially unchanged in permeability in other modalities. There may be compensatory tightening of the boundary in other areas as the family initially reacts homeostatically—to maintain the existing equilibrium—much as the uprooted family closes in on itself.

Consensual adultery, the "Agreement," represents a similar, largely isolated increase in permeability. Extramarital affairs permit much more than the simple exchange of sex, but if they insist on little sharing of experiences, the couple keep the exchanges largely outside their boundaries.

Swinging, in its sexual party form, and consensual adultery are not systemic modifications which are very likely to be generally viable responses to family-boundary pressure over the long term. Both represent very limited boundary changes because each is partially self-canceling in its contemporary form. Each depends on the ability of participants to isolate and compartmentalize certain aspects of their lives. Increased openness about participation, social acceptance of the lifestyle, or greater numbers of people participating makes compartmentalization more difficult. Permeability can be limited to essentially physical sexual encounters only so long as participants do not meet and have to interface in other contexts—as neighbors, business associates, or friends, for example—for then they will have to interact in other modalities, thus tainting the sexual exchange with an involvement of person. Similarly, separate affairs are more difficult to keep separate and beyond the family boundary when they become an open part of the common community in which the marital partners are imbedded.

Even today, many swingers seem to drop out of the social scene into small more or less stable networks of mutually involved family units, sharing much more than just the sex among the parents.[2] An unknown percentage of swingers are involved in this exodus to intimate friendships; they leave behind a hard core of long-term partygoers for whom the limited boundary changes may be the only or best adaptation.

Intimate networks—clusters of families intimately and mutually involved in many aspects of living—are an emerging family form also being sought directly. For the family imbedded in such a network, family boundaries become much more diffuse and permeable, directly altering the family situation for the children as well as for the parents. For expanded families—intentionally enlarged family units with chosen members—the traditional nuclear family boundaries are even more diffuse, the mutual involvement even more pervasive. The marital unit in both intimate networks and expanded families is still essentially the dyad, but there is every reason to expect that in many such family configurations, multiple sexual involvement will be accepted.[3] A sizable fraction of those who are now seeking to establish these lifestyles desire or have already made this alteration to their marital contract.

The single, open-ended marriage has boundaries which are less diffuse than those between nuclear units in an expanded family, and does not have the additional boundary which must inevitably form around the expanded family as a unit.[4] Open-ended marriage is more a pattern being sought directly for itself than the outcome of participation in other marital forms.

Multilateral marriage is, of course, an ideological extreme in which the traditional family boundary is completely eliminated, while a new, similar boundary is erected around the multilateral unit. But our research does not show this to be happening; internal boundaries are present, though highly diffuse; primary dyadic relationships are recognizable.

The commune as a contemporary family model is a special case. Not all communes are family models, and the variability in internal marital and family structure is great. In terms of family boundaries, communes are similar to, and spread along the same continuum as, intimate networks, expanded families, and multilateral marriages. Communes, however, have already been seen to serve a special function of major import to future families. Communes often serve as temporary or alternate families. This function is of special significance to the children of tomorrow's families.

For young people emerging from their families of origin, the options have always been quite limited. A broader range of intermediate alternatives is needed between the family in which children grow up and the one they start themselves.

One of the most common options is widespread though not fully legitimized today. Premarital living together—cohabitation is a convenient shorter term—can be expected to be even more common, open, and accepted in the future. Cohabitation is a kind of intermediate family. A later age at marriage creates the demand for intermediate options the availability of which facilitates late marriage. If the trend among the young to accept sex in committed friendships also continues, then most people will have had several committed sexual relationships by the time they make an official or essentially permanent commitment, i.e., when they marry. With experience in more than one relationship, probably on more than one basic model, more people will start off their first marriage with attempts to create a uniquely personal structure with the precedents for sexual openness.

THEME. Thus many different threads can be seen to be converging under the reinforcement of numerous social forces and changes. When the effects are tallied, the results seem to indicate that the majority of the families of the future, while differing in structural details, will be built around pairs who share a primary but not exclusive commitment. The boundaries of these family units will be significantly more diffuse and permeable, permitting all members of the family freer passage in and out, and enabling the formation of broadly based voluntary (non-kin) intimate ties with other families.

If nothing more were to happen than a general adaptation of an ethic of openness and honesty about the extramarital sex which already occurs, then tomorrow, many of today's conventional marriages would be open-ended. When the possibilities of more general adaptation of ethical congruence are combined with the trends in emerging family forms, it seems almost certain that most of the marriages of the future will be sexually open, allowing or even seeking alternate intimacy and sexual involvement as a contribution to the primary relationship.

A generation seems none too distant a horizon on which to project these changes.

VARIATIONS. The family's future is certain to be pluralistic. The predicted modal pattern is a characteristic of families rather than a complete family model. Sexually open primary marital dyads can exist in variations derived from any of the models now emerging. And diverse family structures without this characteristic may continue to be viable through other adaptations.

The most important insurance of future family pluralism is the individual. Individuation is growing; each individual defines himself through a growing multiplicity of constructs and dimensions of existence. Unique, idiosyncratic lifestyles are necessary to match highly refined and differentiated self-concepts. The quest for fulfillment of individual potential also favors creation of personal family models.

Today even innovators follow models. The influence of the Rimmer models is evidence. Only a very few of the most innovative families have deliberately undertaken to construct their own family model suited to their special individual and collective needs. Tomorrow, large numbers of people may be creating highly personalized family variations. Whereas useful definitions and adequate characterizations of distinct phenomena are difficult now, future families may be all but impossible to categorize by distinct models.

We do not expect that more than a small minority of families will be based on multilateral marriage. In many ways, it is the most difficult and extreme departure from prevailing models. Surprisingly, in its purest form its moral base is not at all distant from conventional morality. Sex and intimacy remain tied to marriage, and the boundaries of several of the intact groups in our knowledge are traditionally tight. Some couples have felt comfortable about cross-marital sex only after they regarded themselves as "engaged to be group married."

If our thesis regarding the convergent nature of changes in family structure is correct, then the ramifications of multilateral marriage and other emerging family forms will reach to the very foundations of modern family life. Few families will not ultimately be affected. For the emergence of new, more viable, more fulfilling, more healthy family variants, the marriage experiments will need the broad support of new services and acceptance or at least tolerance by society.

We do not forecast the demise of the family, not even the passing of the family as most of us have known it. Far into the distant future we expect to see some families which even traditionalists would label traditional. Lifetime partnerships will become much less common, but even conventional, sexually exclusive relationships will appeal to a sizable minority. That will be possible through cultural pluralism. For people whose fulfillment lies in nontraditional settings, there will be an ever-growing system of family models.

The family is alive, and well, and growing!

REFERENCES

1. Rosabeth Kanter, "Commitment and Social Organization: A Study of Commitment Mechanisms in Utopian Communities," *op. cit.*
2. Charles and Rebecca Palson, "Swinging in Wedlock," *op. cit.*
3. James Ramey found that nearly half of informants interested in group marriage had had sexually intimate friendships ("Communes, Group Marriage, and the Upper-Middle Class," *op. cit.*).
4. The O'Neills clearly note the greater viability associated with the more diffuse boundaries of open marriages (*Open Marriage* [New York: M. Evans, 1972]).

Epilogue

 $W_{\text{E HAVE SHARED}}$ a good deal of ourselves in this book, though it is not really our story. With the complicity of our publisher we would share one last thing, a dream.

We certainly hope the research we reported here is merely the beginning. There remain extensive and essential analyses of the data already gathered. We would like, for example, to be able to do a complete study of personality in relationship to group functioning, an analysis far beyond our present resources. New research is needed to investigate other emerging family patterns and to reexamine basic assumptions about marriage, family, and sex. Services are needed for families which do not conform to the working models of social agencies and legislation. Families in transition will need specific, personal help. Society will need more adequate information to deal with the transitions it faces.

No agency is in sight which could undertake the needed innovative research and services. We see the need for an autonomous organization, a National Center for the Advancement of the Family, dedicated to the changing family. Such a Center would do its own research, stimulate research by other organizations and individuals, promote the exchange of up-to-the-minute information and insights among professionals and with the public, develop and disseminate skills appropriate to new lifestyles, and provide and promote services to changing families.

This is an undisguised and unabashed appeal for support of the dream.

APPENDICES

I

Notes on Statistical Procedures

W<small>E HAVE ENDEAVORED</small> to use statistical techniques as appropriate and to the extent that they enhance the value of the study by separating results which are probably spurious from those in which we can place some confidence. For the most part what we have done is straightforward, but in one or two instances our application of techniques might be called into question. It is our purpose in this appendix to rationalize some of these uses.

We have used nonparametric (distribution-free) statistics almost exclusively.* In our opinion, the data achieve ordinal or ordered metric measurement at best and much of these are nominal scale data. The issue of measurement level is more important to us than whether or not the parametric t-test is sufficiently robust to work with whatever distributions might be found in our data. On this we have been very conservative. Both Shostrom's Personal Orientation Inventory and Edwards' Personal Preference Schedule are usually analyzed with parametric techniques, yet neither was developed by methods which would assure the required

---

* The reference for all statistics, unless otherwise stated, is Sidney Siegel, *Nonparametric Statistics for the Behavioral Sciences* (New York: McGraw-Hill, 1956).

interval or ratio measurement, and EPPS scores are not normalized. At the expense of some loss in efficiency, the nonparametric tests give greater general confidence in our findings.

Mechanical considerations were of equal importance. The counting and sorting required for many nonparametric techniques were easy for us to do by hand compared with some of the repetitive calculations associated with parametric techniques. Even aided by a small electronic calculator, the chi-square (χ^2) analysis of problems and motivations took hundreds of hours—to produce only very limited results. Many interesting comparisons which we would like to have done were simply beyond our computational means. For nominal data we generally used the χ^2 test, but were frequently forced to the more tedious computation of the hypergeometric (Fisher) probability because of low cell frequencies. The two-sample Kolmogorov-Smirnov test was our choice for most ordinal data.

If there is anything potentially controversial in our statistical analyses it would be that we often treated individual responses as statistically independent. Strictly speaking, each individual is not an independent draw from some "population" of multilateral-marriage participants, not only because of sampling biases (see Chapter 5 and Appendix II) but because the inclusion of one person in most cases implies the inclusion of a spouse as well as other members of the same group. Yet it was an essential methodological feature that we were interested in separate, independently reported information from each individual. To select randomly some individual response to represent each group for statistical purposes would have defeated a central purpose. On the other hand, by including all individuals we could be accused of having inflated the sample sizes.

Clearly some criterion measures will not be independent as obtained from each individual; for example, whether or not a person has had a group sexual encounter within the group. Other measures are not necessarily statistically dependent even though individuals were not included by a proper sampling procedure. In order to use all the data but not render the results meaningless because of inflated samples, we devised a two-step approach to statistical tests.

Before conducting any test of significance where the measures might be challenged as not being independent, we first tested the statistical reasonableness of treating them as independent. As appropriate to the main hypothesis under test, the preliminary step either dealt with pairs of individuals from existing dyadic marriages or with individuals from the same group. We considered that we were justified in regarding each individual score or return as independent if scores within groups or pairs were not significantly correlated. If these were significantly correlated, then we considered independent treatment as justified provided the correlations between pairs not in the same group were about as high, meaning that the correlation was a function of membership in the population rather than in a particular group or dyad.

For example, we regard spouses' individual assessments of a marriage as capable of varying independently. Thus we desired to use each separate Burgess-Cottrell score in our analysis.* For couples where both scores were available we set up a two-by-two table of husbands' scores versus wives' scores, dichotomized at the median. If scores were not independent, husbands and wives would tend to fall on the same side of the median. For prior B-C scores and present B-C scores the exact (Fisher) probability of results at least as extreme as the ones found were .595 and 1.00 respectively, under the null hypothesis that they are statistically independent. For gains versus losses in scores, the probability was .405. Thus there is no reason to reject the hypothesis of statistical independence even at a very high α.

Similar preliminary tests with similar results were conducted for the other analyses in which each individual score was treated as independent. For personality measures, yet another argument is presented in an earlier paper.[1]

One-sample runs tests failed to produce significant results on randomly selected items from questionnaires taken in the order in which original referrals occurred. We feel justified in treating each set of group returns and measures as independently obtained.

REFERENCES

1. Larry L. and Joan M. Constantine, "Sexual Aspects of Multilateral Relations," *op. cit.*

* See Chapter 9.

II

Further Notes
on Methodological Issues

IMPACT. We are acutely aware of the possible distorting effects of our reciprocal involvement with respondents. We have no wish to control for these effects in that controlling them would require an uninvolved methodology. All we can do is try to be sensitive to the impact we have.

From a scientific standpoint the most serious effects would be those introduced by our expectations and prior disclosures to groups. Insofar as we had previously formed opinions and hypotheses, open dialogue with new respondents could lead them, consciously or not, to fulfill our expectations. Such influences of experimenter bias are well-documented experimental effects. It is our contention that it is the entire experimental milieu which forms the biasing "set" with which any subject enters a reporting or test-taking situation. It is at least plausible and consistent with theory that there are forms of experimenter disclosure which facilitate rather than interfere with authentic self-disclosure. In our interactions with respondents we have never hidden our feelings or guesses on a particular area of investigation, but we have also always emphasized the great range and variability of respondents and the personal and subjective nature of our intermediate guesses. If we combine this with what we regard as strong *unbias-*

ing effects of an accepting, trust-based relationship, then distortions due to our expectations do not loom so large.

On another level there is no denying that our presence and involvement with groups must have influenced their *behavior* even if we were certain it did not bias their *reports* of behavior. In several cases we have made active interventions in a counseling or therapeutic capacity at a group's request. Moreover, certain of the data-gathering procedures were designed to give facilitative feedback to groups. The system that we study is not the system that an uninvolved researcher interested in minimizing his influence would study, for in our case the system includes us. Again, we have no desire to "control" for these effects. If through our intervention as people other people can be facilitated in their pursuit of growth and happiness, then we will intervene.

On several occasions we heard groups mention what amounts to a Hawthorne Effect.* They felt that in participating in the study they had been accorded some special status or recognition, that in some way they were "representing" multilateral marriages and therefore had to live up to some projected ideal. But the context in which this was always presented to us is important. This is typical:

"You know, it was a real strain at first. We felt sort of special, like because we were in the study we had to live up to something. Even though you two weren't here, you added to the tension. But now we realize that, shit, we don't have to live up to *anybody's* expectations!"

As soon as we became aware of this as a pattern, we apprised newly entering groups of the possible effects on their relationship and stressed our interest in them as themselves. Since this prophylaxis became policy, no other groups have had the problem.

VOLUNTEERS. Overall, the scoreboard looks good. In all we have identified 101 groups which we have confirmed to be multilateral marriages or for which there is independent reason to believe that the group would meet our operational definition. The ultimate

---

* Named after the Hawthorne Plant where electrical assemblers were found to increase their production spontaneously simply as the result of being studied.

"disposition" of these groups may clarify the issue of volunteer biases in the study.

Of the 101, five simply were formed or came to our attention too late to be included in the study. Two of these have unanimously decided to participate in the study, two are delaying a final decision pending meeting with us, and the fifth has become involved in parapsychic phenomena and "gone beyond group marriage" in the words of one member. They feel that only by "becoming part of" the parapsychic aspects of the group would we be able to understand.

Similar views were expressed by one of the only three outright refusals we have received. They were into a heavily mystical trip and did not believe that their relationship could be understood by anyone who was not. Of the other outright refusals, one came by mail without explanation and with no response to our attempts to follow-up. The last involved a split decision within a tetrad. One group within a commune objects strongly to the very word "marriage" or to the idea of marriagelike commitments in interpersonal relations. They appear, nevertheless, to be mutually committed but could not be included in the study under our basic criterion. A similar borderline case opted into the study, then withdrew, as the perceptions of one woman wavered. One triad hesitated committing themselves to the study, though we met with them several times. The group dissolved before reaching a decision. Four groups which chose to be in the study dissolved before we could meet with them and begin gathering data. One group dissolved almost immediately after our first meeting with them. An additional seven groups, qualified on technical criteria, could not be included because of conflicts involving participation in other research, privileged communication, or professional status.

Thus most (nineteen of twenty-eight) of those who could become respondents did so. Only two chose to leave the study, and both concluded that they did not have a multilateral marriage. The remaining sixty-six groups were dissolved before we heard of them and could not become part of the study. We should mention that we have exchanged letters or spoken with members of more than half of the groups not in the study. Fifteen of those not in the base study are represented in the nonrespondent survey.

The obvious summation of all these factors is that respondents are likely to represent a longer-lived subset of all groups coming to our attention but not one seriously misrepresentative by virtue of volunteer bias.

"SAMPLING." We made no attempts to control for possible bias in the methods by which groups were identified. We simply contacted every group we could identify by whatever means possible. From other indirect evidence (such as from counselors and other written accounts of group marriages) we can offer some plausible guesses as to the sources and nature of unrepresentativeness, if it exists.

Respondents and survey informants may *under*-represent college-campus-based experiments. We have used our campus presentations throughout the country as sources of leads, but Kilgo's report suggests that collegiate multilateral marriages are very short-lived (and thus less likely to appear in our population). Kilgo's observations are based on a few cases from a single campus, however, which is no more a representative sample than is ours. Neither our data nor personal knowledge permit us to refute or to support her contention; therefore this remains one possible source of bias.

Respondents and survey informants may be unrepresentative racially. Only two respondents were from racial minorities and no racial minority groups have ever been located. We made some unsuccessful efforts to identify groups in the black community in several areas in response to professional conjecture that the alleged traditions of amorphous or extended-family relations would facilitate black participation in multilateral relations. In talks with black students we came away with the impression that many more black women than men were receptive to the idea. ("Mmm, sounds okay having two or three husbands. Most I know can't keep one man home. Maybe with two or three at least one of them'd be around when you want him.") Numerous times we were told that the black community had more essential concerns (survival, economic advancement, political power, etc.) than to make heavy investments in such marital experiments as multilateral marriage. People working in black communities have suggested to us that, not being black, we are less likely to be trusted with a lead. Thus there exists the possibility that black or other minority-based groups are more common than would be suggested by their absence among the twenty-six groups in our study.

So many leads derive from published notices of our work that there could be a class or educational bias. A priori we believe that people in the lower socioeconomic classes and with less formal education are less likely to attempt multilateral marriages. The lower averages and greater spread in socioeconomic indicators for our groups compared with the only other available data (Ramey) would argue against such a built-in class bias due to "sampling," but it remains a tenable hypothesis. Our use of selective publicity to enable groups to contact us could also have biased our groups in the direction of those with a higher interest in growth, education, and self-knowledge. This is also a potential result of volunteer bias.

III

Basic Characteristics
of Respondents
and Survey Informants

Table III–1. Sizes of multilateral marriages.

SIZE	SURVEY INFORMANTS $(N = 15)$	RESPONDENTS $(N = 11)$	TOTAL PERCENT $(N = 26)$
Triads (3 partners)	4	2	23
Tetrads (4)	8	8	62
Pentads (5)	2	–	8
Hexads (6)	1	1	8

Table III–2. Durations of multilateral marriages. .

DISSOLVED GROUPS[a]

DURATION OF GROUPS IN MONTHS	SURVEY INFORMANTS $(N = 13)$	RESPONDENTS $(N = 8)$	ALL INTACT GROUPS $(N = 5)$	TOTAL PERCENT $(N = 26)$
0–3	2			7.7
4–6	5	2		27.7
7–12	5	1		23.0
13–24	1	2	1	15.4
25–36		1	2	11.5
37–48		2		7.7
49–60			2	7.7

[a] Difference between durations of dissolved survey and respondent groups is significant by the median test ($p = .00218$, Fisher exact probability).

Note. No significant association between either duration or intact/dissolved status and group size, number of children, marital status of partners, duration of previously established marriage, age of partners, or group economic status.

Table III–3. Duration of existing legal marriages for couples in multilateral marriages.

YEARS MARRIED AT GROUP FORMATION	SURVEY INFORMANTS (N = 23)	RESPONDENTS (N = 15)	TOTAL PERCENT (N = 38)
0–2	3	2	13
3–5	3	5	21
6–8	10	4	37
9–11	4	3	18
12–15			—
16–20	3	1	11

Table III-4. Number of children by legally married couples in multilateral marriages and by multilateral marriage.

NUMBER OF CHILDREN	COUPLES			MULTILATERAL FAMILIES[a]		
	SURVEY INFORMANTS (N = 25)	RESPONDENTS[b] (N = 15)	TOTAL PERCENT (N = 40)	SURVEY INFORMANTS (N = 15)	RESPONDENTS[c] (N = 11)	TOTAL PERCENT (N = 26)
0	7	5	30	2	2	15
1	5	3	20	2	2	15
2	7	4	28	2	4	23
3	3	2	13	3	2	19
4	1	1	5	1		4
5	2		5	3		12
6				1	1	8
7				1		4

[a] Including children by divorced or separated partners, by unmarried pairs, and born into group.
[b] Difference with survey not significant.
[c] Difference with survey not significant.

Table III–5. Ages of participants in multilateral marriage.

AGE OF PARTNERS AT GROUP FORMATION	SURVEY INFORMANTS (N = 60)	RESPONDENTS (N = 40)	TOTAL PERCENT[a] (N = 104)
21–23	7	5	11.5
24–26	11	10	20.2
27–29	17	9	25.0
30–32	9	4	12.5
33–35	5	5	9.6
36–38	3	5	·7·7
39–41	6	2	7.7
42–44	2		1.9
45–47		1	1.0
48–50		1	1.0
51–53		1	1.0
54–56			—
57–59		1	1.0

[a] No significant difference between survey and respondents. Median age of 54 females = 28; 50 males = 31, difference not significant.

Table III–6. Year of formation of multilateral marriages.

YEAR GROUP FORMED	SURVEY INFORMANTS (N = 15)	RESPONDENTS (N = 11)	TOTAL PERCENT (N = 26)
Prior to 1967	1		4
1967		4	15
1968	1	1	8
1969	5	5	38
1970	6	1	27
1971	2		8

Table III–7.   Education of participants in multilateral marriages.

HIGHEST EDUCATIONAL LEVEL	SURVEY INFORMANTS $(N = 29)$	RESPONDENTS $(N = 33)$	TOTAL PERCENT[a] $(N = 62)$
Secondary school		3	5
Some college	4	17	34
B.A. or B.S.	13	9	35
M.A. or M.S.	5	3	13
Ph.D. or Sc.D.	7	1	13

[a] Difference between survey informants and respondents is significant ($p < .005$, $D_{max} = .468$, two-sample Kolmogorov-Smirnov test, two-tailed hypothesis).

Table III-8. Occupations of multilateral-marriage participants[a] compared with United States population and members of an expanded-family interest organization.[b]

OCCUPATIONS[c]	FEMALES[d] Group Marrieds (N = 44)	MALES[e] Group Marrieds (N = 43)	MALES[e] Interest Group (N = 76)	FEMALES U.S.	FEMALES Group Marrieds[f] (N = 24)	MALES U.S.	MALES Group Marrieds[g] (N = 33)
I—Professional, scientific, and kindred workers	43.2%	44.2%	72.4%	13.0%	79.2%	11.9%	57.6%
II—Managers, officials, proprietors, etc.	6.8	4.7	18.4	4.4	12.5	13.2	6.1
III—Clerical, sales, and kindred workers	4.5	2.3	1.3	38.7	8.3	13.0	3.0
IV—Craftsmen, foremen, and skilled workers	—	14.0	1.3	1.1	—	19.0	18.2
V—Operatives, services, farmers, and laborers	—	11.6	—	42.8	—	42.9	15.2
VI—College students	15.9	23.3	2.6	(students and housewives excluded from census data)			
VII—House spouses	29.5	—					

[a] Respondent and nonrespondent survey informants for whom occupational data were available.

[b] Members of an organization for people interested in expanded family, reported in Ramey (op. cit.). Data furnished by author.

[c] Collapsed U.S. Census Occupational Classification categories after Ramey, "Communes, Group Marriage, and the Upper-Middle Class," Journal of Marriage and the Family 34, 4 (November 1972).

[d] Females among respondents/informants and interest group not significantly different.

[e] Significant difference between group marrieds and interest group (p < .001, $x^2 = 33.85$, d.f. = 3, categories III, IV, and V collapsed for two-sample x^2 test).

[f] Significantly different from expected percentages (p < .001, $x^2 = 92.34$, d.f. = 2, categories I and II, IV and V collapsed for one-sample x^2 test).

[g] Significantly different from expected percentages (p < .001, $x^2 = 27.97$, d.f. = 3, categories I and II collapsed for one-sample x^2 test).

Table III-9. Interests and experience of nonrespondent survey participants in multilateral marriages (N = 29).

EXPERIENCE	TRIED OR BEEN IN	NOW IN OR TRYING	VERY INTERESTED	SOMEWHAT INTERESTED
	(100%)			
Group marriage	4%	15%	48%	7%
Rural commune or intentional community	30	26	30	44
Urban/suburban commune or intentional community			37	18
Close but *not* sexually intimate emotional relationships outside marriage	33	11	44	26
Close, sexually intimate emotional relationships outside marriage	48	19	22	26
Casual sexual relationships outside marriage	37	4	11	4
Close network of separate families	30	4	44	30
Sexual parties and swinging	7	4	—	19
Encounter groups or sensitivity training	63	15[a]	19	33

[a] Eliminating duplicates who also indicated "have tried."

IV

*Family Summary
and Individual Summary*

Table IV-1. Economic structure by groups.

(N = 8, joint households)

	None	1/10	1/4	1/3	1/2	2/3	3/4	All	No Answer
What portion of individual income is pooled?	1				2	3		1	
What portion of household expenses are met by pooled income?	1				1		2	4	1
What portion of small assets are purchased from pooled income?	1				1		1	5	
What portion of major assets are purchased from pooled income?	1				1		1	5	

Live in: house (6), apartment (1), complex (1)
Which is: rented (2), owned outright (2), mortgaged (6)
Lease/deed/mortgage is in: one name (2), two names (6)

	Informal	Consensus	Meeting	Fixed Rules	Individual	Any Way
Household budget is administered by	3	3			1	1
Small asset purchases decided by	4	2			1 (1 sometimes)	1
Major asset purchases decided by	1	6	1		(2 sometimes)	

Problems: shortage of money (6), budgeting (2), agreeing on specific purchases (2), agreeing on general plan (1), none (1)

Table IV-2. Child-rearing by groups.

(N = 9, 6 with children)	ONLY BIOLOGICAL PARENTS	PRIMARILY BIOLOGICAL PARENTS	ALL ADULTS	NO CHILDREN
Discipline is administered by	—	2	4	3
Rules are set by	—	4	2	3

Discipline is characterized as: flexible (6), consistent (4), permissive (2), informal (2), free (1), strict (1)

Children by cross-marital pairs are: now (1), hoped for in future (4), remotely possible (2), not wanted (1), would have, but group broke up (1).

Caring for children is: easier than before group (5), about the same (1).

Relating to children is: easier than before group (5), about the same (1).

EFFECTS ON CHILDREN	YES	YES (STRONGLY)
Been jealous of parents' other relationships	3	
Been jealous of cosiblings	2	
Shown insecurity as result of larger group	2	
Had difficulty accepting multiple parents		1
Been confused by relationship		1
Not related well with cosiblings	1	
Had problems in school or neighborhood as result of group	1	
Responded well to multiple adult models	3	3
Shown increased security or confidence	2	2
In general shown progress and growth in transition to group	3	1
Regarded most or all adults as parents	3	
Related well in school or neighborhood	3	
Got along well with cosiblings	1	
Called other adults "Mommy" or "Daddy"	1	

Table IV–3. Sexual structure by groups.

(N = 9)

Have all opposite-sex adult pairs had intercourse?   yes (9), no (0)

Homosexual activities occur in group: never (9)

Group sex has occurred in group: never (4), one man, two women (3), one woman, two men (3), two men, two women (3), other (1)

How often has group sex occurred?   rarely (2), occasionally (2), often (1)

Was overt same-sex sexual expression involved?   no(3), yes (2)

Sexual partners/sleeping arrangements: strictly fixed rotation (1, later changed), fixed rotation with exceptions (5, 2 later changed), unstructured/informal (2), group decision process (3), other (1)

Sleeping arrangements provide for: heterosexual pairs (9), sleeping alone (7), groups (4), some priority or veto by legal spouse (3), homosexual pairs (0)

Sex within primary pairs occurs: about as often as other pairs (3), more often than other pairs (2), less often than other pairs (2), most of the time (1), occasionally (1)

Table IV–4. Social relationships by groups.

(N = 9)

The group has outside contacts/friends with whom it interfaces as a group: yes (8), no (1)

The neighborhood knows of the group marriage: probably nothing (5), some suspicions (2), probably guess (2), (2 also said "some know for certain")

Relationships with neighborhood/community are: good (5), excellent (2), fair (1), some hostility (1), some harassment (0), considerable harassment or hostility (0)

Table IV–5. Most important reasons given for participation in multilateral marriage (indicated by approximately one-half or more of respondents).

REASONS[a]	TOTAL PERCENT[b]	PERCENT STRONG REASON
More companionship	82	42
Variety of sexual partners	88	18
New aspects of personality emerge relating to more people	73	27
Feeling desired and wanted more	76	21
Opportunity for personal growth	73	24
Personal fulfillment	76	18
Increased self-awareness	73	21
Intellectual variety	67	27
Loved the particular people involved	64	30
Being loved more	73	18
New experiences	70	18
Richer environment for children	55	27
Sense of "community"	61	18
More people to talk to	64	12
Improvement over rigid, arbitrary morality	60	15
Multiple adult models for children	52	24
Sense of belongingness	64	9
Sense of sharing	58	15
No one has to bear full weight of another's need	58	12
More personal freedom	52	18
Opportunity to express existing love or friendship sexually	48	18
Satisfy missing elements in present marriage	52	9
Same as two-person marriage but more	52	9

[a] Listed in decreasing rank order by weighted sum of number indicating reason or strong reason.

[b] N = 33; percent indicating either reason or strong reason.

Table IV–6. Least important reasons given for participating in multilateral marriage (indicated by less than half of respondents).

REASONS[a]	TOTAL PERCENT[b]	PERCENT STRONG REASON
Greater economic power of group	42	12
Sense of completeness	48	3
Realize potentials	45	6
Overcome aloneness of two-person relationship	36	15
More security	42	6
Avocational variety	39	9
Child-rearing easier	39	3
More chance for vocational variety	33	9
Relax and be oneself	33	9
Sense of oneness	36	3
Boredom/staleness eliminated	36	
Strengthen bond with present spouse	33	3
Emerge from ruts in present relationship	33	3
Overcome discontent with single spouse	27	3
More stability than two-person marriage	27	
Less individual responsibilities	21	3
Avoid having to choose between two (or more) partners	21	
Group sex	21	
Recovery of individual identity lost in two-person relationship	18	3
Protesting establishment	18	
Fortress/protection from outside world	15	
Bisexual opportunities	9	3
Retreat from outside	9	
Religious principles/ beliefs	9	

[a] Listed in decreasing rank order by weighted sum of number indicating reason or strong reason.

[b] N = 33; percent indicating either reason or strong reason.

Table IV–7.   Most common problems in multilateral marriages (indicated by approximately half or more respondents).

PROBLEM[a]	TOTAL PERCENT[b]	PERCENT SERIOUS OR RECURRING PROBLEM
Communication	82	33
Friction in personalities	72	36
Jealousy	79	24
Commitment	79	18
Lifestyles	64	18
Daily tension	67	12
Personal hangups	61	30
Lack of openness	45	21
Sleeping arrangements	58	6
Manipulation	48	15
Sexual compatibility	48	12
"Game"-playing	45	15
Complexity of group situation	48	9
Group decision-making	52	3
Simple misunderstandings	48	6
Choice of sex partners	48	6
Competitiveness	45	6
Budgeting	42	9
Time to be alone	42	9
Privacy	48	
Selfishness	48	

[a] Listed in decreasing rank order by weighted sum of number indicating problem or serious/recurring problem.

[b] N = 33; percent indicating problem or serious/recurring problem.

Table IV–8. Less common problems in multilateral marriages (indicated by less than half but more than one quarter of respondents).

PROBLEM[a]	TOTAL PERCENT[b]	PERCENT SERIOUS OR RECURRING PROBLEM
Incompatibility	36	12
Dysfunctional "cycles" of behavior	36	12
Love, difficulty or lack	36	9
Frequent fighting	39	3
Lack of freedom	36	6
Money	36	6
Sex	36	6
Immaturity	36	6
Dominance or leadership	33	9
Empathy	33	3
Understanding	33	3
Food preferences	30	6
Work sharing	30	6
Philosophies	27	9
Sharing	30	3
Group pressure	30	3
Neuroticism	27	6
Envy	27	6
Use of leisure	27	3

[a] Listed in decreasing rank order by weighted sum of number indicating problem or serious/recurring problem.

[b] N = 33; percent indicating problem or serious/recurring problem.

Table IV–9.   Least common problems in multilateral marriages (indicated by less than one-quarter of respondents).

PROBLEM[a]	TOTAL PERCENT[b]	PERCENT SERIOUS OR RECURRING PROBLEM
Existing marriage	24	6
Rules and rule-making	24	6
Getting to know each other	24	6
Growing to love each other	21	6
Housekeeping practice	24	
Caring, concern	21	3
Interruptions	18	6
Discipline of children	21	
Dishonesty	21	
Inexperience	21	
Work scheduling	18	3
Relating to children	18	
Lack of enthusiasm	15	3
Group activities	15	3
Parental roles	12	6
Lack of knowledge	9	
Planning	3	

[a] Listed in decreasing rank order by weighted sum of number indicating problem or serious/recurring problem.

[b] $N = 33$; percent indicating problem or serious/recurring problem.

Table IV–10. Sexual experience of multilateral marriage participants.

SEXUAL PRACTICE	PERCENT INDICATING EXPERIENCE $(N = 33)$
Premarital intercourse	91
Extramarital intercourse (prior to group)	55
Extramarital affair	48
Swinging or wife-swapping[a]	48
Petting to orgasm	82
Variety of intercourse positions	97
"69"	94
Fellatio	95
Cunnilingus	97
Anal intercourse	42
Homosexual sex	33
Three-person sex (2 females, 1 male)[b]	52
Three-person sex (2 males, 1 female)	36
Two-couple sex	52
Other group sex	33

[a] Interpretation of percentage indicating experience is difficult because the original questionnaire did not define these terms.

[b] 64% indicated some group sexual experience.

Table IV–11. Significant associations between reported reasons/
problems and sex, group size, number of children, age of respondents,
duration of prior marriage, and duration of group (see note below).

PROBLEM OR REASON	YULE'S Q^a	LEVEL OF SIGNIFICANCE[b]
SEX OF RESPONDENT[c]		
Reasons:		
Strengthen bond with present spouse	.89	$< .01$ $(\chi^2 = 6.74)$
Variety of sexual partners (strong reason)	− .79	.0533
Recovery of individual identity	.75	.0726
Avoid having to choose between partners	.75	.0726
Problems:		
Use of leisure time	.84	.0183
Caring, concern	.75	.0726
AGE OF RESPONDENT		
Reasons:		
Sense of oneness	− .78	$< .05$ $(\chi^2 = 4.72)$
Improvement over rigid, arbitrary morality	.67	$.10 > p > .05$ $(\chi^2 = 3.02)$
Problems:		
Jealousy	− 1.00	.0434
Frequent fighting	− .82	$< .025$ $(\chi^2 = 6.01)$
Selfishness	− .73	$< .05$ $(\chi^2 = 4.92)$
Budgeting	− .67	$.10 > p > .05$ $(\chi^2 = 3.02)$

PROBLEM OR REASON	YULE'S Q[a]	LEVEL OF SIGNIFICANCE[b]
SIZE OF GROUP (triads, tetrads)		
Reasons:		
Group sex	− .90	.011
Fortress/protection from outside	− .90	.0247
Opportunity for personal growth	− 1.00	.0627
Loved particular people involved	− .78	.0667
Increased self-awareness	− 1.00	.0917
Opportunity to express existing love or friendship sexually	− .74	.098
Problems:		
Neuroticism	− .95	.0039
Food preferences	− .90	.011
Existing marriages	− .84	.0239
Dysfunctional cycles of behavior	− .85	.0265
Lack of enthusiasm	− .81	.0560
Friction in personalities	− 1.00	.098
NUMBER OF CHILDREN (none, one or more)		
Problems (other than concerning children):		
Communication	.83	.0059
Housekeeping practice	1.00	.023
Work scheduling	1.00	.0673
Time to be alone	.73	$.10 > p > .05$ ($\chi^2 = 3.44$)
DURATION OF PREVIOUS MARRIAGE (below median, above)		
Reasons:		
Multiple adult models for children	.83	.022
Satisfy missing elements in present marriage	.85	.0263
Opportunity for personal growth	1.00	.0402
Increased self-awareness	1.00	.076
Problems:		
Neuroticism	1.00	.00957

PROBLEM OR REASON	YULE'S Q[a]	LEVEL OF SIGNIFICANCE[b]
DURATION OF GROUP (dissolved groups: below median, above)		
Reasons:		
Variety of sexual partners	− 1.00	.00957
More people to talk to	− .91	.0109
Intellectual variety	− .91	.0109
Child-rearing easier	− .89	.0119
Multiple adult models for children	− .83	.022
More companionship	− 1.00	.0364
Richer environment for children	− .81	.062
Problems:		
Incompatibility	− .89	.0119
Philosophies	− .75	.0860

[a] Yule's Q is a measure of the degree of association varying from 0 to a maximum of ± 1 depending on how closely two dichotomized variables are associated. We are using it largely because of ease of computation. A minus sign indicates that the "greater" group was less likely to check the reason or problem.

[b] Probabilities given alone were calculated by the Fisher exact formula; others employed the χ^2 test. These probabilities can only be taken as a very rough indication of the approximate degree of statistical significance, since the proper assumptions of independence cannot be met in all cases.

[c] A positive Q indicates females checked reason or problem more often than males.

Note. The number of associations which would be statistically significant if they were from independent responses is small enough to be within the number which could be expected by chance. The statistical independence of responses cannot be assumed for most of the comparisons. Consequently this table should only be taken as indicating strength of association and not be interpreted statistically.

Table IV–12. Reasons for interest or participation in multilateral marriage for male and female nonrespondent survey informants, and respondents.

Reason	Non-respondents % checking (N = 27)	Respondents % checking (N = 33)	Males Rank[a][b] — Nonrespondent (N = 11)	Males Rank[a][b] — Respondent (N = 15)	Males — Total % (N = 26)	Females — Total % (N = 34)	Females Rank[c] — Nonrespondent (N = 16)	Females Rank[c] — Respondents (N = 18)
Sense of isolation in conventional relationship	78	36***	9.5	13	46	62	2	20
Variety of sexual partners	63	88*	6.5	1	85	71	17	6
Greater economic power of larger group	74	42*	6.5	16	50	62	13	15
More chance for vocational variety	59	33†	14	19	35	53	11	18
New aspects of personality emerge relating to more people	81	73	1	4	77	76	9	4
Less individual responsibility	19	21	23.5	21.5	12	26	21	21
Sense of belongingness	74	64	13	11	54	79	7	13
Feeling loved, desired, and wanted more	52	76	15.5	5	54	74	14.5	2.5
Greater intellectual variety	63	67	11.5	10	62	68	8	7
Multiple adult models for children	85	52**	4.5	23	54	76d	6	14
Protesting establishment	22	18	19	3	15	24	23	22
Personal fulfillment	93	76	3	9	77	88	1	5
Richer environment for children	85	55*	3	17.5	62	74d	3	8.5
More stability than conventional family/marriage	11	27	22	17.5	23	18	24	23
Satisfy missing elements in my present relationship	33	52	23.5	23.5	23	59**	18	16
Strengthen bond with my present spouse	19	33	21	21.5	12	38*	22	16
Sense of "community"	85	61	4.5	8	62	79	4	10.5
Increased self-awareness	63	73	9.5	6.5	58	76	10	2.5
Opportunity for personal growth	81	73	15.5	6.5	65	85	5	1
More personal freedom	52	52	20	14	38	62	14.5	12
Easier child-rearing	52	39	18	15	31	56d	16	19
Eliminate boredom or staleness	41	36	11.5	20	27	47	19	17
Expression of existing love or friendship for certain people	56	55	16	12	50	59	12	8.5
Religious principles/beliefs	26	9	17	24	12	21	20	24

[a] Rank order by weighted sum of number indicating reason and strong reason.

[b] Spearman rank correlations for males, $r_s = .72$ ($p < .01$).

[c] Spearman rank correlations for females, $r_s = .535$ ($p < .01$).

[d] Correlation with sex on "easier child-rearing" is greater ($C = .211$) than on either "multiple adult models" ($C = .198$) or "richer environment" ($C = .0911$).

* $p < .05$ (χ^2 test).

** $p < .02$ (χ^2 test).

*** $p < .01$ (χ^2 test).

† $.10 > p > .05$.

V

Family Background
and Orientation

Table V–1. Family background of participants in multilateral marriages.

	MEN (N = 13) %	WOMEN (N = 16) %	TOTAL (N = 29) %
Mother living:	77	100[a]	90
Father living:	62	81	72
Parents were divorced:			
respondent 12 or younger	23	6	14
respondent 13–20	8	6	7
respondent adult	8	6	7
Respondent was adopted:	—	19	10
Other residents of home:			
friends	8	19	14
relatives	15	56	38
boarders	15	13	14
Left home for:			
college	15	38	28
job	—	25	14
marriage	31	31	31
service	23	—	10
other	23	19	21

[a] Approaches significance, $p = .0783$ exact (Fisher) probability.

Table V–2. Evaluations by adult multilateral-marriage participants of child-rearing in their families of origin.

DISCIPLINING CHARACTERIZED AS	MEN (N = 13)	WOMEN (N = 16)	TOTAL (N = 29)
Strict	31	50	41
Lax	15	19	17
Consistent	88	38	38
Inconsistent	38	50	45
Flexible	46	44	45
Authoritarian	31	63	48
Permissive	31	—[a]	14
Free	15	6	10
Formal	15	—	7
Informal	38	44	41

[a] Significant difference, $p = .0301$ exact (Fisher) probability.

Table V–3. Religious orientation of multilateral-marriage participants as children and as adults.

RELIGIOUS ORIENTATION	TOTAL PERCENT (N = 29) THEN	NOW[a]
Strongly religious	21	3
Religious	34	14
Nonreligious	38	76
Antireligious	7	7
	THEN	NOW[b]
Orthodox	17	—
Conservative	7	3
Middle-of-road	21	3
Liberal	31	41

[a] Decrease in "religiosity" is *significant* ($p < .001$, $n = 14$, $x = 1$, sign [binomial] test).

[b] Increase in religious liberalism is *significant* ($p < .02$, $n = 9$, $x = 1$ sign [binomial] test).

	TOTAL PERCENT $(N = 29)$	
	THEN	NOW[c]
Protestant	59	—
Roman Catholic	3	—
Jewish	7	—
Humanist/Ethical Humanist	7	34
Agnostic	7	24
Atheist	3	—
Other: mysticism/metaphysics	3	7
"my own"	—	17
Mormon	3	—
Unitarian		3

[c] Change to humanist/agnostic/atheist from all others is *significant* ($p <$ .005, $\chi^2 =$ 8.1, $d.f. =$ 1, McNemar test for the significance of nominal changes).

Table V–4. Political orientation of participants in multilateral marriage.

	TOTAL PERCENT $(N = 29)$
Not politically oriented	21
Democrat	10
Republican	10
Other (Peace and Freedom Party)	10
Not party oriented	62
Proestablishment	0
Antiestablishment	31
Reactionary	0
Strongly conservative	7
Middle-of-road	21
Liberal	21
Radical	31
Revolutionary	17

VI

Selected Attitudes

Table VI-1. Selected attitudes of multilateral-marriage participants compared with a general liberal population.[a]

Attitude	Mean Rating[b] (X = participants, * = survey[a])	D$_{max}$[c]
The law has no business regulating sexual relations between consenting adults.	X * (1.0) (1.6)	−.224†
Religious groups should not attempt to impose their standards of sexual behavior on others.	X * (1.0) (1.5)	−.241*
Sexual behavior should be judged on the quality of relationship between people and not on whether or not they are married.	X * (1.1) (2.0)	−.441****
Women should be free to initiate sexual activity.	X * (1.1) (1.5)	−.218†
In general, women do not enjoy sex as much as men.	* X (4.6) (5.2)	.262**
Often couples who have sex together and then marry wish they had waited.	* X (4.1) (4.8)	.325***

The header columns labeled: Strongly Agree / Strongly Disagree span the Mean Rating column.

Table VI-1. cont.

Attitude	Strongly Agree	Mean Rating[b] (X = participants, * = survey[a])	Strongly Disagree	D$_{max}$[c]

Easy access to birth-control devices increases promiscuity.

         *   X   .272**
         (4.2) (4.7)

Homosexuals should be considered no better than criminals.

         *X   .102
         (5.6)(5.8)

Most of us can sincerely love any one of several people equally well.

  X   *   —.432****
  (1.3) (2.4)

Lovers ought to expect a certain amount of disillusionment after they marry.

       *   X   —.352***
       (2.6)   (4.1)

Love is more important than practical considerations.

      X *   —.052
      (3.4)(3.6)

True love seldom lasts forever.

          *   X   .162
          (4.1) (4.7)

[a] Readers of *Psychology Today*. See Athanasiou, *et al.*, "Sex," *Psychology Today* 4.2 (July 1970).

[b] On a scale from 1 = *strongly agree* to 6 = *strongly disagree*.

[c] Statistic used in two-sample Kolmogorov-Smirnov test. $N_1 = 25$-29, $N_2 = 1937$-2045, depending on item due to unusable responses. N_2 is random 10% sampling of 20,000+ returns. Asterisks indicate significance of difference for one-tailed hypotheses.

* $p < .05$.
** $p < .01$.
*** $p < .005$
**** $p < .001$

† approachs significance, $.10 > p > .05$.

Table VI-2. Attitudes of multilateral-marriage participants on "traditional" values as applied to multilateral marriage.

Attitude	Mean Ratings[a]
	Strongly Agree · · · Strongly Disagree
Sexual involvement outside a group marriage means something is wrong with the marriage.	X (4.6)
Intimate involvement outside a group marriage threatens the stability of the group.	X (3.5)
A partner in a group marriage should strive to love all the others equally.	X (2.9)
A group marriage should be a lifetime commitment.	X (3.9)
If a group marriage dissolves it means it was a failure.	X (5.2)
For the sake of the children, partners should strive to keep a group marriage together.	X (4.6)
Early sexual involvement among potential group-marriage partners creates problems.	X (5.0)
I would like to see my children eventually enter a group marriage.	X (1.6)

[a] On a scale from 1 = *strongly agree* to 6 = *strongly disagree*. No significant differences between male and female attitudes.

Table VI-3. Attitudes on sexual equality of multilateral marriage participants.

Attitude	Mean Ratings[a] Strongly Agree → Strongly Disagree
Women should be free to initiate sexual activity.	X (1.1) at Strongly Agree
In general, women do not enjoy sex as much as men.	X (5.2) near Strongly Disagree
Men and women should have completely equal rights and opportunities.	X (1.2) at Strongly Agree
Most socially prescribed sex roles for men and women are artificial or arbitrary.	X (1.3) at Strongly Agree
Men should be free to do housework and raise children if they desire.	X (1.0) at Strongly Agree
Women should be free to hold jobs and pursue careers if they desire.	X (1.0) at Strongly Agree
Group marriage allows greater freedom from stereotyped sex roles than does conventional marriage.	X (1.8) near Strongly Agree

[a] On a scale of $1 =$ *strongly agree* to $6 =$ *strongly disagree*. Differences between ratings by males and females did not differ significantly, but men were more equalitarian on five of the six equalitarian attitude items $(p = .109)$.

Table VI-4. Attitudes on sexual practices of multilateral-marriage participants.

Attitude	Mean Ratings[a]		
	Strongly Agree		Strongly Disagree
Sexual involvement between parents and children is not necessarily bad.		X (3.0)	
Sexual involvement between brothers and sisters is not necessarily bad.[b]		X (2.2)	
People should be able to express affection physically to individuals of both sexes.	X (1.3)		
The ability to relate sexually to individuals of both sexes is healthy and desirable.[c]	X (1.8)		
Group sexual activity is desirable within a group marriage.		X (2.5)	

[a] On a scale from 1 = *strongly agree* to 6 = *strongly disagree*. No significant differences between male and female attitudes.

[b] *Significantly* stronger agreement on this item than on preceding item ($p = .006$, $n = 11$, $x = 1$, sign [binomial] test).

[c] *Significantly* weaker agreement on this item than on preceding item ($p < .001$, $n = 21$, $x = 2$, sign [binomial] test).

Table VI-5. Selected attitudes on legal issues of participants in multilateral marriage.

Attitude	Mean Ratings[a]
	Strongly Agree ←→ Strongly Disagree
Group marriage should be legalized.	X (1.6)
Any form of marriage that individuals find fulfilling should be legal.[b]	X (1.1)
The law has no business regulating sexual relations between consenting adults.	X (1.0)
Public as well as private sexual behavior between consenting adults should be legal.	X (2.9)
Social nudity in public places, such as "free beaches" is acceptable and should be legal.[c]	X (1.4)

[a] On a scale from 1 = *strongly agree* to 6 = *strongly disagree*. No significant differences between male and female attitudes.

[b] *Significantly* stronger agreement on this item than on preceding item ($p < .001$, $n = 18$, $x = 1$, sign [binomial] test).

[c] *Significantly* stronger agreement on this item than on preceding item ($p = .025$, $n = 17$, $x = 4$, sign [binomial] test).

VII

Marital Adjustment and Satisfaction

Table VII–1. Marital-adjustment scores for respondents' prior and present dyadic relationships.

	First Quartile	Median	Third Quartile	Range
Prior individual[a] scores (N = 25)[b]	117	132	151	57–174
Present individual scores (N = 24)[c]	138.5	153	163.5	89–182
Burgess-Cottrell norms[d]	114	152	171	0–199

[a] See Appendix I for justification of use of individual scores.

[b] *Significantly* different from norms ($p < .025$, $D_{max} = .309$, two-sample Kolmogorov-Smirnov test, two-tailed hypothesis).

[c] *Not significantly* different from norms ($D_{max} = .191$). For 20 individuals reporting on same prior and present relationship, increase in scores is *significant* ($p < .025$, $T = 39$, $n = 18$, Wilcoxon matched-pairs signed-ranks test).

[d] Derived linearly from norms in E. W. Burgess and L. S. Cottrell, *Predicting Success or Failure in Marriage* (Englewood Cliffs, N.J.: Prentice-Hall, 1939) as used in statistical analyses.

Table VII-2. Mean self-ratings of marital happiness/satisfaction of twenty-nine participants in multilateral marriage.

	Very Happy	Happy	OK	Somewhat Unhappy	Very Unhappy
How do you see your happiness with your dyadic-marriage relationship prior to entering the group marriage?	▼	▼	▼	▼	▼

├───────────────X───────────────┤
                (3.7)

Are you still married or in a similar dyadic relationship?
yes (24)   no (5)

If yes, how do you feel now about that relationship?

├──────X──────────────────────────┤
    (4.4)[a]

With respect to your *group* marriage as a whole, how do you feel? (How *did* you feel, if your group has dissolved.)

├───────────────X───────────────┤
                (3.4)

How do you think each of the others in the group feel (felt) about the group?

├───────────────X───────────────┤
                (3.3)

	Very Satisfactory				Very Unsatisfactory
I feel my sex life is:	▼				▼

├──────X──────────────────────────┤
   (4.1)

	Increased Greatly	Increased Some	Stayed Same	Decreased Some	Decreased Greatly
My satisfaction with my sex life, after entering the group marriage:	▼	▼	▼	▼	▼

├──────X──────────────────────────┤
   (4.2)

My frequency of intercourse, after entering the group marriage:

├───────────X──────────────────────┤
           (3.9)

If your group marriage should dissolve (or has already), would you try to form or be in one again?

perhaps [depending on people] (17), yes (10), no (2)

[a] Increase in self-ratings *significant* ($p < .005$, $T = 6$, $n = 13$, Wilcoxon matched-pairs signed-ranks test, one-tailed hypothesis).

VIII
Personality

Table VIII-1. Shostrom's Personal Orientation Inventory scores of
forty participants in multilateral marriages.

SCALE	DESCRIPTION	FIRST QUARTILE	MEDIAN	THIRD QUARTILE	D^a_{max}
Tc	Time-competence. Lives in present	17	18.5	20	.103
I	Inner-directedness. Independent, self-supportive	90	95.5	103	.317**
SAV	Self-actualizing values	20	20.5	24	.143
Ex	Existentiality. Flexible in applying values	24	25	27	.38 ***

ᵃ Statistic used in two-sample, one-tailed Kolmogorov-Smirnov test, $N_1 = 40$ (multilateral-marriage participants), $N_2 = 158$ ("normal" adults, derived from Shostrom, *Manual for the Personal Orientation Inventory* [San Diego: Educational and Industrial Testing Service, 1968]). Asterisks indicate level of statistical significance if less than .05.

    ** $p < .005$.
    *** $p < .001$.

SCALE	DESCRIPTION	FIRST QUARTILE	MEDIAN	THIRD QUARTILE	D^a_{max}
Fr	Feeling reactivity. Aware of own needs and feelings	16	18	21	.254*
S	Spontaneity. Freely express feelings behaviorally	14	15	16	.428***
Sr	Self-regard. Self-worth.	11	13	14	.11
Sa	Self-acceptance. Acceptance of own weaknesses	14	18.5	20	.095
Nc	Nature of man seen as constructive	11	13	14	.094
Sy	Synergy. Synergistic perception	7	7	9	.104
A	Acceptance of aggression.	15	18	20	.103
C	Capacity for intimate contact	20	22	24	.35 ***

* $p < .05$.

Table VIII–2. Edwards Personal Preference Schedule scores of forty-two participants in multilateral marriages, expressed as percentiles of General Adult Norm

EPPS SCALE	H_1[a]	MALES ($N_1 = 19$, $N_2 = 4031$)[c] D_{max}[b]	First Quartile	Median	Third Quartile	FEMALES ($N_1 = 23$, $N_2 = 4932$) D_{max}	First Quartile	Median	Third Quartile
ach		.159	46	65	91	.165	40	70	88
def	lower	− .609******	2	8	18	− .606******	3	5	19
ord	lower	− .446******	3	8	47	− .506******	4	14	30
exh		.212	47	57	75	.143	42	42	89
aut	higher	.366***	37	88	92	.336***	64	79	97
aff	higher	.249	48	75	87	− .194	20	44	63
int	higher	.335**	61	77	95	.335***	42	84	95
suc		.176	42	71	83	.295*	46	78	94
dom		− .212	37	50	63	.103	40	64	85
aba	lower	− .432******	4	17	41	− .553******	2	23	29
nur		.156	26	70	86	− .342***	13	24	47
chg	higher	.294*	18	82	94	.269*	37	76	87
end		− .419*****	7	23	37	− .428******	2	11	39
het	higher	.585******	80	89	91	.780******	91	94	96
agg		− .342**	22	29	46	.205	46	71	83
con		.122		70		.120		66	

[a] A priori hypotheses, if any, of direction of difference of participants' scores with respect to normative population. One-tailed tests were employed for scales with a priori hypotheses; two-tailed tests for the others.

[b] Statistic used in two-sample Kolmogorov-Smirnov test. Asterisks indicate level of significance, if probability less than .05.

[c] N_1 is multilateral marriage participant population, N_2 is "General Adult" population used in standardizing EPPS. See Edwards, *Manual for the EPPS* (New York: Psychological Testing Corp., 1968).

* $p < .05$.   ** $p < .025$.   *** $p < .01$.   **** $p < .005$.   ***** $p < .001$.   ****** $p < .001$.

IX

Substudy on Children

Table IX-1. Observational definitions for rating families on restrictiveness-permissiveness in child-rearing.

1. Restrictive child-rearing practices:
   Parents treat the child as a blank slate they must make an imprint upon.
   Parents put their own expectations upon their child.
   Parents dominate their child, are authoritarian, promote dependency, insist upon obedience, impose many regulations, suppress a child's aggression, suppress a child's sexual play, administer harsh punishment, encourage their child to seek approval from them.

2. Free child-rearing practices:
   Parents allow the child to be a unique individual, yet are able to express openly limitations necessary for their own comfort and maintenance of their own individuality. There is an acceptance of the child's innermost self.
   Parents help their child reach his own expectations for himself.
   Parents provide reinforcement for their child, support growth and new struggles, support their child's autonomy, allow their child to be dependent in certain areas while independent in others, allow their child to express his emotions openly and express their own emotions openly to the child.

3. Permissive child-rearing practices:
   Parents treat the child as if he had the capacity to make adult decisions and functioned at the adult level.

   Parents have no expectations for their children, nor play an instrumental role in the child's own expectations.

   Parents put no or few limitations on their child, even if the child's behavior limits the parent's own individuality and comfort.

   Parents don't allow for dependency, avoid playing an instrumental role in their child's life, provide little or no supervision of their child's activities, are a bit neglectful of meeting the child's needs and opening channels of communication, seldom administer punishment or reward, have lack of contact with their child.

Table IX-2. Observational definitions for rating families on consistency-inconsistency in child-rearing.

1. Consistent child-rearing practices:
   There are a set of clear, consistent rules, policies, or decisions about the treatment of the child, that all adults in the home are aware of and practice. There are consistent rewards for desirable behavior and consistent punishment for undesirable behavior used by all adults in the home.

2. Generally consistent child-rearing practices:
   There is a vague underlying set of rules, policies, or decisions about treatment of the child which most of the adults follow through on, even though there are a few exceptions from the normal pattern. Occasionally policies, rules, and/or decisions are readjusted to meet unusual circumstances. There is a general reward for desirable behavior and general punishment for undesirable behavior, but sometimes this depends upon the person and situation involved.

3. Generally inconsistent child-rearing practices:
   Although there are no normal, understood set of rules, policies, or decisions about the treatment of the child, there are specific areas where adults in the home consistently treat the child in a certain way. Exceptions and modifications are frequent and require the child's readjustment. Although normally each adult in the home or each situation demands its own method of reward or punishment there are specific incidents or people that allow for similar patterns of reward and/or punishment.

4. Inconsistent child-rearing practices:
   Rules, policies, and decisions about the treatment of the child vary from situation to situation and from one adult to another. There is no clear, normal, dependable pattern or reward or punishment in the home. The child can never know what to expect.

Table IX–3. Observational definitions for rating families on high child-orientation/low child-orientation.

1. The whole household revolves around the child, his needs, wishes, demands. Many major sacrifices of pleasure, convenience, opportunity, etc., are made by the adults in an attempt to benefit the child.

2. Consideration of the child clearly predominates, but not to the exclusion of the interests and needs of the adults. The child's welfare gets slightly more attention than the welfare of others. The family includes the child in trips, affection, family councils, even when it is difficult or represents some sacrifice.

3. The child gets proportional consideration, but is as often disregarded as sacrificed for.

4. Although given attention in critical matters, on the whole the child is neglected in favor of other interests.

5. The household is organized around interests of the adult members. The child's needs, desires, and interests definitely are neglected even in essential matters.

Table IX–4. Observational definitions for rating families on acceptance-rejection of children.

1. Intimate and inseparable partner:
   The child is accepted for his innermost self, valued for his contributions to the family and accepted for his needs from the family. The child is an integrated member of the family.

2. Accepted as a member of the family:
   The child is included in family councils, trips, affection, and even when it is difficult or requires considerable sacrifice on the part of adult family members to include him/her.

3. A charter member of the family:
   The child is "kept in his place," excluded from certain phases of family life, but accepted in the areas of family life he is to be included in.

4. Excluded member of the family:
   The family predominantly avoids or excludes the child from many phases of family life, but without open rejection.

5. A rejected burden of the family:
   The child is openly resented and rejected by the family and has become a burden.

Table IX–5.   Intercorrelations of four child-rearing scales for thirteen[a] families.

SPEARMAN'S RANK CORRELATION R_s[b]

RATING SCALE	Consistency-inconsistency	High Child-Orientation– Low Child-orientation	Acceptance-rejection
Restrictiveness -permissiveness	.48	− .30	− .36
Consistency -inconsistency		− .28	.06
High Child-Orientation -low Child-Orientation			.82[c]

[a] Fragments of dissolved groups were evaluated independently.

[b] Based on mean ratings by three judges. All correlations are in the predicted directions.

[c] Significantly intercorrelated ($p < .01$). Other scales may be argued to be independent as rated by these judges. Both high-low and acceptance-rejection are inversely correlated with restrictiveness-permissiveness to about the same degree. The influence of restrictiveness-permissiveness may be partialed out using Kendall's τ (no partial correlation formula for r_s is available). The correlation between high-low and acceptance-rejection is $\tau = .67$. When the correlations with restrictiveness-permissiveness are partialed out, the correlation only drops to $\tau._{restrictive-permissive} = .64$, calling into question restrictiveness-permissiveness as the common factor.

Table IX–6.   Inter-rater correlations for ratings of thirteen[a] families on four child-rearing scales by three judges.

RATING SCALE	Kendall's Coefficient of Concordance (W)	Mean Spearman Rank Correlation ($\bar{r}_s$)	χ^2 (d.f. = 12)[b]	p
Restrictiveness -permissiveness	.74	.61	25.14	< .02
Consistency -inconsistency	.62	.43	20.77	.10 > p > .05
High child-orientation -low child-orientation	.82	.73	26.81	< .01
Acceptance -rejection	.82	.73	26.81	< .01

[a] See footnote *a*, Table IX-5.
[b] Test of significance of W by χ^2 test. Associated probabilities, *p*, are given.

Table IX–7.   Rogers' Personal Adjustment inventory scores for seventeen children ages seven to thirteen whose parents are or were in a multilateral marriage.

	MEAN SCORES[b]		
	Personal Inferiority	Social Mal-adjustment	Family Mal-adjustment
Normal range[a]	12–15	10–14	7–10
Total children ($N = 17$)	8.8	16.8	11.4
Girls ($N = 9$)	8.9	17.8	12.8
Boys ($N = 8$)	8.6	15.6	9.7
Children in intact multilateral-marriage families ($N = 11$)	7.2	16.0	9.3
Children of dissolved multilateral-marriage families ($N = 6$)	11.7	18.2	15.2
Older children, ages 11–13 ($N = 6$)	9.1	16.8	9.8
Younger children, ages 7–10 ($N = 11$)	8.6	16.7	12.2

[a] Suggested norms from Carl Rogers, *Personal Adjustment Inventory: Series of Character and Personality Tests* (New York: Association Press, 1961).

[b] Differences are reported only for reference, *not significant.*

Bibliography

Bibliographies can be many things. They can be personal recommendations, evidence of scholarly intent, or merely filler. To us, the real end has always been to be useful. We have selected items for relevance and availability without striving for either completeness or complete selectivity. We have not listed fiction or unpublished papers. We have included a few items which we regard as being of limited value because we have found that if we leave them out people assume we do not know about them and write to remind us of our inadequate scholarship. Since including items in bibliographies is often taken as tantamount to recommendation, we have "X-rated" those items. For unpublished items and more complete annotation of many of the entries, see our "Group and Multilateral Marriage: Definitional Notes, Glossary and Annotated Bibliography," listed below. Reprints are available from the Multilateral Relations Study Project, P.O. Box 674, West Acton, Mass. 01720.

Key: pb—paperback
t/p—technical or oriented to the professional
X—of limited value
*—especially recommended
**—highly recommended

GROUP AND MULTILATERAL MARRIAGE

Anonymous. "Group Marriage: How It Really Works," *Sexual Freedom* 1 (January 1969).

Anonymous. "Letters on a Group Marriage," *The Modern Utopian* 4, 2 (Spring 1970).

Constantine, Larry L. "Alternative Life Styles and Family Life Education," in Baird and Keenan (eds.). *Family Life Education Reexamined.* Washington, D.C.: American Home Economics Association, 1972. pb.

———. "Emotional Health of Participants in a 'Deviant' Family Form." Report available from Multilateral Relations Study Project.

———. "Personal Growth in Multiperson Marriages," *The Radical Therapist* 2, 1 (April–May 1971).

Constantine, Larry L. and Joan M. "Counseling Implications of Comarital and Multilateral Relations," in Clifford T. Sager and Helen S. Kaplan (eds.). *Progress in Group and Family Therapy* New York: Brunner/Mazel, 1972. t/p

———. "Dissolution of Marriage in a Non-conventional Context," *The Family Coordinator* 21, 4 (October 1972).

———. "Group and Multilateral Marriage: Definitional Notes, Glossary, and Annotated Bibliography" *Family Process* 10, 2 (June 1971).

———. "The Pragmatics of Group Marriage," *The Modern Utopian* 4, 3–4 (Summer–Fall 1970).

———. "Group Marriage: The Prognosis Depends on Society's Maturity in Permitting Differences." Comment on Kilgo (see below).

———. "Marital Alternatives: Extended Groups in Modern Society," in Jacob Crist and Henry Grunebaum. *Marriage Problems and Their Treatment* (in preparation).

———. "Multilateral Marriage: Alternate Family Structure in Practice" (plenary address, 1970 meeting, Indiana Council on Family Relations), in Robert H. Rimmer, *You and I Searching For Tomorrow.* New York: Signet, 1971.

———. "Sexual Aspects of Multilateral Relations," *Journal of Sex Research* 7, 3 (August 1971).

———. "The Group Marriage," in Michael Gordon. *The Nuclear Family in Crisis.* New York: Harper & Row, 1972.

———. "Where Is Marriage Going?" *The Futurist* 4, 2 (April 1970).

Constantine, Larry L. and Joan M., and Edelman, Sheldon K. "Counseling Implications of Comarital and Multilateral Relations," *The Family Coordinator* 21, 3 (July 1972). t/p

Ellis, Albert. "Group Marriage—A Possible Alternative," in Herbert A. Otto (ed.). *The Family in Search of a Future: Alternate Models for Moderns.* New York: Appleton-Century-Crofts, 1970.

Fairfield, Dick. "The Family," "C.R.O. Research," and "Harrad West" in *Communes U.S.A.* Baltimore: Penguin Books, 1971. pb

Gourley, H. Wayne. "Group Marriage: "Utopian Ethics," *The Modern Utopian 2*, 1 (Winter 1968). X

"Harrad West," *The Modern Utopian 4*, 1 (Winter 1970).

Henriksen, A. J. N. "An Alternative to Monogamous Marriage," in Rimmer, 1971 (below).

Kilgo, Reese Danley. "Can Group Marriage Work?" *Sexual Behavior 2*, 3 (March 1972). [Includes several commentaries. See also reply in "Letters," *Sexual Behavior 2*, 6 (June 1972) p. 2.]

Malinowski, Bronislaw. *The Family Among the Australian Aborigines.* New York: Schocken Books, 1969; reprint of 1913 edition. pb

McKern, Sharon S. and Thomas W. "Will Group Marriage Catch On?" *Sexology* (June 1970).

Ramey, James W. "Communes, Group Marriage, and the Upper-Middle Class," *Journal of Marriage and the Family 34*, 4 (November 1972). t/p, *

Rimmer, Robert H. (ed.). *The Harrad Letters to Robert H. Rimmer.* New York: Signet, 1970. pb, X

———— (ed.). *You and I Searching for Tomorrow.* New York: Signet, 1971, pb *

Smith, David E., and Rose, Alan J. "A Case Study of the Charles Manson Group Marriage Commune," *Journal of the American Society of Psychosomatic Dentistry and Medicine 17*, 3 (1970); similarly in *Psychedelic Drugs 3*, 1 (1970). [A very nonrepresentative case.]

Solis, Gary. "Group Marriage and California Law," *Harrad 1*, 1 (January 1970). [An excellent paper, unfortunately only published in a now-dead periodical.]

Stein, Ruth. "Not Just an Ordinary Family," *San Francisco Chronicle* (August 28, 1970), p. 19.

Walley, David. "Getting It Together," *Scenes 2*, (December 1969).

SWINGING, EXTRAMARITAL SEX

Bartell, Gilbert D. *Group Sex: A Scientist's Eyewitness Report on the American Way of Swinging.* New York: Peter H. Wyden, 1971. Also pb, *

————. "Group Sex among the Mid-Americans," *Journal of Sex Research 6*, 2 (May 1970).

Breedlove, William and Jerrye. *Swap Clubs: A Study of Contemporary Sex Mores.* Los Angeles: Sherbourne Press, 1964. [First serious study, flawed, somewhat dated.] X

Denfeld, Duane. "How Swingers Make Contact," *Sexual Behavior 2*, 4 (April 1972).

Denfeld, Duane, and Gordon, Michael. "The Sociology of Mateswapping: or the Family That Swings Together Clings Together," *Journal of Sex Research 6*, 2 (May 1970). Reprinted in Skolnick and Skolnick, *Family in Transition*, Boston: Little, Brown, 1971. *

Hunt, Morton. *The Affair*. New York: Signet, 1969. pb

Johnson, Ralph E. "Extramarital Intercourse: A Methodological Note," *Journal of Marriage and the Family* 32, 2 (May 1970).

Lewis, Richard Warren. "The Swingers," *Playboy* 16, 4 (April 1969).

Neubeck, Gerhard (ed.). *Extra-marital Sex*. Englewood Cliffs, N.J.: Prentice-Hall, 1969.

O'Neill, George C. and Nena. "Patterns in Group Sexual Activity," *Journal of Sex Research* 6, 2 (May 1970).

Palson, Charles, and Palson, Rebecca. "Swinging in Wedlock," *Society* 9, 4 (February 1972). *

Rubenstein, Paul, and Margolis, Herbert. *The Groupsex Tapes*. New York: David McKay, 1970.

Smith, James R., and Lynn G. "Comarital Sex and the Sexual Freedom Movement," *Journal of Sex Research* 6, 2 (May 1970).

Trimble, John F. *The Group Sex Scene*. New York: Pinnacle Books, 1971. pb, X

Walker, Brooks R. *The New Immorality*. Garden City, N.Y.: Doubleday, 1968. X

Walshok, Mary Lindenstein. "The Emergence of a Middle-Class Deviant Subculture: The Case of Swingers," *Social Problems* 18, 4 (Spring 1971).

Wells, John Warren. *The Wife-Swap Report*. New York: Dell, 1970. pb, X

COMMUNES, INTENTIONAL COMMUNITIES

Only a few especially selected items. See also chapters in entries under PERSPECTIVES.

Fairfield, Dick. *Communes U.S.A.* Baltimore: Penguin Books, 1971. pb

Fonzi, Gaeton. "The New Arrangement," *Philadelphia Magazine* (January 1970). Reprinted in Michael Gordon. *The Nuclear Family in Crisis*. New York: Harper & Row, 1972. pb

French, David. "After the Fall—What This Country Needs Is a Good Counter Counterculture Culture," *The New York Times Magazine* (October 3, 1971).

Holloway, Mark. *Heavens on Earth: Utopian Communities in America 1680-1880*. New York: Dover, 1966. pb

Houriet, Robert. *Getting Back Together*. New York: Coward, McCann, and Geoghegan, 1971. *

Kanter, Rosabeth M. "Commitment and Social Organization: A Study of Commitment Mechanisms in Utopian Communities," *American Sociological Review*, 33, 4 (August 1968). t/p *

———. "Communes," *Psychology Today* 4, 2 (July 1970). Reprinted in Gordon, *Perspectives*.

————. *Commitment and Community: Communes and Utopias in Sociological Perspective.* Cambridge, Mass.: Harvard University Press, 1972. pb, *

Robertson, C. N. *Oneida Community: An Autobiography 1851–1876.* Syracuse, N.Y.: York State Books, 1970.

PERSPECTIVES

Broad views of marriage, family, and sex relations, many emphasizing alternatives and the changing nature of the family.

Baird, Joan, and Keenan, Dorothy (eds.). *Family Life Education Reexamined: Applications for Teachers.* Washington, D.C.: American Home Economics Association, 1972. pb

Beach, Frank. *Sex and Behavior.* New York: Wiley and Sons, 1965.

Beck, Dorothy Fahs. *Current Challenges to the Traditional Family and Some Newly Emerging Alternate Forms for Family Living: Summary Outline.* New York: Family Service Association of America, 1972. [Includes bibliography.]. pb, *

Brecher, Edward M. *The Sex Researchers.* Boston: Little, Brown, 1969. *

Brecher, Ruth and Edward. *An Analysis of Human Sexual Response.* New York: Signet, 1966. pb

Broderick, Carlfred, and Bernard, Jessie. *The Individual, Sex, and Society.* Baltimore: Johns Hopkins Press, 1969. pb, *

Christopherson, Victor A., and Jacobsen, Ralph Brooke. *Family Dimensions.* New York: Simon and Schuster, 1971. pb

Cox, Frank D. (ed.). *American Marriage: A Changing Scene?* Dubuque, Iowa: William C. Brown, 1972. pb

Cuber, John, and Harroff, Peggy. *Sex and the Significant Americans: A Study of Sexual Behavior among the Affluent.* Baltimore: Penguin Books, 1969. pb, *

De Lora, Jack and JoAnn (eds.). *Intimate Life Styles: Marriage and Its Alternatives.* Pacific Palisades, Calif.: Goodyear Publishing, 1972. pb

Edwards, J. M. *The Family and Change.* New York: Alfred A. Knopf, 1969.

Ford, Clellan S., and Beach, Frank A. *Patterns of Sexual Behavior.* New York: Harper & Row, 1951. pb, **

Gagnon, John H., and Simon, William (eds.). *The Sexual Scene.* New York: Transaction Books, 1970. pb

Goode, William J. *World Revolution and Family Patterns.* New York: The Free Press of Glencoe, 1964.

Gordon, Michael (ed.). *The Nuclear Family in Crisis: The Search for an Alternative.* New York: Harper & Row, 1972. pb

Kirkendall, Lester A., and Whitehurst, Robert N. (eds.). *The New Sexual Revolution.* New York: Donald Brown, 1971. pb

LeShan, Eda J. *Mates and Roommates: New Styles in Young Marriages*. New York: Public Affairs Committee, 1971 pamphlet. **

Marshall, Donald S., and Suggs, Robert C. *Human Sexual Behavior: Variations in the Ethnographic Spectrum*. New York: Basic Books, 1971. **

Nimkoff, M. F. (ed.). *Comparative Family Systems*. Boston: Houghton Mifflin, 1965. t/p, *

Otto, Herbert A. (ed.). *The Family in Search of a Future: Alternate Models for Moderns*. New York: Appleton-Century-Crofts, 1970. **

———. *The New Sexuality*. Palo Alto, Calif.: Science and Behavior, 1971.

Shiloh, Ailon. *Studies in Human Sexual Behavior: The American Scene*. Springfield, Ill.: Charles C. Thomas, 1970. t/p, *

Skolnick, Arlene S. and Jerome H. (eds.). *Family in Transition: Rethinking Marriage, Sexuality, Child Rearing and Family Organization*. Boston: Little, Brown, 1971. pb, **

Stephens, William N. *The Family in a Cross-Cultural Perspective*. New York: Holt, Rinehart and Winston, 1963.

Udry, J. Richard. *The Social Context of Marriage*. Philadelphia: J. B. Lippincott, 1971.

Ullerstam, Lars. *The Erotic Minorities*. New York: Grove Press, 1966. pb

Wiseman, Jacqueline P. *People as Partners*. New York: Harper & Row, 1971. pb

FUNDAMENTALS, SKILLS

Selections about being, growing, and relating which are relevent to emerging family patterns.

Allport, Gordon W. *Becoming: Basic Considerations for a Psychology of Personality*. New Haven: Yale University Press, 1955. pb, t/p

Bach, George, and Wyden, Peter H. *The Intimate Enemy: How to Fight Fair in Love and Marriage*. New York: Avon, 1970. pb, *

Berne, Eric. *Games People Play*. New York: Dell, 1967. pb, *

———. *Transactional Analysis in Psychotherapy*. New York: Grove Press, 1961. pb, t/p

Burton, Arthur (ed.). *Encounter: The Theory and Practice of Encounter Groups*. San Francisco: Jossey-Bass, 1969. t/p

Ginott, Haim G. *Between Parent and Child*. New York: Macmillan, 1965. Also pb. [Not only a model for effective parent-child relations but for many adult-adult encounters.]

Gordon, Thomas. *Parent Effectiveness Training*. New York: Peter H. Wyden, 1970. [No-lose model for adult-adult as well as adult-child relations.] **

Harris, Thomas A. *I'm OK—You're OK: A Practical Guide to Trans-actional Analysis.* New York: Harper & Row, 1969. [Easier and more directly useful than Berne.] **

Jourard, Sydney. *The Transparent Self.* Princeton, N.J.: Van Nostrand, 1964, pb, *

Maslow, Abraham. *Eupsychian Management: A Journal.* Home-wood, Ill.: Irwin and Dorsey Press, 1965.

———. *Motivation and Personality.* New York: Harper & Row, 1970; 2nd edn.

———. *Toward a Psychology of Being.* Princeton, N. J.: Van Nos-trand, 1962. pb, *

Montagu, Ashley. *On Being Human.* New York: Hawthorne, 1966; 2nd edn.

O'Neill, Nena and George. *Open Marriage: A New Life Style for Couples.* New York: Evans, 1972. **

Otto, Herbert A. *A Guide to Developing Your Potential.* North Hol-lywood: Wilshire, 1967. pb

———. *More Joy in Your Marriage.* New York: Hawthorne, 1969.

Otto, Herbert A., and Mann, John (eds.). *Ways of Growth.* New York: Viking, 1968. pb

Perls, Frederick S. *Gestalt Therapy Verbatim.* Lafayette, Calif.: Real People Press, 1969. pb, *

Perls, Frederick S., Hefferline, Ralph F., and Goodman, Paul. *Gestalt Therapy.* New York: Delta, 1951. pb

Rogers, Carl. *Carl Rogers on Encounter Groups.* New York: Harper & Row, 1970. pb, *

Rubin, Theodore Isaac. *The Winner's Notebook.* New York: Trident, 1967.

Schutz, William C. *Joy: Expanding Human Awareness.* New York: Grove Press, 1967. pb

Shostrom, Everett L. *Man, the Manipulator.* New York: Bantam Books, 1967. pb, *

FUTURES

Views of others on the future of marriage and the family. See also individual chapters in entries under PERSPECTIVES.

Bernard, Jessie. "Women, Marriages, and the Future," *The Futurist* *4*, 2 (April 1970).

———. *The Future of Marriage.* New York: World Publishing, 1972 (We feel this misrepresents our work but is a significant feminist view.)

Cancro, Robert. "Preserving the Species," *Saturday Review* (March 6, 1971).

Constantine, Larry L. and Joan M. "Where Is Marriage Going?" *The Futurist 4*, 2 (April 1970). Reprinted in DeLora and DeLora.

Intimate Life Styles, op. cit. Also reprinted in Christopherson and Jacobsen, *Family Dimensions, op. cit.*

Davids, Leo. "North American Marriage: 1990," *The Futurist* 5, 5 (October 1971).

East, Margorie, "Family Life by the Year 2000," *Journal of Home Economics* 62, 1 (January 1970). Reprinted in Christopherson and Jacobsen. *Family Dimensions, op. cit.*

Farson, Richard E., *et al. The Future of the Family.* New York: Family Service Association of America, 1969.

Francoeur, Robert. *Eve's New Rib. Twenty Faces of Sex, Marriage and Family.* New York: Harcourt, Brace & Jovanovich, 1972.

Gagnon, John H., and Simon, William. "Prospects for Change in American Sexual Patterns." Reprint available from SIECUS, 1855 Broadway, New York City, 10023.

Hill, Reuben. "The American Family of the Future," *Journal of Marriage and the Family* 26, 1 (February 1967).

Hunt, Morton. "The Future of Marriage," *Playboy* (August 1971). X.

Keller, Suzanne. "Does the Family Have a Future?" *Journal of Comparative Family Studies* (Spring 1971).

Kubie, Lawrence S., *et al. The Future of the American Family: Dream and Reality.* New York: Child Study Association of America, 1963.

Mead, Margaret. "Future Family," *Transaction* 8, 11 (September 1971).

Orleans, Myron, and Wolfson, Florence. "The Future of the Family," *The Futurist* 4, 2 (April 1970).

Otto, Herbert A. "Has Monogamy Failed?" *Saturday Review* (April 25, 1970).

Pollak, Otto. "The Outlook for the American Family," *Journal of Marriage and the Family* 29, 1 (February 1967).

Rainwater, Lee. "Post-1984 America," *Society* 9, 4 (February 1972).

Ramey, James W. "Emerging Patterns of Behavior in Marriage: Deviations or Innovations," *Journal of Sex Research* 8, 1 (February 1972).

Rogers, Carl. "Man-Woman Relationships: U.S.A. 2000," *Journal of Applied Behavioral Science* 4, 3 (1968).

Roy, Rustum and Della. "Is Monogamy Outdated?" *The Humanist* (March/April 1970). Also in Kirkendall and Whitehurst. *The New Sexual Revolution, op. cit.*

Sussman, Marvin B. "Family Systems in the 1970's: Analysis, Politics, and Programs," *Annals of the American Academy of Political and Social Science*, 396, (July 1971).

Time staff. "The American Family: Future Uncertain," *Time*, December 28, 1970. pp. 34–38.

Toffler, Alvin. "The Fractured Family," *Future Shock*. New York: Random House, 1970.

Weiss, Robert. "Marriage and Family in the Near Future," *Ciba Foundation Symposium on the Family and Its Future*, 1970. London: J. & A. Churchill, 1970.

Winch, Robert F. "Permanence and Change in the History of the American Family and Some Speculations as to Its Future" (with comments by Hope J. Leichter), *Journal of Marriage and the Family* 32, 1 (February 1970).

Zimmerman, Carle C. "The Future of the American Family: I. The Revolution," *International Journal of Sociology of the Family* 1, 1 (March 1971).

———. "The Future of the American Family: II. The Rise of the Counter-Revolution," *International Journal of Sociology of the Family* 2, 1 (March 1972).

———. "The Future of the Family in America," *Journal of Marriage and the Family* 34, 2 (May 1972).